# Bomber

## Behind the Laughter

## Herol Graham with Stuart Wilkin

Behind the Laughter

First Published in the United Kingdom by TH Media in Derbyshire

2011


ISBN number 978-0-9559534-4-6

Design by Jonathan Stansfield


Printed in Great Britain by Impressions Print and Publish 93 High Street,
Somersham, Cambridgeshire.


Pictures reproduced with thanks to Tom Bootyman and the Sheffield Star

# Contents

Behind the Laughter

To my children who are the loves of my life
And to Karen my Earth Angel,
For the inspiration she gave to me to carry on.

Behind the Laughter

# Foreword

Seldom do we have the chance to look at the world through the eyes of an iconic sports personality, but we're less likely still to go on such a journey with a man as warm and humble, as he is hilarious and troubled. Herol Graham tells his story with an emotional intelligence rarely seen in this genre and reveals as much about his personal demons as he does his view of his professional record and the boxers he met. And the conclusion we inevitably arrive at is that Herol is as mad as a box of frogs.

But his passionate fans from Sheffield and further afield knew that anyway. Anyone who saw him box with hands down, sticking his tongue out at opponents and kissing his glove before delivering a knockout blow knew that there was something different about Herol. His whole philosophy of boxing was at odds with many of his contemporaries and his artful ability to keep his face away from the sledgehammers aimed at him wasn't to everybody's liking. Fight fans who revelled at the prospect of two brawlers standing virtually still, trading punches and slugging it out until one of them fell over didn't follow Herol Graham, because his speed and craft frustrated many a street fighter.

Rival trainers and boxers worldwide suggested that he'd be better suited to a running track than a boxing ring, although the twenty seven professional fighters he stopped within the distance wouldn't necessarily bear testament to that. In truth the true edge that Herol had over his contemporaries was in his almost inhuman levels of fitness and lightning speed. And at his height he was named by Harry Carpenter as Britain's most skilful boxer.

As a youngster growing up in Nottingham he first caught a glimpse of Muhammad Ali on a snowy black and white television and the boy was transfixed. Here was the man who Herol wanted to emulate and in the end he didn't half do a bad job of it.

The christening of 'Bomber' sounds like the product of a promoter's limited repertoire but it was bestowed on Herol at the age of eight, before he'd ever set foot in a boxing gym. And it had nothing to do with his punching ability. He looks back to events at that age which arguably took him down the path he followed and there are suggestions that he never actually lost some of the naivety of childhood. He had his trust betrayed far more than most of us would before he eventually began to suspect that not everybody inside and outside the world of boxing are philanthropic. And that cost him dearly.

For a while Herol was one of the biggest sporting names in Yorkshire along with Sebastian Coe and Tony Currie, and he fought at a time when the middleweight boxing world was festooned with stratospheric talent. Marvellous Marvin Hagler, Thomas Hearns and Sugar Ray Leonard took the world stage and began to look across the pond at the emerging British fighters, and Herol Graham was up there with the best.

He enjoyed true celebrity status and became the only fighter in Sheffield to own a pink leather settee. And he will reveal more explosive detail such as who came closest to landing a knockout blow on him – Roberto Duran or a twenty four year old female police officer?

His vaunted partnership and ultimate split with his trainer Brendan Ingle is the stuff of legend, and both men have wondered what may have happened if Herol's head hadn't been turned by the bright lights.

Like countless sports stars before him he has experienced the heights of success and the depths of despair. Each of his world title fights were a mirror of the rollercoaster that he has travelled on outside the ring. And he has the grace and humility to tell us which of the fighters who beat him really deserved to.

In a different age or in a different place he may have scaled even greater heights in the boxing world than he did. But the sheer entertainment and joy that he gave countless fight fans over almost two decades will be hard for us to repay.

Herol Graham was one on his own, swimming against the tide, and winning and losing in equally spectacular measures. He always wanted to please from a very young age, and he still does. But that single part of his nature has not always been his true friend. He has known the best and the worst of times and is thankfully willing to tell the tale. Herol has been a pleasure to work with.

An exceptional fighter and a wonderful man.

*Stu Wilkin*

Behind the Laughter

# 1

# <u>Who Switched the Lights Out?</u>

## Spain, 24<sup>th</sup> November 1990

*"Not in the clamour of the crowded street,*
*Not in the shouts and plaudits of the throng,*
*But in ourselves, are triumph and defeat."*

## H W Longfellow.

Out of the darkness I saw a tiny chink of light and it bloody hurt. It made me squint and felt like it was burning right through my brain. It was almost like someone was shining a torch in my face. As I opened both of my eyes to meet the light it began to hurt less and within seconds, in amongst the garish coloured walls, I could make out some blurred figures and hear them mumbling.

Waking up can be a strange sort of thing in any circumstances. The nicest way to do it is in your own bed on a Sunday morning in summer when there's no alarm and you gently come around. Then there's the way where you struggle to open your eyes, your head's banging and your tongue feels like a dried out rat's arse, because you lost count of your drinks the night before. Being woken up by an alarm isn't great either, and waking up after surgery's kind of weird. But all in all waking up is generally a good thing because it means you're not dead.

On this occasion I couldn't focus my eyes properly no matter how hard I tried. You know when you see a cartoon character who has taken a wallop and they are surrounded by a ring of stars or tweeting birds? Well I could see the stars as clear as day but not much of anything else. The room I was in had bright red and yellow walls which added to the whole surrealistic vibe. Then as I strained to focus I finally made out a figure I could recognise. It was Brendan.

My vision was very sketchy and everything was still kind of hazy. The whole thing felt like a dream. I wasn't sure if I was waking up or I was still asleep. But as I strained further I could make out the blurred outlines of three or four people and I recognised Brendan for sure because he was only a couple of feet away. I was awake. But I had no idea what had happened, so I asked:

*"Did I win?"*

Brendan just shook his head.

*"I want a rematch."*

In all honesty I still had no real recollection of what had gone before over the last few hours and I struggled to keep my focus. The medical staff wanted to check me out as soon as I had come round, so when I managed to get to my feet I was ushered out of the changing room and taken to hospital. Once I had woken up this time I didn't lose consciousness again but everything was scanty. I was trying my hardest to visualise, but it was all still like some surreal dream. I was surrounded by a cloud. I was walking okay but I felt absolutely like I was floating on air ….. and not through any sense of happiness.

At that very moment I didn't have a sense of anything at all. The truth of the matter was that I had been hit by something so hard that all sense had gone.

♦

## Sheffield, August 1990

1990 was an amazing year in history. After being in prison in South Africa for 27 years Nelson Mandela was released in February and it seemed like the whole world was having a party. It was a bit grim back in the UK though, we were heading towards a recession and hundreds of thousands of people were demonstrating against the Poll Tax - the riots lasted for weeks. Mrs Thatcher seemed to have a knack of getting people to riot. She had beaten the miners a few years earlier but this looked like it might be a fight too many for the Iron Lady.

In July the country was hit by World Cup fever. There weren't the flags on cars and houses that we see nowadays, all strung up and then taken down the minute we go out. But even so, everyone was up for it. And it even looked like we were going to win the World Cup having missed out for far too long (24 years). When Gary Linekar scored the equaliser in the semi finals against Germany we were as good as home and dry. We were on top and our opponents in the final were going to be Argentina, who were much weaker than the 'Hand of God' team that stiffed us in 1986. At the final whistle the only thing in our way was a penalty shoot out. This was the first time we'd had a shoot out but we were bound to beat the Germans surely, they probably wouldn't be that good at them. Well it seemed so at the time!

After Chris Waddle narrowly missed the floodlight with his attempt we could all get back to normal and see what was happening elsewhere in the world. It wasn't all good news by any stretch of the imagination. In August Iraq invaded Kuwait to start the first Gulf War and then Timmy Mallett reached number one with that bloody Itsy Bitsy Teeny Weeny crock of shit.

In the boxing world Buster Douglas had taken Mike Tyson's unified heavyweight titles and the legendary Roberto Duran had just left the WBC world middleweight championship vacant. For my part I'd had a bit of a lay off at the beginning of the year because I'd hit Rod Douglas in a fight and he ended up needing some serious brain surgery after he'd got a blood clot. That had upset me a lot. I got pretty low about the whole thing. It was a dark time and I had lost all my enthusiasm for the sport. I seriously considered retiring then, and it was months before I wanted to get back in the ring even to spar. But when Timmy Mallett appeared on Top of the Pops I somehow regained my motivation to smack someone again.

♦

I had just finished a workout at the gym in Sheffield; I'd done some weights, a bit of sparring and finished off with a five mile run. It was pretty warm weather, which is rare in England even in August, so I had to work hard and I had been sweating like a donkey. After I'd showered down I was about to set off home when Brendan called me over. He'd been on the phone most of the afternoon, he was smiling, and he had something to tell me.

*"So Herol, we've got you another shot,"* he said in his Irish drawl.

*"What's that then?"* I asked.

*"WBC Middleweight championship of the fucking world that's what!"*

*"Okay, who's it against?"*

*"Julian Jackson,"* he replied.

*"Who?"*

I didn't know who Julian Jackson was. I had never spent that much time looking around myself to see what everyone else in the world was doing, I had always just concentrated on what I was doing. That was my way. I just wanted to get better and better at what I did and didn't give much thought to anyone else. That was up to Brendan. He told me that Jackson was originally from the British Virgin Islands but he'd been boxing in the US for a while and now he was based there.

He carried on:

*"He's a very good fighter but there's one big thing in your favour."*

*"What's that?"*

*"He's blind as a fucking bat!"*

*"What?"*

*"He wears glasses that look like fucking milk bottles so he does!"*

What Brendan didn't tell me was that he was the main contender for the vacant WBC world title and, despite his eye defects, he'd spent the last three years merrily knocking out anyone that came within his range.

As Brendan and the others talked to me about him over the next few weeks they said that he'd knocked this guy out and knocked that guy out, and it started to seem to me like he was knocking everybody out. But they were giving me the real impression that he'd had a fair amount of luck. They weren't emphasising to me that he was a big hitter; just that he'd knocked a few guys out. But then so had I.

Because I hadn't heard of Jackson I was happy to listen to what the guys were saying, particularly the bit about luck. Maybe there was a subconscious part of me that didn't really want to know if he was a dangerous fighter. I just wanted to concentrate on myself and didn't want to be distracted.

This was a massive chance for me. The year before I'd lost a WBA World Title fight to Mike McCallum on points and I was determined to make amends and pick up a World Title this time. To be honest I had been running out of patience. I'd had 44 professional fights by this time, and I had reached the grand old age of 30. If I'd been a London based fighter I would have had at least three title shots by now. I tried not to think about that too much but it had been at the back of my mind that I wouldn't get another title shot, so this was the best news I'd had in a long time.

Brendan told me that Jackson had quite a few knockouts but I still wasn't getting the clear information as to just how dangerous he was. But then maybe I wouldn't have listened if I had. Sometimes I listened and sometimes I didn't. I wasn't being arrogant, but sometimes I simply wasn't interested. But as time went on I became conscientious enough to start reading about Jackson and as the fight drew nearer I started to listen to people who were talking about him. He'd boxed loads of guys …. and punched them.

But I don't think I was properly taking it all in. I had never worried about my opponents and what they could do, and I always knew what I had to do. I just do my thing. But, with hindsight, this was probably the first time that I had wished that I had really listened to what was being said around me. Jackson had knocked some good people out. I did find out that his nickname was 'The Hawk' but I assumed that was because he only had one good eye!

I'd been waiting longer than I'd wanted for a title shot because no one else who was around at the time wanted to give me a go; even Marvin Hagler didn't want to. Promoters had been trying to get me to defend my British Title against Chris Eubank, but he was showing no interest at all. I felt like some managers didn't want to get a fight on, because they were scared that I'd beat their man. After I missed my chance against McCallum I had been getting more and more frustrated, up until the sad fight with Douglas, which kind of put things into context for me for a while.

But when I stepped back into the ring I hoped it was just a matter of time before I'd get my chance again and it was a case of hanging in there. And now I'd got the shot.

But sometimes it seems in life that nothing's ever easy. The British Board of Boxing Control wouldn't allow the fight to be staged in the UK because of Jackson's eye defect. Then the US promoter Don King muscled in and said that he'd get the fight on over there and offered me $25,000. I thought that was taking the piss and I told him. And then King said if I didn't want that he'd offer the fight to someone else.

But soon after, Barry Hearn, the snooker promoter, won the bidding to stage the fight and I was absolutely delighted with that as he was one of the top names in the sport. And I knew that I'd get three times the amount that King had offered. So when Barry got the fight all he had to do was find a venue. He planned to get it on in Monte Carlo, a fantastic place to stage it, and we all wanted to go back to Monte Carlo because we'd had such a great time there before. They love a boxing match and there were plenty of famous people hanging out and lots of money around. But soon we discovered that even the French had an uncharacteristic attack of safety awareness and they too baulked at the fight.

Shit – if the French were worried then Barry Hearn may have a problem. But not so. The answer came, unsurprisingly, from Spain, the home of tomato festivals and the most brutal entertainment on the planet – bull fighting. I suppose the lovers of ritual murder of dumb animals for mass entertainment probably found the idea of a fight involving a half blind man quite appealing. So the fight was set for November in Benalmadina.

I didn't have any other fights scheduled between August and November, so it was all preparation for the World Title.

♦

I'd been with Brendan Ingle ever since I'd moved to Sheffield some fourteen years earlier. He'd taken me in his house when I was sixteen and looked after me ever since. Our relationship had been pretty straight forward in the early days, but as things took off Brendan decided to let someone else in, and in 1985 he sold my contract to Barney Eastwood who took over the management while Brendan did the training. Barney had made a name for himself looking after Barry McGuigan. So Barney was managing me and Brendan was training me, but sometimes the lines of responsibility seemed to blur.

It was an odd sort of triangle. It felt to me like they were both training and managing me and you could often tell that they were at loggerheads with each other. One of them would talk to me then the other would come and talk to me and say something completely different. They were both very keen to talk to me but they didn't seem to be all that good at talking to each other. To be fair to them they were often saying the same thing, but in a certain way, so it didn't sound the same.

When Barney had bought Brendan out, part of the contractual details meant that Brendan stayed with me. But nevertheless, it was often an awkward relationship. The manager, trainer and boxer all need to be working together if you're going to get optimum performance. But with these two, sometimes one of them would try to pull me one way and the other would go the other way. And I was aware of the friction between them. They used to have little arguments all the time in training sessions. And on one occasion they actually started arguing in the corner at a fight. There was a better battle going on in our corner than there was on the canvas!

I don't think it really helped that they were both Irish, Brendan was from the Republic in the South and Barney was from Northern Ireland. In all honesty it was a business arrangement between them and nothing more. But it didn't particularly help me because I could see what was happening between them and it became a distraction. Maybe if I had been hearing just one clear voice I would have taken more information in. The tension was always there and I would either want to go to one side or another. They'd be arguing and then one of them would look at me and say:

*"Herol – isn't that right?"*

*"If you say so."*

In many ways it felt like I was a kid being pulled two ways by bickering parents – they'd put me in that position, but they didn't always act like mature adults.

As far as I was concerned Barney was the man with the money and Brendan was the trainer so I had to listen to them both for different reasons. At the time I trusted Brendan more than I trusted Barney simply because I knew him more – we'd been through an awful lot together.

♦

So it was Brendan who told me that I'd got the Julian Jackson fight. And I had over three months to prepare, which was easily enough time. I had a fairly happy-go-lucky lifestyle in those days and even with a World title fight coming up everything carried on as normal. At the time of the fight I had a girlfriend called Claire, who I lived with in the Hillsboro area of Sheffield with our baby Son Oliver, who was a sheer delight to both of us.

My routine didn't change much at all at the beginning. I started with an early morning run, at about 4-30. I was strict with myself in that if I'd had a late night out and came in after midnight then the following day would be a run day and not a rest day. If I came in at one then I knew I'd be out running in four hours. That was a deal I kept with myself which I've always kept.

After my run, I'd get a shower, have something to eat, a sandwich or some cereal and then I'd go back to bed and have a sleep. Then I'd get into the gym about ten to do some weight training, and repetitions and combinations with weights, and then bag work and sparring. I was comfortable with my training routine and always relaxed, and I made my life easier for myself. A lot of the time I stayed at Brendan's house, even though I had my own, because the gym was across the road from where he lived.

I didn't go too far overboard on the late nights but I did used to go clubbing Friday and Saturday nights in Anabellas and Josephines, two 'classy' nightspots in Sheffield. They weren't heavy nights on the booze, just late. Everyone around me who I went to the clubs with were okay. The sports fans knew that I had a World Title shot coming up so they didn't try to get me drunk. Other people were often surprised if they asked me what I wanted to drink and I said 'lemonade'. Those who knew me well enough knew that I'd have a sneaky brandy now and again.

As we got nearer the fight I started to work on quicker stuff in the gym and on my runs and I did less repetitions. The runs, which at the longest had been 18 miles, were cut down to 10 or 12 miles and then down to about a five mile run, then three miles and then sprinting. It was hard work but I was determined to get as fit and fast as I could. I had a lifetime chance to achieve everything that I had sweat blood and shed tears for over the last ten years.

I had fantastic support from my friends at the gym. Johnny Nelson, a Sheffield cruiserweight, who at the time was well on the way to making a big name for himself, did a lot of work with me and I had a mate called Brian Anderson who trained long hours with me, and he stopped at my house as well. The nearer the fight came, the faster the work was. It all became quicker stuff, working on my legs just as much as my upper body and I carried on with this routine right up until the week before the fight.

On the medical side I was looked after by a guy called Doctor Wynne. He had a surgery down at the bottom of the road near the gym and he came round to help us whenever we needed it. Massage work wasn't all that sophisticated, or fun, as it was usually done by Brendan, and he was hardly anyone's ideal image of a masseuse. But you get what you get in life I suppose! I could go to a local centre to get some expert massage on my back or neck if there was something that Brendan's bricklayer's hands were not up to.

But, apart from his massaging, from the moment I had got the fight Brendan was the most important man to me. I'd been with him for so long. He'd known of me almost from the time when I began boxing in Nottingham as an eight year old, and we'd been very close to each other for all my adult life. From when he took me to Sheffield at the age of 16 he'd always been in my corner, for 14 years. I saw Brendan every single day and I lived at his house for a lot of the time.

My diet was tried, tested and pretty simple. It was always based around the holy trinity of chicken, peas and rice, the three things that I had eaten the most of for all my life. As my diet became more and more focussed around protein and carbohydrate we just increased the chicken and rice. I always made sure that I had very lean meat which was usually chicken. I was always careful to take away any of the fat on the meat but once I'd done that it was okay. At Brendan's we used to have a lot of red meat but when I stayed at my house I could do what I wanted. So that was chicken. We didn't have all the nutritional advice that athletes get nowadays, but I always had a healthy diet passed down to me from my parents.

♦

As the fight drew nearer I didn't have a worry in the world. Other than watching Brendan and Barney bickering and the usual girlfriend and boyfriend happenings at home I didn't really have any concerns, I was just getting focussed on the job in hand. And when we came within a month of the fight I felt I was ready and I just wanted to get it on.

The atmosphere in the gym was relaxed and happy. We were still joking about Jackson's bin lids and Brendan and Barney were happy to play down his ability, saying that he'd been lucky. Barney said that his eyesight was so bad that he could only see you properly from about two feet away. The way they were talking you'd have thought I was going to fight Mr Magoo. To be fair they were probably saying things that I wasn't actually listening to, I just heard the things that interested me.

As we moved into November I still didn't know all that much about Jackson. To be fair I had caught on that he was sort of a big hitter, but still had the distinct impression that he had been lucky. So I knew that I had to be careful, but if I was, then I didn't have anything to worry about. He wasn't a big guy at all, about 1.76 metres and quite a slight build, he was lean, but he'd handed out a few knockouts and he clearly had muscle and technique. What I didn't know until weeks later was that in 41 fights he'd knocked over 38 of his opponents.

We'd known for a while that the fight was getting on in Spain. I hadn't fought in Spain before but I had been there on holiday and I loved the place. It had been sorted out in good time so I was relaxed. To be honest, because I had always enjoyed my holidays there I was quite excited to be going there to fight.

We arrived in Benalmadena about a week and a half before the fight to give me enough time to get acclimatised. It was a lot hotter than Sheffield so I had to keep my body temperature stable and keep hydrated. Brendan travelled with me with a couple of his sons, along with Tony Green, my corner man. It was a cool hotel, brand spanking new, with a good pool, nice views and lovely staff. I was sharing a room with Brendan, he always wanted to do that to check that I was okay and doing the right things (not emptying the mini bar), but I didn't mind because it was a big room. We were looked after very well and had everything we needed to relax and prepare. I liked to chat to the staff there, which was a bit of a challenge because I couldn't speak any Spanish. I can speak some French but as the French Boxing Authority had been more safety conscious than the Spanish, that wasn't all that helpful. But I decided that French and Spanish are pretty similar. And I could understand some of the Spanish words. In any case the staff spoke pretty good English, so with me chucking bits of French in we could get by fine and the conversations went something like:

*"Que aproveche Signor Graham."*
*"What?"*
*"Enjoy your meal."*
*"Oh merci."*
*"De rien"*
*"Gracias"*
*"Good."*

You should always make an effort when you're abroad!

There was a fair amount of press attention for the fight and the TV and newspaper guys were there for their holiday too. With us being in Spain I think there'd been a clamour in the press rooms to get the job. In the days leading up to the fight I tried to avoid reading and watching the press coverage. I was always careful not to read too much of the press. On one hand, I guess it might have given me an idea that I hadn't already had, but on the other, I didn't want any added pressure of the expectations on my shoulders or read anything that could get into my head. But I had to do a few interviews, just talking about general stuff like how I felt, what I was doing, whether I liked being over here and all that. I did an interview with the Star where I said I wasn't really worried about Jackson's eye because he could look after himself. The story came out that I WAS worried about Jackson's eye – but then as the press guys always say, why let the facts get in the way of a good story. The guys from Look North were there and joined in when we held the pre fight press conference. I was always pleased to see the chaps from Look North, and the Sheffield Star had even forked out for one of their reporters to come over. I asked him where he'd parked his donkey.

A lot of boxers and other sports guys start to shit themselves before going into press conferences but it never really bothered me. I didn't mind doing the press conferences or interviews. I guess I wasn't nervous because I thought there were plenty of other things in life to get nervous about so I didn't mind just talking to people, I actually enjoyed it. So it was cool.

And a lot of fans came across from England too. Just like the journalists, for boxing fans it was a great opportunity to combine a sporting trip with a holiday, so a lot of fans had been over for the full week before the fight. It was good to see them around and gave me a real lift. Because they were in holiday mode they were having a lot of fun as well as getting pumped up for the fight so it was the perfect kind of atmosphere – excited, happy and energetic, if sometimes a bit pissed.

In the final two or three days before the fight I still felt relaxed. Brendan was staying with me everywhere I went and just talking to me calmly, telling me what I needed to be thinking about and just going over the same messages as ever. When we walked past some fans they were always asking how I was and I'd say:

*"I'm okay, okay, okay".*

I was confident, but as the fight drew nearer I began to find my edge. That's so important in the run up to a fight, because you can't go in without any tension, you'll just get battered. I was the bookies favourite to win but I always held the view that anyone could win a fight at any time so I wasn't taking a win for granted. But I knew that my opportunity was now and I had to do everything in my power to take it. Anything could happen but if I did the right things then I'd win and if I did the wrong things I wouldn't – it was just that simple. As far I was concerned everything - my training, the mental side, diet - was going okay, and I've always had the relaxed approach anyway, so outwardly and inwardly things were cool.

On the day before the fight I went with Brendan to see the venue and it was absolutely amazing. It was a casino and sports stadium and had a brilliant, massive arena - as good as anything I'd seen in the US. It wasn't just huge, it was really smart as well – the whole place had a velvety feel about it and I knew that the atmosphere in there was going to be electric. It gave me a shiver just thinking about it.

On the Saturday morning of the fight I woke up at about eight o' clock and immediately knew that I felt a bit more tension than the previous days, but I was still in a good place. That was pretty natural I guess, I wasn't frightened but I was definitely nervous. I couldn't have any breakfast because the weigh-in was booked for eleven so I just wandered round my room, shadow boxing, and walking around a bit fretfully. I was hungry and wanted something to do so I weighed myself, but that only confirmed that I still couldn't eat. Bollocks. I put the banana down and just carried on wandering around. I didn't want to mess about by eating something and making it too tight for myself so I just took it as easy as I could and kept moving around. I mixed it up a bit by walking over to the balcony ….. and then back again. Brendan was still asleep.

At about a quarter to eleven I went along with Brendan, Barney, Tony and the guys for the weigh-in. This was the first time I'd properly met Julian Jackson. On the way we were still joking about him and I was kind of looking forward to seeing just how thick his milk bottle glasses were! Everyone and anyone were at the weigh in; press, officials and the teams, it was absolutely packed and for the first time I had a sense of reality that the fight was here. But when I saw Jackson he seemed fairly unremarkable, similar height and build as me, same reach, and disappointingly he wasn't wearing glasses. He didn't trip or bump into anything so I guess he was wearing lenses. When I stepped on the scales I was absolutely smack on my weight and Jackson was a pound below.

We didn't speak to each other, other than to say 'hello' and shake hands. That was it. Just one word. These moments are never the best time to strike up a conversation. I always think it's funny when boxers have a row at the weigh-in or start insulting each other. I think it's as much for the telly and the hype as real. We're here to do a job, and the way I saw it there was never much point in making your opponent angry before you got in the ring.

To be honest, when I left the weigh in I didn't really have any impression of Jackson at all. And as I was so hungry, as soon as the weigh in was over I said:

*'Right let's get something to eat'*

We went to the restaurant and I had some cereal and orange juice:

*"Zumo de naranja Signor Graham?*

*"What?*

*"Orange juice?"*

*"Merci."*

*"De nada."*

*"Gracias."*

Virtually bi-lingual.

And then I went back to the room for a sleep. I woke up at about two, had another wander around before going with Brendan and the guys for a mid afternoon meal of chicken and rice and vegetables – of course. After that I went for a walk around outside with Brendan. You could tell that the atmosphere was building up; there were fans all over the place, wearing massive shorts and sombreros, waving bottles of beer, dropping chips and shouting:

*"Hey Herol, how're you doing?"* and *"Good luck Herol."*

It was great to see them all there and some familiar faces that I knew from when I'd done exhibitions in the Yorkshire working men's clubs. They were having a fantastic time already and that sort of relaxed me a bit and took my mind off what I was doing. But as I spent the afternoon listening to Brendan and chatting to the fans, the time went pretty quickly and when I realised it was nearly six o'clock I knew we were almost there. The boredom of the morning listening to Brendan snore and looking at the fruit bowl was long gone. As the time came closer and closer I could start to feel my heart beating *'bubum, bubum'*. Brendan was talking all the time, just saying:

*"You know what you have to do.... keep moving .... keep your hands up... do this ... do that..'*

I was kind of listening. It was all technical stuff, all boxing, no clever psychological or motivational words – just business as usual. I knew I had to keep Jackson at arms length and that way he couldn't see me – let alone get near me!

With the benefit of hindsight I think maybe they purposefully hadn't built Jackson's punch up too much because they didn't want to spook me. But 'forewarned is forearmed' as they say. Any way, I knew that he'd had a string of knockouts and I wasn't stupid, I just maybe didn't know quite how big his punch was. Either way I wasn't going to change my style or the way I fought for anyone.

♦

The fight was on at eleven and we arrived at the stadium just under two hours before. It gave me the chance to get used to the place, feel the atmosphere and understand what was about to approach me. I had been getting a bit restless during the afternoon and it made me feel more relaxed being in the stadium, watching a couple of fights and seeing the crowd and the ring. I took in the atmosphere and what was happening and then an hour before my fight I made my way to the dressing room.

Having been seemingly wandering around for days, all of a sudden the time started flying. One hour became fifteen minutes in a flash. I got my shorts on. My shorts were always made by a lady called Brenda back in Sheffield, and for this fight I was wearing orange and black flowery type shorts, sort of multicoloured. Brenda did some great designs.

At about quarter to eleven, Brendan and one of his sons, Brendan, helped me to put my gloves on. They strapped my hands and then put tape on the laces on the gloves to secure them. The gloves we used weren't that different to gloves they have now, they're better padded these days but that's just about the only difference.

Brendan was the only person to speak to me in the last few minutes before I went out, he was just going over and over what he'd been saying all day, all week in fact.

And then my time came.

As I walked out into the arena all that was going through my head was, '*Fucking Hell, I'm here.*' I was completely in awe of where I was and everything that was around me. The stadium was packed with thousands of fans and the atmosphere was incredible – it was bedlam. As I got down to the ring I could hear people talking, but there were several voices at the same time so I didn't listen. I didn't really know who was saying what.

Then as I climbed in the ring I heard the announcer…

*"Ladies and Gentlemen...."*

Then the same thing in Spanish. And when he stopped talking I knew that the time was almost here.

I was absolutely there, I was in the right place and I was ready. I knew that this was my chance and while I didn't really hear everything that was going on around me. I knew what I was going to do and I had to take the chance.

Brendan, Barney and Tony were in my corner. Brendan said something else which I didn't hear properly (I hope to this day it wasn't *'oh by the way Bomber, he's got a fucking howitzer on his right hand)*. And then the bell went.

I came out in the first round and simply started doing my thing. I was moving around and getting my feet used to the canvas. I found my feet straight away and I was moving quickly and started to jab and jab. Within a minute or so of the start I found myself thinking, *'bloody hell this is easy'!* Very early on I was well into it. Jackson wasn't really doing anything, just chasing me, now and again jabbing me, but not with any menace at all. And soon I started taking some blood from his mouth. I hadn't used much effort by the time the bell went and I sat down. The nerves had gone; I was pumped, focussed and ready to listen. Brendan just said:

*"Keep it going, keep the shots going, move him from left to right and right to left..."*

The second round was more of the same but I was getting much cleaner shots in on him. He was getting cut up and I started to be able to pick him off where and when I wanted.

By the middle of the third round his left eye had started closing. Jackson's left eye was his good one and his right eye was near to useless so if it closed he wouldn't be able to hit a barn door. I was hitting him and hitting him and the eye was closing up more. By the end of the third round he still hadn't touched me.

As I sat down I heard the crowd roar but I carried on focussing and listening to Brendan. The referee came over to our corner and told us that this was going to be the last round.

Jackson's good eye was a mess and the referee said he wasn't going to take any risks – even in Spain! Brendan said:

*"Just keep moving, keep moving, and keep jabbing, the refs going to stop it at the end of the round."*

What hadn't really registered with me was that as well as talking to us, the ref had told Jackson's corner that he was stopping the fight at the end of the next round too. So he was loaded up. But if he couldn't catch me, and he could hardly see me, I could just pick him off. I couldn't afford to be lackadaisical and had to keep focussed. It was mind over matter. I had to keep my head and finish the job.

It had been such an easy fight and I was confident and I was nearly there. The bell went and as the fourth round unfolded I was still well in control; Jackson hadn't hit me with a telling shot all the way through and didn't look like he could stay with me. All I had to do was keep going. I had to just keep moving around and moving him around. I was still connecting and he was back on the ropes. He knew that I was taking his title away from him if he couldn't do anything. I was way ahead on all three and a half rounds and the truth of it was I just had to stay on my feet.

But I wanted to stay on the attack and finish the fight. Jackson was more than half blind and he was reeling on the ropes. But was I too relaxed? Who knows?

I knew that I was less than a minute away from the World Title and as Jackson rested on the ropes I saw he was open, so I tried to connect with my left hand. As I leant forward he threw my shot over. I was forward too far. You should never have your head over your knees because you lose your sense of balance, and I was slightly off balance. I had been watching him like a hawk all the way, and then for that split second I took my eye off him. Every boxer in the world knows that you never ever take your eyes off your opponent. But I had left myself open, especially my jaw. When I did look at him the last thing I saw was his right hand come over. BANG. I was down and everything went dark.

Why didn't I stay out of his way for twenty seconds? If I could answer that I would. I guess it was just too simple.

I was unconscious before I hit the canvas and I didn't come round for five minutes. There was quite some panic in my corner so I'm told. Then I blacked out again on the way to the dressing room.

After I'd been to the hospital I went back to my hotel ……. and Jackson offered a prayer of thanks.

Fair enough.

# 2

## Run Fatboy Run

### Nottingham, 1960

*"Before you judge me, try hard to love me, look within your heart.*
*Then ask, - have you seen my childhood?"*

### Michael Jackson

Hubert and May Graham moved from Jamaica to Nottingham in the middle of the nineteen fifties along with a lot of other families from the West Indies who were hoping for a better life. When I say a better life, if you've been on holiday in the Caribbean then you might think I'm off my head. The crystal clear blue sea, the white sands, the Reggae and the rum or ...... the cold rain, the mud, Come Dancing and warm beer. Not a difficult choice really - unless you're looking for work.

Jamaica was, at that time, still a British colony and so all the inhabitants were officially British up until independence in 1962 in any case. The word 'Jamaica' means 'Land of Wood and Water' – and, like many of his mates, Hubert trained to be a joiner, and that became his trade for the rest of his life. But by the nineteen fifties, work in the Caribbean had become very hard to find.

When wealthy people from around the world started to holiday further afield, Jamaica became known as a tropical paradise, and soon enough it became the location for James Bond films like Dr No and Live and Let Die, so it had a glamorous image in the UK. But there was a wild side to the place as well; the island was crawling with crocodiles and alligators, and Kingston became notorious for its rising culture of drugs and violence. So there was a dark undercurrent to the beautiful land of sun, sea, dolphins and flamingos. Either way, other than the tourist industry growing, it became increasingly evident to young families that work was getting harder and harder to find. Many Jamaicans emigrated to the USA and England - so many that emigrants had their own collective name – 'the Jamaican Diaspora'. And England, being the motherland for the Grahams, was an obvious destination. So that's where Hubert and May, and their baby Winston, set off to find a better life.

It was a very difficult decision for them to make. Life in Jamaica was easy come easy go, and the people there have a much more laid back approach to life. They soon found out that life in England wasn't quite so relaxed, and certainly not as warm.

As an adult I've been over to Jamaica a couple of times and I love the pace of life, it's a great place to go for a holiday. But there's no way that I can pass off for a local. The locals would always look at me and say:

*"He's an Englishman."*

I guess it's obvious by the way I stand and the way I walk. I haven't grown up with music in my steps - I don't walk slowly enough - and I'm paler because I've missed the heat of the sun over there. But while I stand out physically, I can get myself into the Jamaican way of thinking easily enough.

And I always thought it was kind of weird that such a relaxed and laid back country is so close to the USA, the global hub of the heart attack and home of the incredibly uptight Tea Party movement. You get these American guys coming over for a holiday like we go to France or Spain or Greece, and they're so neurotic about their service standards. It's always a laugh to see a big guy from New York shouting:

*"What do you have to do to get a cold beer around here?!"*

- with his blood pressure visibly shooting upwards every time the bar tender fixes him with slanted eyes and a knowing grin and saying:

"*Irie Man ... chill owt ....I'm comin' ......jus' relax...*"

So it's a cool place to live, but the only problem is that you have to work of course. In the nineteen fifties there was no government support or welfare at that time in Jamaica and the only way to legitimately get money was to work. And if there wasn't employed work available you had to work the land. Hubert and May made their decision to leave their home when Winston was born. The Caribbean was a fantastic place to live outdoors but with a growing family you can't live on sea air and bananas! So they decided to try to make the most of their lives somewhere else.

One certain thing that Jamaicans can give to the world is physical strength. Even now, the worlds' fastest man, Usain Bolt, is from Jamaica. But for many years the island has had a rich history in sport, particularly cricket and basketball, and more recently the 'Reggae Boys' have hit the headlines at the football world cups. And there are some pretty impressive fighting genes in the Caribbean too. Chris Eubank, Frank Bruno and David Haye all have Jamaican parents, so if Hubert and May settled in England and had more children there was a fair chance that one would end up as a boxer I guess!

♦

Hubert and May got used to life quite easily over here in Nottingham, and were genuinely welcomed by the English people. The only thing they really missed was the heat of the sun. So they kept themselves warm on the cold dark evenings any way they could - and as a result when Winston was one and a half he got a little brother, Noel. Two years later, Winston and Noel had a sister, Leonie and two years after that another brother, me. We already had an extended family over here in England, brothers and sisters of Hubert and May. And when I was born I already had some cousins in my family and we had relatives living in London.

I can remember from a very early age, Mum and Dad talking about Jamaica and always saying how cold it was over here. But all I ever knew was Nottingham, so it just seemed like normal to me. Cold, but normal.

We grew up in the Radford area of Nottingham in 43 Guthrie Street, which was a corner grocery shop with room for us all in three bedrooms - one for Mum and Dad, one for the boys and one for the girls. There were two beds in each room so at first there were enough beds for everyone. But when I was two I had a little sister Elaine, and then another brother Paul. So sleeping arrangements became a little more cramped, but we managed okay. Dad was getting plenty of work but he was frequently away, he was self employed and was often contracted as part of a gang on big jobs, which meant he had to go to where the work was, and sometimes he was away for weeks at a time.

Mum ran the shop and the house, as well as holding down a job at the local Raleigh bike factory. She worked extremely hard to keep us all in order; she was kind of like a black Wonderwoman.

The shop sold sweets, meat, household goods, tins, vegetables and all kinds of stuff, and it was 'open all hours'. As we got older sometimes we helped Mum in the shop, alongside Auntie Bet and Uncle Tom. They were like our second parents. I soon found where the sweets were and that became a powerful magnet to me, like any kid let loose in a sweet shop, the temptation was often too great.

And it was difficult for Mum to see what we were up to all the time. So at times we resorted to the kids 'law of the jungle'. I used to fight with my older brothers and sister almost as soon as I could walk. When I was three or four they started to torment me and say that I had to do what they said. I got pushed around a lot, as the little ones always do. Winston's okay now but he was a bully to me then, getting me to do his jobs and generally shoving me round. Noel would push me around as well but he was more subtle than Winston. He was and is a very creative and artistic guy, and at that early age it was harder for me to convince Mum that he was being mean to me. If I said it was

Winston then that was easily believable for Mum, but Noel 'was such a good boy'. Clever sod.

So they all knocked me about as and when they felt like it, even Leonie had fights with me. In fact she hurt the most when she slapped me! But by the time I was six I could hold my own. Then, when I'd given her a slap she would tell Mum and Dad and then they'd slap me as well! It was like the old Lenny Henry sketches with his Caribbean Mum shouting and then whacking! It was made very clear to me at an early age that if you hit your sister you were in big trouble. It didn't seem all that fair at the time but rules are rules and a slap is a slap. And I soon stopped fighting with Naomi, not only to avoid the additional slaps, but also because as she got older she became more of a mother figure to us, and she used to help to run the house when Mum and Dad were working.

Mum and Dad gave us a loving home and we didn't want for anything. But discipline was always pretty tough in the house and we all knew exactly where our place was. We had to do jobs like washing up, and there was a strict rota of who did what on each day of the week. And you knew you'd get into trouble if you hadn't done your job. And trouble was, of course, a whack.

As the oldest, Winston was the first to get into real trouble. He used to hang around with the bad boys and gangs and they'd get themselves into a lot of grief. Mum and Dad were furious if they found out what he'd been up to and they'd give him hell. But I quickly learned never to laugh when either of my brothers got into trouble with Mum and Dad because I always knew that I could be next. I knew that anything that could happen to them could just as easily happen to me. Every now and then you rat on each other to save your own skin, but it always comes full circle in the end.

I got some of my comeuppance on the first time that I tried my hand at shoplifting (outside our own sweet shelf). I'd pinched an apple from a shop round the corner not thinking that the lady who owned the shop had seen me. She knew who I was of course, and kids of seven or eight always think they can do stuff without the grown ups seeing them. But they rarely get away with it and on this occasion I certainly didn't. When she inevitably heard about it Mum gave me both barrels:

*"Why in God's name did you do that Herol?"* She had always taught us not to steal and I'd let her down big time. She'd also told us that honesty is the best policy so that's the plan I pursued:

*"Because I was hungry..."*

Wrong answer. So Mum hit me. And when Dad arrived home a couple of hours later and I heard him screech:

*"WHAAAT?!"*

I knew exactly what was coming.

♦

Although we were being brought up in the middle of England we had a very West Indian upbringing in every way – not just in the hands on discipline. We ate the same kind of food as Mum and Dad had always done back in Jamaica, or at least we ate what they could get their hands on in Nottingham, which was pretty similar. We had potatoes and yams and bananas and the staple was rice and peas and chicken. Every day we'd have the balance of the protein, the carbs and the greens (although we didn't have the nutrition knowledge that's around now) and it was always a combination of rice and peas and chicken. Often we had a soup before our meal, and sometimes we'd have the soup as the meal with the chicken, rice and peas in it. That was all I ever knew and I loved it.

The first time I went to my friend Gary's house for tea it was a hell of a shock for me. Sometimes we'd have a sandwich when I went round there, but on this first occasion his mum put the plates and knives and forks out and then a massive roll of newspaper in the middle of the table. As she opened the newspaper, steam started to come out and my eyes widened. I couldn't believe what I was seeing and I nudged Gary:

*"Wow! What's this man?"*

*"It's fish and chips,"* he replied.

*"Fish and chips? Chips? Wow!"* (This could catch on).

And the really amazing thing was that Gary's mum hadn't even made them herself. There was a shop round the corner that sold just fish and chips and pickled eggs. So why should she make it herself? Brilliant.

Then when Gary came round to my house it was chicken, rice and peas - or peas, chicken and rice. After a few years we started eating fish and chips in our house too, but we mainly stuck to our Caribbean diet.

We didn't have holidays when I was a kid, as Mum and Dad were working all year round. Mum worked in the shops and at Raleigh on shifts between two and ten or six and two. Dad was working anywhere and everywhere on his building contracts as a carpenter. And then we had someone helping Mum to look after the shop. We were comfortable but we were certainly not awash with cash. And I didn't feel hard done by not going on holidays – lots of my mates didn't either, and in any case, you don't miss what you've never had. And we always seemed to have plenty to do in the school holidays.

♦

At the age of eight most of you wouldn't have recognised me at all. I was a fat kid, which you may find hard to believe as I've already told you that I spent the whole of my childhood eating rice and peas and chicken. That's true enough but it wasn't all I was eating. At Guthrie Street I was always in my Mum's corner shop helping out or, more often than not, just helping myself to the chocolate. So I grew to quite a size, so big that people called me names and made fun of me. So nowadays, when I see people who are big, I understand what they feel like. People look at me now and don't believe me but my friends from Nottingham in the early years knew me just as a fat barrel. And when I talk to people who are trying to get fit and say 'don't eat this and don't do that', they think I'm patronising them. But I'm not - because I've been there - so I really think it's easier for me to help them. Everyone knows that there's nothing worse than a skinny bloke telling you to eat less cake!

Back in the sixties living in a shop made it even worse for me because not only was I visible to everybody, I was surrounded by crisps and chocolates. I had a real sweet tooth and I nicked everything from Hundreds and Thousands to Mars Bars. I often loaded myself up to go and eat my stash with my friends, but I'd end up eating most of them myself, and by the time I was eight I'd grown to an unhealthy tubby size.

I got some stick at my school, Radford Primary, but I still liked going there and I had some good mates. I was quite good at school on the whole, as was Noel and my sisters. At the age of seven or eight I was always asking questions and wanting to learn. I was good at geography but, even though I was overweight, I guess my best subject was sport. I was always running, so I dread to think how many sweets I must have been eating to make me so fat. My metabolic rate at the time was slow, so I wasn't burning anything off, which happens to certain people. It all depends on your physical make up. Some burn fat off quicker. But I'd eat anything that was made out of chocolate and by the time I was seven it really showed. It also makes me wonder how much of Mum's profits I was scoffing. I can't believe how much I got away with. I must have been going through ten bars of chocolate some days. Every now and then Mum would say:

*"We're going to have to watch this. We should be making more profit than this – something's not right."*

Nobody pointed the finger at me and I could eat loads of chocolate in one go, and then eat my tea as well. If I told Mum now just how much I was eating then I'm sure it would dawn on her how fat I was getting on rice, peas and chicken. Winston and Noel took bits as well but I was prolific. Hardly a criminal mastermind, but a world class and dedicated choc nicker. .

At one time we used to help in the shop every day, but eventually Mum kept me out when she had a suspicion just how many sweets I was nicking. I think my last chance was when I was in the shop one day and this bloke called Terry Miles was talking to my mum. Out of the corner of his eye Terry saw me nick a Bounty Bar and hoof it out of the shop. He shouted:

*"May, Herol's just shot off down the street with a chocolate bar!"*

Terry ran down Guthrie Street after me but even though I was fat I was still pretty quick. I was too fast for Terry who, as a navy guy, was no slug himself. Eventually he gave up chasing me and went back to May and gasped:

*"He's bombed off!"*

And so a nickname was born.

People think that 'Bomber' was a manufactured boxer's name, a name to depict fast shots, or a name I came up with - but not so. It was Terry who first called me the 'Black Bomber'.

♦

When I look back on my life, I realise that some pretty important things happened to me when I was eight years old. Things that would have a lasting effect on what I was going to do and the person I was going to be for the rest of my life.

I was a happy kid and we all liked where we lived. Radford was okay, it was quite a big area and on the whole it was cool. There wasn't a lot of trouble at all. Like any town or city there were little gangs wandering around but nothing really nasty. Through my childhood I had generally happy memories there … in the main. Every child faces demons or trolls of some sort now and then, but usually when they're asleep. But the demon I faced was horribly real.

As I got more into sport I used to run around the block a few times every day. Mum didn't worry about me because she always knew that I wouldn't go further away from our block and it was pretty safe around there. There was a man who lived just across the road from us and he used to watch me running past his house and often told me how well I was doing. He was a friendly man and was always nice to us. And all the encouragement I was getting kept making me feel stronger and want to run further and faster.

This particular man befriended me more and more and as he knew I helped Mum in the shop he asked me if I wanted to do some little jobs for him. And, like most eight year olds, I was keen to help. He asked me if I wanted to do some cleaning and I said:

*"Yeah, yeah I'll do some cleaning Mister."*

When I went inside his house it turned out that it wasn't cleaning he wanted me to do.

♦

When you're an adult you think you're strong enough to talk about something like this without crying, but you aren't. As I tell you this now, my eyes are filling up with tears.

Little kids have amazing imaginations; they have incredible and wonderful dreams and they can have vivid nightmares. If your little one tells you about his dream you listen to every fantastic detail of his story with a loving smile. If he tells you about his nightmare you cuddle him and tell him that it's all gone away now because he's awake – and he's safe in your arms. But what if the demon won't go away?

Eight year olds should be playing marbles, learning rhymes, drawing pictures and singing songs. They should be running in the park, learning to ride a bike, going to school with their friends, trying to make their Mum and Dad proud.

Eight year olds should be looking forward to Christmas; they should be learning how to share. They should be breaking their toys, learning how to mend them, they should be getting dirty and scuffing their knees, on which Mum can put a plaster and make it better.

Eight year olds should be eating fish fingers and baked beans and then ice cream, and trying to keep it all on the plate or in their mouths. They love fish fingers but they don't know how they turn from a fish to a box of fish fingers, but it doesn't really matter. For an eight year old, nothing like this should matter too much. Life will throw all manner of triumphs and troubles at you from when you are in your teens to old age. Adults have day to day pressures that children don't, and shouldn't have the faintest idea about. For eight year olds life should be about excitement, security, fun and discovery.

This man raped me. He's dead now and I'm not. But either way, eight year olds should not be fighting a demon.

# 3

# <u>Growing Pains</u>

## Nottingham, 1968

### *"I never think I have hit hard, unless it rebounds."*

## Samuel Johnson

It's very hard for a child of eight to understand why someone who is much older would want to hurt them. And it's very hard to come to terms with this type of horror. As I look back now I know that what happened affected me profoundly, but at the time, like any small child I simply felt frightened and confused. I told my mum what had happened and tried to explain it as well as I could. And it was clear that I had been crying. But there was something at the time that made people push certain things under the carpet, not through lack of concern, but simply because people didn't, and sometimes still don't know how to cope with the most difficult things in life. I knew Mum and Dad loved me and I needed them more than ever, and they were there for me. But nothing was ever said again.

I can trace an awful lot of things that have happened through my life back to when I was eight. It isn't just the terrible thing that happened, but there were good things happening too, that were going to help me determine the path I could eventually go down. And for every bad man in the world there are a hundred good men, and I was lucky enough to be looked out for by one of the best. I had strong moral guidance and schooling from Mum and Dad but they weren't all that interested in the physical side of things. They were too busy, in all honesty, looking after all us kids, holding a job down and running a business. And it was all that Mum could do to keep my rapidly escalating chocolate habit in some kind of check.

I came to realise that the guy who had nicknamed me 'Bomber' after he'd chased me down the street when I nicked the Bounty bar was a close family friend.

Terry Miles was a top bloke. He was a lieutenant in the Royal Navy and was really fit and had an impressive appearance, tall and slim, with smart light coloured hair; and he looked imposing in his Navy uniform. He used to go to a gym near us and one day he suggested to Mum that I could come down with him. I guess he could see that for an eight year old I'd grown a pretty big stomach, but on the other hand, he had first hand experience of just how quick I was. I didn't know at the time that he was my godfather but he had taken me under his wing. When he was on leave he used to take me to the park to run around or play football, which was great because Mum and Dad didn't have the time. And I was happy when he said that I could go down to his gym with him. He told me that it had a boy's boxing club there and that was even more exciting to me. At the time we had a small black and white television in the lounge and one of my first memories was seeing Muhammad Ali, or Cassius Clay as he was then. I saw him skipping around the ring with a smile on his face, while the guy he was fighting was chasing him, swinging at him and getting slower and slower. I was completely mesmerised. I wanted to do that and I said to myself that one day I would.

When I was eight I knew what I had to do to get out of being a fat kid - and it was literally by doing more exercise and training. Terry thought it would do me some good and help me to lose some weight if I started boxing as part of my training. He could see I had plenty of mischief in me, and thought that boxing would give me some discipline, which as a military man, he was well qualified to judge. In any case, despite my tubby gait, I was already pretty sporty anyway. By the time I was eight I was frequently running around the block ten or fifteen times a day, which I guess if I hadn't I'd have been the size of a house.

So Terry knew that I'd more than likely respond to a physical challenge. Sometimes when we were out walking down the street Terry would see a car and shout 'Chase it!' to me, which I did, not realising at the time that that was a pastime more commonly enjoyed by dogs!

One weekend Terry took me along to a gym called Radford Boys Boxing Club, attached to the White Horse pub. The gym was about a mile away so we could walk it and I was fascinated, not knowing what to expect. But when we arrived and Terry took me into the boys club I was a bit underwhelmed to be honest. It was much smaller than I'd imagined and kind of dark with a musty smell. It was just about the size of a decent living room. One side of the gym was entirely taken up by a fourteen foot boxing ring and along the other side there were six punch bags. And that's all there was there.

The gym was run by three brothers, Roy, Alan and Frank. Their sons came down to train and box along with about six other kids. The three of them had all been in the army, so they had a military background and that kind of aura that goes with it. Frank did a lot of the coaching but Roy was in charge and Alan was always on hand to offer advice.

Roy told me to get in the ring and my heart began to race, but it soon slowed down. He handed me a skipping rope and told me to get going, so I started by doing some skipping as well as I could, which was kind of, 'right yeah okay'. I was getting a bit bored of that and wondering whether boxing was actually the thing for me, when after about twenty minutes we started to do some hitting on the bags. Better. But the bags were big heavy things and I was starting to get a bit tired of that when the real fun started. Roy tapped me on the shoulder and said:

*"Right Herol, let's see how you do with a bit of sparring."*

Fantastic. Roy laced some gloves on me and I climbed through the ropes. This was it; Muhammad Ali has arrived in the ring! But instead of Smokin' Joe Frazier or even a kid my size I was faced by old man Frank who had a pair of pads on his hands. So I launched myself at him and for the first time I heard the true passion and adrenalin of a boxing man in the ring. Right from the off, Frank was barking instructions at me:

"*'Keep your hands up Herol, go on hit them, fucking hit them! Go on, go on.'*

Which was easier said than done, because the gloves I had on were the size of balloons and weighed a ton. Gloves only benefited from new technology about ten years later when Rays came out in the late seventies, and then technology advanced so quickly that the speed of boxing increased dramatically in the eighties. But in 1968 they were bloody huge to a little kid like me - about six pounds in weight and absolutely enormous.

But despite the comedy gloves I'd loved the whole experience, and I pestered Terry to take me back to do some more, and he, being the top man he was, took me back two days later. This time, after skipping and hitting the bags for half an hour or so, Frank told me to get in the ring to do some sparring with one of the other boys, a lad called Mick. This was the first chance of my life to see if I could have a go and do the things that I had seen Ali do on the black and white telly. I hadn't had any formal boxing training like the other boys there; some of them had been boxing since they were six. So I did what I always did - I just made it up. I stepped into the ring with my balloons attached to the end of my arms and wandered over towards Mick. Straight away he had a couple of hits at me but they both missed. I could see them coming, and moved my head quickly enough to get out of the way. Other than Mum and Dad, with the back of their hand, no one had ever hit me before, and while I wouldn't dare get out of the way of a rebuke from them, this was purely instinctive. And when I hit back at Mick I connected. This was brilliant, I started to dance around the ring like I'd seen Ali doing and as I looked around the gym I noticed that Roy had stopped his training and had joined Frank watching us spar. I was having a great time, I'd found my feet and I was zipping around the ring and occasionally catching Mick with a punch. For his part Mick had a few swings at me but when Frank called us out after three minutes I hadn't been hit once. Roy put his hand on my head and said:

*"You are coming back again aren't you?'*

I don't think that Frank and Roy had ever seen anyone move around the ring so quickly and be able to land some punches without getting hit. And it wasn't as if I was a small target at that stage. All my instinct that I'd used now and then on the streets of Nottingham in avoiding getting hit had come into play in a fourteen foot boxing ring. In a ring you can't run off around the corner, so you have to be more agile within a close area. Over the next few weeks I learned quickly to move my neck around in a circle, which allowed me to stay firm on my feet and move the six or so inches you need to avoid a punch.

In the gym we did some exercises to help strengthen our neck muscles and the health and safety guys that are around these days would have had heart failure if they had seen what we did. Basically, all we were told to do was to arch our backs and put our heads on the floor, with the neck taking most of your weight. If you slipped you could break your neck, which was a distinct possibility with the amount of sweat on the floor! Suffice to say it's not standard practice for eight year olds any more.

But my neck stayed intact and a few weeks after my first sparring session with Mick they put me in with a lad called Andrew Tarr – and he was a real hard nut. He was a proper fighter and about two years older than me and he was the hardest lad I'd come across in my eight years. But I wasn't too frightened. Terry was often there watching and encouraging me and in any case Frank and Roy always had good control of the place, and made sure that kids didn't get hurt. If someone was struggling or someone was dishing out a lot of pain they'd step in very quickly. So I knew that the very worst thing that could happen to me was that he'd hit me a few times and I'd get pulled out.

But he didn't. In fact he didn't hit me at all. And as the three minutes went on Andrew got more and more frustrated, you could almost see steam coming out of his nostrils. I had started dancing around with my hands down by my side like I'd seen Ali do, while Frank was shouting:

*"Get your fucking hands up!"*

So I did now and then to hit Andrew. I was a good mimic and a good copier and I was doing my best to copy Ali. And, combined with that, I didn't want to get hit. I hated getting hit because it hurts, and you have to be a special kind of idiot to like that.

Every now and then I did get hit in sparring but I always said to myself, 'you're not going to get me next time.'

♦

I kept at the boxing and I really loved the sport. Terry could see how well I was getting on and as I was putting more effort and energy into my boxing I was putting less effort into nicking and eating chocolate so the fat gradually fell away from me. And by the time I was eleven I was pretty lean. The guys at the gym didn't really advise us what to eat it had just happened to me as, at the age of eight, I had found a new hobby that helped me to lose weight rather than put it on! Roy just told us to look after ourselves, and Mum made sure I was eating well. She did all the cooking at home and had a never ending variety of combinations of chicken and rice and peas.

The thing that had got me out of the whole fat thing was the boxing gym. And from the very first day I went boxing at the age of eight I made sure I was running round the block every day, and soon I was running half an hour at a time. As my weight just dropped off me I don't think my family could believe that I was sticking to my new way of living with such determination. I had learned a lesson that anybody could. Roy and Frank, Terry and my parents could help me and advise me but, at the end of the day, you can only really do something like that for yourself.

♦

Mum and Dad could see that I was growing up; I was sticking to my training and getting into soul music. I still love that now. But we didn't have a lot of soul music in the house. Mum and Dad were very religious. Dad was a lay preacher and not all that long ago he went back to university to do a theology degree. So naturally most of the music in the house was religious and gospel rather than Jamaican reggae and English soul.

Discipline was still pretty firm and I knew exactly what constituted pushing my luck. If I was supposed to be in at nine o 'clock and I came in at ten then that was certainly pushing my luck. But it didn't stop me. One Friday November evening I lost track of time and I turned up at ten. Mum and Dad had already gone to bed but I didn't know how I could get in the house if they knew I'd come home late. So I just waited and waited. And waited. I didn't go in because I was too scared, but on the other hand I was freezing cold. That was kind of stupid, but I was still stood outside at midnight. Deep inside I knew what was going to happen when I eventually got in. I tried to wake Noel up by throwing stones up to the window and eventually he appeared at the window:

*"What the hell are you doing Herol?. It's after midnight!"*
*"Shhhh! I know, help me in."*

Noel hung out of the window and dragged me up and in, shaking his head as I quietly climbed into bed. Had I got away with it?

Less than two minutes later there was a knock on the door and I jumped out of bed in a flash. Dad walked over to me, dragged me out of the room and then BAM, BAM, BAM.

*"Aaaaaagh ....I'm sorry Dad .... I won't do it again."*

Dad looked after us with a firm hand and Mum was just as tough, so there wasn't a whole load of respite for anyone who wanted to be naughty and do their own stuff. And I learned pretty quickly that I couldn't play one off against the other. Mum would hit me for something and then when Dad came home and I told him he'd ask:

*'What's that got to do with me?'*

And then he'd hit me again for bringing him into it.

He always used to say to us:

*'If you have trouble you deal with it. And if you bring trouble I will deal with you. If you listen you'll feel. If you don't listen to me you'll feel what I'm going to do.'*

And as we got older and cockier and started to say,

*'yeah, yeah, yeah'*

we still got hit, he'd say:

*'Well, I did warn you.'*

All in all it was pretty clear.

Mum and Dad were very devout and we all went to church every Sunday. So swearing in the house was a big 'no no'. And I usually managed to keep my mouth clean because I knew how important it was to Mum. But as always in life you're bound to slip up somewhere along the way, and when it came to swearing I did so fairly spectacularly.

I was walking up the stairs one day without wearing my slippers and there was a drawing pin on the step. As I landed on it with my full weight and the pain shot up through my leg I let out a loud yelp of:

*"FUCK!"*

At which point Mum, doing her best Lenny Henry impression, appeared at the top of the stairs and shouted:

*"WHAAT did you say?"*

Before I could muster my answer Mum's shoe clattered off the top of my head.

*"Whaaat did you say, whaaaat did you say?"*

*"My FOOT"* I lied.

*"You liar!"* she confirmed as her other shoe sailed down towards my head like a keenly trained guided missile.

I didn't even bother trying to pull the wool over Dad's eyes. Quick learner!

At the time I was in a little gang in the Radford area. My best mate was Gary, a mischievous guy who had a little brother called Glen, and we spent a fair amount of time together. They lived next door to us and we played a lot with a boy called Keith. All my mates were white, largely because we were one of only two black families in the area, along with Dad's brother's clan. We never had any trouble and me and my mates never thought about the colour of our skin – just the stuff we could do to have fun. Obviously, against the backdrop of increasing immigration there was some racial suspicion around in the sixties, but we never had any bother.

We got in some fights with other gangs but even then, on the street, I didn't get hit much at all. Once I'd been hit once we usually ran away. I was pretty cool about it, I didn't get upset when I was hit, I just didn't particularly like it and couldn't see the point of sticking my face in the way when I didn't have to. Rather than get hit twice, brighter kids run away and don't get caught. And if you could land a couple of nice hits as well then that's a win all round!

We lived near to the Raleigh bike factory where Mum used to work part time and sometimes we climbed over the walls to see if we could get some bikes, but with limited success. A few years later they got some proper security in there, but at that time, if you jumped on to the six foot wall you could just flip over. There was no CCTV and the night guard was invariably reading his copy of Razzle with too much concentration for him to spot any wrongdoings as we stumbled, sniggering, in to the yard. Because Mum worked there I had a bit of inside information and we knew where the bikes were stored. But we couldn't get to them, let alone get them back over the wall.

So we branched out and started nicking bikes from off the streets and changing them over, changing and painting them, and then selling them or keeping them for ourselves. We never got caught. But Mum was getting wise to me. When I brought one bike home she asked:

*"Where did you get that from?"*

*"I bought it."*

*"What with, you haven't got any money?"*

I realised my answers were getting less convincing the bigger the hole I dug:

*"Well, I kind of made it!"*

But Mum kept coming back to me asking where it was from. I think she kind of knew and was just letting me know that in her own way. As I was getting older it wasn't just a case of getting a whack. Mum started to make me think. So that was the end of that particular enterprise. I got away with it but looking back it's a good job that I had boxing to pull me away from the naughty stuff.

♦

By the time I was twelve I was old enough to get my first amateur fight, against a guy called Nick Lee who was from Leicester. It was one of the most exciting things to happen to me in my short life and when Roy told me I'd got the fight I was on top of the world. It was in three weeks time and Roy told me I had to work hard and be absolutely ready. I was really ecstatic but I didn't go to tell Mum and Dad straight away. They were always kind of supportive, but in all honesty they weren't really interested in my boxing. Terry was the man who had pushed me down this route. Mum and Dad were keen to know I was okay and studying hard and learning to be a good man, but boxing just wasn't their thing. It isn't fair to say they weren't at all interested but they weren't outwardly so. They had always made it clear that they'd rather I went to college.

I'd never heard of Mick Lee, as he was a Leicester lad and that was a long way away from Nottingham there was no reason why I should have. Roy told me he was about the same age as me but with a bit more experience, he'd already had four fights and, by all accounts, he wasn't half bad.

I did what Roy told me and went to the gym almost every day for the next three weeks, and carried on running, sometimes an hour at a time. And when the night of the fight came I was desperate to get started. I was so proud to be fighting and representing Radford Boys. I loved it at Radford. The previous year, while Terry was away, I had briefly been to Nottingham Boys because someone told me they had a better gym, but I quickly came back to Radford. Nottingham was different, not as tight as Radford and I only stayed for a few months. So I was representing Radford when I got my first fight.

Roy and Alan drove us down from Nottingham in an old minibus full of all the lads from Radford. Andrew Tarr was fighting as well so there were two of us from our club on the bill.

We arrived in Leicester and made our way into an old civic hall and I stared wide eyed at the scene in front of me. There was a boxing ring in the middle of the hall and about a hundred people sat around it. This was a new experience for me to have so many people watching and it gave me an enormous buzz. You could smell the atmosphere, quite literally.

There were 12 fights on the bill, all of three rounds, which were scheduled for three minutes, two, or one and a half. Because I was one of the young ones my fight was three rounds of one and a half minutes and it was pretty early on. The organisers always put the youngest fighters on first because they didn't want the apprehension to get to us, and the sixteen year olds could cope with that better. I did feel nervous. And as I watched the first fighters enter the ring the butterflies arrived. The first two bouts seemed to pass quickly and I physically jumped when I heard my name:

*"Bout three representing Leicester Boys, Nick Lee, and representing Radford Boys, Her...Herol Graham!"*

As I climbed in to the ring I looked around and saw all the faces of grown ups and kids watching the fight and my heart was going 'Boom Boom'. I felt the part. I was wearing the Radford club colours of blue satin shorts with a big blue stripe down the sides. Other than that it was just the massive gloves and a gum shield. Although it looked big to me, it wasn't actually such a big hall and so it was a packed house and as we were on his territory Nick had a loud backing. Roy, Alan and Frank were in my corner and that was a comfort for sure. Even though I was in a different city, where I had never been, I had all the familiarity I needed with the three guys there who I had known for four years and trusted implicitly. They were all different the way they worked and the way they looked. Roy was skinny with a keen and critical hardness, Alan was considered and insightful, and Frank was a big guy and a loud and passionate motivator. As I sat in the corner Alan put his hands on either side of my head and quietly said:

*"Just go out and do what you do the best son."*

The bell went, I stood up and thankfully my legs didn't buckle. Nick was a good fighter and backed by his local supporters came straight over to me and aimed a jab. And missed. I moved in time. That was it, I could start to do my thing now and even at that young age I wanted to show the purest of boxing. Nick could box as well but soon I was just moving around him and jabbing and jabbing. By the end of the first round I had forgotten about the people watching and I was full of confidence, but not cocky. As the fight continued I carried on moving and moving. I wasn't being flash, I had my hands up, but I was moving quickly and although it was a good contest, by the end I had enjoyed the fight more than I had hoped. In the third round some people in the crowd were starting to applaud me and my corner was praising me and eventually I won by a unanimous decision. Frank gave me a big hug and one of the Leicester coaches came over to me and told me I boxed great while some guy took a photo.

So that was it. On that 1972 night in Leicester surrounded by middle aged, sweaty blokes sporting some pretty ace comb overs, I decided for sure what I wanted to do. I wanted to be a boxer.

The following day as I put on my school uniform I came back down to earth pretty quickly, but back at school my mind was still in the civic hall in Leicester. And when I got home from school and dropped my bag in the hallway Noel stuck his head round the door, grinned and said:

*"Hey Herol - I've seen you in the newspaper already. You're in the Post!"*

♦

Over the next year I got a few more fights but then all of a sudden it started to become harder. I had gained a reputation for being a quick mover and as a south paw pretty awkward, so it became more complicated for me to get fights even at that early age. This was something that from time to time was going to plague me throughout my career. I was unbeaten for the first 20 fights and I think some coaches kept their kids away from me, because they didn't really know how to box a different kind of fighter. I was too hard to hit.

I managed to get championships and medal fights because guys wouldn't avoid me there, because if you want to get a championship you have to fight. So within a couple of years it was mainly in championships that I fought.

And I liked getting in the newspaper and having my photo taken. Every fight I had I appeared in the Nottingham Post in that week and I always made sure I got a copy. And with my new purpose in life, I was training hard and eating well. I still had a craving for chocolate but I also had a new discipline and all my weight had gone. And there was a big part of me that believed that no one could hurt me as long as I learned to box and to defend myself properly.

Mum and Dad could see that I was getting a buzz from what I was doing as well as getting in the newspaper. They were appreciative of my progress and would say 'well done' but always insist that they wanted me to go to university. It wasn't long before I started to say:

*"I don't want to do that. I want to box."*

♦

When I was thirteen I got a job on the market in Nottingham on a stall that sold pots and pans and cups and saucers and all that kind of stuff. It was owned by a guy called Jack Lee and I was mates with his younger brother, Philip. He'd become a good friend of mine since I went to senior school and he got me the job down there. I worked there for about six months, every Saturday, and it was good fun. It was a chance for me to see all types of people from all walks of life that came to the stall, all with one thing in common – they were looking for a bargain. You could get good stuff off the market at a fraction of the price on the High Street. It was a good crack – and by the time I'd finished, there were some good cracks on the cups as well!

I went to Cottismore Comprehensive, which wasn't a bad old place; it was big and pretty typical of nineteen seventies comprehensives I guess. I carried on with my sports at Cottismore, playing football but more often rugby where I represented the school at sevens as an inside centre. The highlight of my rugby career was when we beat the posh kids at Nottingham High, which we really wanted to do. They were a real rugby school, but we had this lad called Alonso, and he was awesome. He was like Jonah Lomu, about a foot taller than everyone else, a yard faster and if anyone got near him he could swat them away like a fly. The Nottingham High kids shit themselves when they saw him! It was a fantastic victory but it proved, on the back of Alonso, to be the pinnacle of my rugby career.

While I was still training regularly at my boxing, Mum and Dad kept on telling me to work hard at school as well. They were keen for me to go on to further education and I appreciated why. They were working so hard that they didn't want any of us to waste our lives doing this or that.

I was quite well behaved at school, mainly I think because of the discipline that Mum and Dad had already instilled. And I certainly didn't want to get a whack at school because I knew that the chances were I'd get another one at home. Or maybe even two! And in any case I liked school, it was okay.

And despite my obsession with boxing, I didn't get into many fights at all. In all honesty the one or two I did get into were completely unspectacular. There was this one guy, David Sketchley, a quiet boy, and I saw that he was having an argument with another lad. I stuck my nose in and he stuck it back out! Fair enough, I wasn't needed there, but to my surprise, David ignored his initial argument and turned his attention to me. He wasn't a big lad, but he was a bit bigger than me as he was in the year above. After a minor scuffle he pinned me down to the floor and I couldn't get up. He was really strong which is probably why he went for me. After a short stand off where I waited patiently for a whack my mate, Patrick, persuaded him to get off me.

There were a few fights at school but with the exception of Sketchley's technical knockout I wasn't involved in any of them. I just watched them with a passing interest - I wasn't a big fighter by any stretch of the imagination.

When I was thirteen I turned my attention to the girls, and found my first girlfriend in a grocery shop across the road from Radford swimming baths. Her name was Michelle Smith and she was older than me with long blonde hair. She was very pretty. But like most people's first loves I guess, it was quite a fleeting romance. It turned out Michelle had a thing for boxers and she was soon going out with Andrew Tarr. That lasted a lot longer; in fact, I think they may even have got married.

But undeterred by my swift rebuff from Michelle I continued with my strategy of developing my skills as a lover, in case the fighting didn't work. Mum and Dad were still determined that I'd go on to be an academic of some sort, but that was looking increasingly unlikely. I was doing okay at school but not pulling up any trees.

I didn't have any serious girlfriends until I'd made it into the fourth year, and by that time we could fish in a bigger pool and meet girls from other schools. And there was always that extra sense of danger and fun with girls from off our own patch, often fuelled by the rivalry between schools. Our biggest rivals were at a school nearby called Glenbott. It was quite a fierce rivalry between us but not a particularly violent one; there wasn't really a lot of trouble. The rivalry was more on an educational level between the senior teachers, and there was sports rivalry between the PE departments and then the base level rivalry between the kids. At Glenbott they thought they were better than us at everything. Our games field was on their school grounds so the rivalry was always visible. The fact that we had to travel from our school to theirs for games reinforced their upper hand the way they saw it. And they had a nice blue uniform, but we did our best to blend in because we hardly ever wore our black blazers.

We still didn't mix a lot with the kids at Glenbott but we did go to the same venues at the weekend. The nightclubs were happy to let us in on Fridays – there was more attention to an approximation to the age of consent than the legal drinking age. And so the heady cocktail of underage and inexperienced drinking by a hoard of hormone fuelled teenagers was a demographic time bomb!

One Friday night after a steady old week at school I was relaxing with Patrick in the biggest school kids' night spot, where we'd been going for a few weeks. And that was where I met Lilian. I can't say it was love at first sight because it was so dark that I couldn't see her face! But as my eyes became trained to the murkiness (and I had got closer) I saw that she was actually really lovely. I thought she had a beautiful kind of deep red skin, although that may have been the lights. She wasn't mixed race but she certainly had a darker complexion than Nottingham people, and she was extremely good looking, tall and slim with long black hair.

I got on well with Lilian and when we started going out I was pretty well pleased with myself. Over the next few months we got closer and closer and soon we were inseparable. We went to the clubs together, went down the shops together but most of all we used to go to each other's houses all the time just to mess around.

I loved going to Lilian's house, it was funny. All the settees and chairs were covered by throw-overs that her Mum had crocheted to adorn every piece of furniture in the house with. I can't honestly say that these crochet blankets were an aphrodisiac but when Lilian's parents were out, most of our lovemaking took place on something crocheted, largely because there wasn't anywhere comfortable in the house without one. They were very fashionable in the seventies and so I spent a lot of my relationship with Lilian sat on crochet.

I didn't mind it at all because I'd grown up with the West Indian commitment to cover anything with a doily, or something crocheted. It was a form of sanitation I guess. If we got a new chair Mum covered it with something that looked like a giant tablecloth. If we got a new table you couldn't put anything on it for doilies, and of course there was always the toilet roll with a weird woolly hat and a doll on top of it in the bathroom. Nowadays it's trendy to have a little basket of bog rolls in all their brazen exposure in the bathroom and you'd laugh if you saw one with a tea cosy on it. I'm sure in those days tea cosies were interchangeable if you could find a use for the spout hole.

Lilian and I had been seeing each other for ages when one cold February day, as we were walking to her house, talking about this and that, she dropped a cracker, in a very much 'by the way' sort of manner.

As we entered her Mum's living room Lilian said:

*"I'm pregnant."*

I sat down on a crocheted tablecloth with a striking sense of bewilderment:

*"You're pregnant?"*

*"I'm pregnant."*

*"You're pregnant."*

Confident that the message had reached home Lilian sat down next to me. I can't really remember what she said to me, but it didn't really matter – this was a bombshell on a weapons grade scale. Lilian and I had joined the legion of teenagers who had conceived on a crochet covered settee (probably).

♦

My parents and Lilian's knew of each other, but they weren't friends. And now, thanks to yours truly and Lilian, they discovered they had something of an involuntary bond.

I don't actually know when Lilian told her parents, no doubt her Mum dropped her crochet needle, but I thought better not to delay my task with Mum and Dad. Of course they were deeply religious people but they also knew the ways of the world. I picked my moment while the three of us were alone at our house. Mum was doing some ironing and Dad was reading the Nottingham Post. I took a deep breath:

*"Erm, Dad, I've got something to tell you."*

Dad peered over from the top of his newspaper.

*"Erm, I'm going to have a baby..... well Lilian is."*

Dad looked back down at the crossword and gave his considered opinion:

*"Oh right. Hmm, Hmm."*

Mum wasn't quite so laid back:

*"You whaat?"* she snapped with all the venom and speed of a cobra.

I was about to repeat my announcement, which probably wouldn't have gone down that well when Dad proffered, in a mildly conciliatory way:

*"I hope you can look after her and do the right thing"*

This seemed to aggravate Mum and she just carried on with her tirade:

*"YOU WHAAAT?"*

*"Do you want a drink of water?"* I asked uselessly, before sneeking off upstairs.

Actually, I thought that had gone as well as could be expected and I'd be in a lot more trouble than I was. Dad had taken it very calmly, and once Mum had got over the shock all she gave me was her love and support. There was never any blame or recrimination from either set of parents and we know we were lucky in that. Although I know that I, for one, would have struggled to cope with hassle from Mum and Dad at that moment.

I felt scared. And once the reality had hit home I was bloody terrified. Soon I was going to be sixteen years old and I was going to be a dad. Shit. Only eight years ago I was a little fat kid nicking chocolates, only four years ago I had my first ever boxing match in Leicester. Only a week ago I was foot loose and fancy free.

I knew that this whole thing was going to make a massive difference to me but I had no idea how. I was still at school, about to do my O – Levels the following year, and I know that Mum, in particular, would have been worried sick that I had lost my chance.

But I made up my mind that I would have to box to look after Lilian and our baby. I'd already decided a hundred times that boxing was what I wanted to do, and now I had a bloody good reason to go for it. This was actually a huge inspiration for me. It compelled me to take my life more seriously and it was my first real bit of growing up, a monumental turning point in my life. I went around seeing Lilian as much as I could. We were very close and our parents could see that, and that we were trying to be as mature about this as we could. Lilian's mum wasn't well at the time and she spent a lot of her day sat with her pregnant daughter. She often looked at me across the room and in a firm but kindly way she'd say:

*"I hope you're going to look after her Herol."*

This was quite a happy time of my life really. I never had the screaming rows and getting thrown out of the house stuff that many lads in my predicament had. It was all pretty calm. I managed to do my end of year exams and then through the Summer I carried on with my boxing and going round to check Lilian was okay. I had everything in reasonable control. It was better when I wasn't at school during the holidays, because I could train harder and spend more time with Lilian. This is where I saw my future, and I saw no reason why it couldn't work. By this time I still hadn't lost a fight.

♦

On 18th October 1976, Lilian's dad phoned our house to tell us that she had gone into labour. Dad wasn't at home at the time so I flew out of the door and ran, on my own, the two miles to Nottingham Infirmary. As I skidded into the hospital waiting area, a kind lady who must have guessed why I was there and looking in such a panic, pointed me in the right direction and I managed to find Lilian in the delivery room.

Minutes later our baby Natasha was born and I was there, holding Lilian's hand. Natasha was small, wrinkly, dusky, slimy and beautiful. That was the weirdest feeling in the world. I thought to myself, 'I'm a dad. I'm only sixteen and I'm a dad.' But suddenly I wasn't frightened any more. I was sort of relieved that this part of it was all over, and excited that the next stage of my life had just begun. I was a dad and for the first time in my life I had real responsibility. I was sixteen and I had a baby to look after, when I could barely look after myself!

I promised myself that I had to make the boxing work. I was so proud of Natasha and vowed to make sure she'd be okay. I was really proud of Lilian as well. This was a time when both of us had to grow up pretty quickly and I couldn't have had a better friend to do it with.

At that moment in the hospital you couldn't stop me smiling and I said:

*"Wait till I tell my Mum".*

I knew Mum and Dad would be worried for me, but happy too, and they would never let me down. Children were always looked after in our family, and this was Mum and Dad's first grandchild. So they were very proud as well.

This was the opposite end of the scale of emotion and understanding to the trauma I had when I was eight years old. I had all my family around me and, combined with becoming a dad myself, that gave me the strength to confront life and whatever it had to throw at me.

I was round at Lilian's house all the time and we tried together to make Natasha's first year as good as possible. In many ways it was easier for me, because I didn't have the sleepless nights or a lot of the messy stuff, but I did my best to help and be there for them both as much as I could. And when Natasha was two months old it was Christmas. This year was the first one for Natasha and the first for me as a dad so it was a bit different to normal, mainly in that I went round to Lilian's house in the morning, before returning home for Christmas dinner with my family and to listen to Winston taking the piss when Johnny Mathis appeared on the telly singing 'When a Child is Born'!

After I'd been to Lilian's it was a fairly normal Christmas back home. Christmases had always been manic in the Graham household. With six kids hurtling down the stairs in the morning the present opening was always a frenzy with shouts of 'you shouldn't have got that I should have got that ....' With six of us it was inevitable that someone would be annoyed because 'someone else's presents were better'. So there were always tantrums.

For Christmas dinner we did, of course, have rice and peas and chicken, but with a turkey as well. We had all the lot –

sprouts, sausages, carrots – but never without the chicken and peas and rice. We were miles ahead of these 21st century Masterchef types who cook one bird inside another for Christmas, a partridge inside a duck or something like that. The Grahams had a chicken and a turkey four decades ago! We were at the forefront.

The turkey always dried out but we ate it anyway. Mum used to say:

*"It's not easy to cook such a big bird in an oven."*

I wasn't sure where else she thought she might cook it, but thought better of asking. Everyone was used to dry turkey in those days, but we ate it all up with the chicken and gravy. And then we'd have dry turkey sandwiches for days and the carcass of the turkey and chicken was always used for soup.

♦

Over the next weeks and months I kept on seeing Lilian and watching Natasha becoming a proper fun baby. But it was never going to be a long relationship between us, despite how well we got on together. We were still only sixteen, and by now I spent more time in the gym or boxing than I did seeing Lilian. In the spring of 1977 we split up. Lilian got a new boyfriend and that was the end of our relationship, as boyfriend and girlfriend anyhow. We both had and understood our responsibility to Natasha, but for all our attempts at maturity, we were still kids ourselves. There were no bad feelings at all. It was cool.

I was still working reasonably hard at school but I spent all of my spare time at the gym. I'd been boxing competitively for three years by this stage and when I sat my O –level exams I did just about okay. Mum and Dad thought I could have done better, and I knew I could, but it just wasn't top of the list with a little baby and my boxing. There was much too much going on for a sixteen year old and I could only handle two priorities.

Mum used to say:

*"If you had spent as much time on your studies as you did on your boxing then...."*

But I had myself and Natasha to think about. Either way my mind had been made up. I didn't know how far boxing could take me, but at that very moment it seemed to be the best opportunity I had to make something of myself.

I had to finish school but all thoughts of going to university had long gone. I thought I had a way of making money through my boxing and my final year at school was lost amidst the trials and excitement of fatherhood and my focus to become a successful fighter.

Within a year I was off to Sheffield.

# 4

# <u>Ding Ding, Round One</u>

## Sheffield 1976

*"Some of my best friends are white boys. When I meet 'em, I treat 'em just the same as if they were people."*

## Ray Durem

Before I was seventeen I'd had seventy or eighty fights, and still hadn't lost any. I was still training down at the Radford Boys club and one of the lads I boxed with was an Irish boy called Kevin Sheehan. I was mates with both him and his brother. The Sheehans were part of a big Irish community that had moved over, very much like my parents, to find work and big swathes of Irishmen had settled within reach of the M1 where there was a lot of road and construction work available. And Kevin's family knew some of the Irish people up in Sheffield, and one day he told me of this trainer he knew:

*"Herol, there's this guy called Brendan, he's a good trainer, and he wants to see you. If you go over there you can stay at his house."*

I was kind of interested, so Kevin said he'd talk to Brendan and within a week I was packing my bags.

I went up to Sheffield on a cold September Sunday. It had been a lovely hot summer, the best I'd ever known, but by September that was all over and back to normal. The summer holidays had ended and I was looking for something to do and had made up my mind that I didn't want to go back to school. It was freezing when I went up to Brendan's place, the St

Thomas's Gym on Newman Road. I arrived, wrapped up in coat, scarf and hat and made my way inside.

When I stepped in I opened my eyes a little wider. This really was a boxing gym. I'd got used to Radford, but this one was for men and not boys. It was at least four times the size, with loads more bags and weights, and a smart ring. It still smelt of sweat and graft but it was definitely a step up for me. Brendan welcomed me over:

*"Lads, this is Herol. He's come all the way up from a small town called Nottingham. A little birdie tells me he can box so he's going to work with us today."*

Brendan had kept a few of his lads behind to wait for me because he knew I'd be there in the afternoon. So after I'd got changed and hit a few bags for a while he called me over to step in with one of the boys, a lad called Mick Mills. He was a tough looking bloke, solid and with a mean face. So I stepped in and went to shake hands.

Mick looked me up and down and then we started. He began with a regimented stance, with his hands up and a very tight guard, and that didn't change for the ten minutes I was in with him. Mick was pugnacious in his fighting and threw plenty of jabs, but not many connected, and he kept his guard up, just like you see on those boxing photos from the fifties and sixties. For my part, I just did my thing. I moved around, kept on spinning him and tapped him, more and more as the sparring went on. I was getting just the same bemused response that I'd had when I started out back in Radford all those years ago and when I had my first fight in Leicester.

I carried on moving around the ring with my hands all over the place saying to myself, 'this is easy, this is easy,' and Mick looked over to Brendan and said:

*"Fucking hell – what's he fucking doing?'*

They'd never seen anything like it. All of the other three lads I sparred with that day fought in the same way as Mick, hands up and tight guard. I knew in my own mind exactly what I was doing. I was moving around like my hero Muhammad Ali did, and I was picking my shots when I wanted to. Brendan watched me like a hawk and saw how I got out of the way of shots. I still hated getting hit so I did everything I could to make sure that I didn't. Particularly by Mick, because if he landed one then I knew it would hurt. By the end of the session Mick was absolutely shattered. I was tired but I could still keep moving. Mick had worked overtime to stay with me while I just did my normal job.

As we climbed out of the ring Brendan pulled me over and said:

*"Son, if I trew a handful of stones at you, you'd get out of the way of the fucking lot! If I had a handful of pebbles I couldn't touch you with a single one."*

There was another lad there called Robert Wakefield and Brendan told me to get in the ring and have a go with him. He looked a better boxer to me than Mick. He could clearly look after himself but there was more thought and art in what he was doing. You could see when he boxed that he wasn't just after a scrap, he wanted to score points, and he was clever in the way he did it. When we started sparring I soon realised that he was harder to hit than Mick and, as it turned out, any of the others there. He wasn't as tough or as strong but he was a better boxer.

As I sparred with Robert I had to think more, and work a little harder but I didn't mind that. When I sparred with the scrappers I didn't have to think as much, just do my thing. Of course, I had to keep my wits about me and make bloody sure I didn't get hit. When I was in with Mick he had swung shots at me relentlessly and hadn't stopped for minutes on end, so I had to keep moving. But I didn't mind that either because working was my thing, ever since I'd been running round the block in Nottingham I had never stopped moving.

Robert and Mick were both bright lads but they were both blessed with more strength than speed. If you stood still they'd knock you out, so it was a no brainer for me …. keep on moving. I just had to work a little harder to hit Robert. My thinking was he had to try to get me, but I was going to get him first … that's always how it's going to be. Why should I stand in front of anyone with a tight guard and hope that it will stand up to their strength. That's just stupid.

I had sailed a bit close to the wind as I hopped around the ring with Mick or Robert in pursuit. They didn't hit me and when I found the gap, at first I just tapped them on the shoulder. That really pissed them off. Mick said:

*"Fucking hell Herol, why didn't you just hit me?"*

But right from the start I was just playing my own cheeky game of cat and mouse. The stakes were higher the longer I went on and the angrier Mick got, because if I lost concentration and let him get near me he'd probably have buried me!

During the afternoon I sparred for about half an hour or maybe forty five minutes in total. After Mick and Robert I sparred with another two and I enjoyed that just as much. But then I always enjoy it. They were hard men too but they just couldn't hit me. They were fighting just the same as Mick and Robert. When I had them knackered I went in and 'Bing!' – session over.

At the end of the sparring session Brendan came up and said to me:

*"You're staying up here with me son."*

We'd sort of provisionally arranged for me to stay if I wanted to. But there was no way I was going back home to Nottingham now. I'd taken a big step up, sparred with four hard men, including Mick Mills, who was Brendan's biggest hope, and I had absolutely loved it. So the following week I moved in with Brendan and his family.

I went back that evening to Nottingham to pack my bags and say 'so long' to Mum and Dad, and they were really cool about it. When I told them I was going to Sheffield they said:

*"Oh really?*

But I'd already gone.

♦

I didn't really know anything about Brendan Ingle. Kevin Sheehan just told me he was a good trainer and it would be a great step for me to be trained by him. Apparently he didn't have a boxing background. Kevin told me that when Brendan lived in the Wincobank part of Sheffield the local catholic priest had asked him to do some local community work because the youth in the area were running wild. So a few years previously he had set up St Thomas's as a lads and girls club. So I guessed he was well in with the church and lived by the church's code.

I never really found out how Brendan came to leave Ireland for Yorkshire. He was part of a very big family over there and I think he was a businessman of some kind. Someone had told me that when he left Ireland he went to Doncaster at first, but he mustn't have liked it there because, while there was an Irish community in Doncaster who knew his family, he didn't stay there for long and decided instead to set up in Sheffield. He should have gone there in the first place and saved the hassle of moving twice.

He seemed like a friendly sort of bloke and looked like everyone's uncle, unless you're black of course. He had a genial smile and an easy way about him. And as Mum and Dad would have thought, he was well in with the church so there was no reason that I should doubt that he was the right man to look after me.

There were five children already in the house, Brendan Junior, Dominic, John, Bridget and Tara. It was a nice house but it wasn't so big and I shared a room with Brendan Junior. Not such a big change for me there then.

I settled in quite quickly. All the family were okay with me and pretty soon it felt like home. The only big difference I noticed to life back in Nottingham was at mealtimes. Their meals were certainly a departure from what I'd been used to.

In my new home I was eating normal English family food. We had shepherds pie, fish and chips, sausage and mash and stuff like that most of the time. Quite often we had peas, and sometimes on a Sunday we had chicken. In fact, sometimes we had chicken and peas. But we never had rice with the peas and the chicken. In fact, I don't think we had rice at all, just loads of potatoes. Potato after potato, and soon it dawned on me that potato was their national dish. And we often had a cup of tea with our meals. Brendan always told me to be careful what I was drinking:

*"Herol, don't drink too much water, it's not good for you."*

He was a keen nutritionist. So, no matter how much salt we had on our fish and chips and potatoes I tried not to drink too much water.

But I was very grateful that they had taken me in and for the food in front of me, however different it was from what I was used to. No matter what we ate though, it didn't make me feel any different; at sixteen your body will take food in any form.

And whichever family you're in, it's always a great feeling being in a family, particularly at mealtime. Mrs Ingle was a lovely lady to be in charge of this family. And I'm sure she was a good cook at what she cooked! It was all plain, nothing fancy, but then it was the nineteen seventies and we didn't need anything fancy. And, more importantly for the kids it was like clockwork. Half an hour after I came in there was a meal ready for me on the table and I couldn't ask for more. She had all her own children to look after and she was taking on another without a word of complaint. I had wondered how the conversation between Brendan and Mrs Ingle might have gone when he broke the news that he was bringing me home. But she always made me feel welcome and told me to treat the home as my own. And she was a busy woman, not just with the kids, she also worked at the gym, doing the cleaning and washing and other stuff and as well as that she did some voluntary work at the church. She was no Nigella Lawson but she was cool.

Even so it was still kind of a bit weird. This was the first time I'd left home. Even though I already had my own daughter, I was still a kid myself, and leaving Mum and Dad in Nottingham was a big thing. And it's amazing how many cultural differences there are between families and nationalities. I was born in England, but I had a very West Indian type upbringing. My Mum and Dad had brought their culture to the UK and hadn't really changed it. They had merely adapted it to living in a different place. People are comfortable when they live how they always have, so the rice and peas and chicken served to remind them of the sunny place. But they did adapt. And you could go in any West Indian house in the country and see the same things, crocheted blankets, doilies and a Sunday room that was kept clean and you only went into after church. If we bought a new sofa the plastic wrapping would stay on for about six months, such was Mum's obsession with keeping things nice.

But I guess many English households were just the same, certainly the décor, maybe with a few less covers but basically the same. And in England the same type of food had been around for decades without really evolving.

So in 1976 a move from a West Indian family in Nottingham to an Irish family in Sheffield was a much bigger change for me than the thirty miles up the road represented.

My biggest problem was with the Irish dialect. At first I couldn't understand a word they were saying and it took me a while to catch on to the strong Irish brogue. The whole family spoke like that. But then again I sometimes had a struggle with some of the Yorkshire speech in the early days. Whenever someone said to me *'Tha knows'* I wondered what was wrong with my nose. And when I asked what the problem was, did I have snot hanging out or something they just said *'gee oer'*. Wasn't that Winnie the Pooh's donkey?

Just to compound matters, one day a Scottish guy came down to the gym and this was the first time I'd heard anyone say, *'ken?'* instead of *'you know'*. So it went:

*"It's a fucking good gym, ken".*

*"It's Herol."*

*"Aye, ken."*

*"No, it's Herol."*

It would have gone on for days if he hadn't got bored and walked off.

But all the people I met were very friendly. It was easy for me to make friends as everyone seemed willing to talk to newcomers. As I walked down the road people would say, *'good morning'* and I'd say *'are you talking to me?'* I must have sounded like a black Robert de Niro. But once I'd got used to it, I thought it was nice and it definitely helped me to settle in. They were mega friendly, even the boxers, and I guess that's why I still live here three decades later. In the early days the bus drivers would take me to wherever I was going, even if I didn't have the right money. I've since discovered that in London they won't take you to where you're going no matter how much money you have. So it's the North for me every time.

♦

For the first seven or eight weeks I went back to Sheffield to see Natasha and Lilian every week. And I went to see Mum and Dad too. I really missed them all at first, but as I became more settled in Sheffield I started to leave it for a month, then two months and eventually it became a few months at a time before I went back. I don't feel proud about that, but by then I was still only seventeen and I hadn't completely grown up.

At first Lilian came up to Sheffield as well for a few days in the holidays, and as I went down at the weekends we saw plenty of each other. But that got less and less too, and so our contact slowly dwindled.

I had things to do. I was training for championships and Brendan was working me hard. Sometimes I got up at four in the morning to go running, and by the weekend I was very tired. It was tough work and the days were very long. And Lilian was busy too. She was looking after Natasha while she was studying at college. Her parents helped her out, but she didn't have much spare time, and I guess she was pretty exhausted most of the time too. It must have been hard for them. And maybe I should have made more effort to keep in touch.

But as you go through life sometimes you don't understand exactly what makes you do things. There are things I think about still now which can really upset me, and when I look back I had been through quite a lot at an early age, and I just don't know whether that had made me tougher or more vulnerable.

♦

I got pretty well known almost as soon as I arrived in Sheffield because Brendan had got me fighting straight away. I'd already been boxing in competitions for four years so I was definitely ready. It was the right time for me to switch over from Nottingham, because it had been getting more and more difficult for me to get fights back home. Because I hadn't lost any fights fewer and fewer people were willing to get in the ring. So it was definitely worth the risk.

Even after a few weeks in Sheffield I don't think that Brendan could really understand what I was doing. In the early days he wanted to change it, but he didn't know how. I was doing too much freestyle and boxing in a different way to all his other lads. He was afraid to spoil what I was good at but wasn't comfortable watching me jumping around the ring without a tight guard.

I was willing to listen, and in later years I came to learn that sometimes it was best to do what Brendan asked, even if you knew he was wrong, just for a quiet life. But the way I saw it you could be strong, and I could be as strong as you, but that wasn't where I could win every time. I had a better chance of winning fights by making it into a test of speed, skill and endurance. And when I'd won that game I could land my shots and win the fight. It had worked for me so far and that way of fighting, coupled with the fact that I was a south paw made me a very unattractive proposition for anyone who wanted to look good.

There was a science behind how my style developed, and it was different. A lot of boxers still jabbed with their knuckles in a horizontal line. But from the very start I was at ninety degrees and had my knuckles vertically. It wasn't the classic defence of the time, but that way I had the flexibility to get more shots in much quicker. Just try it.

The hard thing for Brendan was to find a formula. And his conundrum was always going to be to work out whether he should apply my formula to the other fighters, or whether he could get me to fight like his other boxers, or simply just leave me to get on with it. The difficult thing in translating the way I fought to others was that it would be like teaching a style and not a method, which is so hard to do. A lot of it was in the mind and my confidence in what I was doing. Quite simply it's what I had always done, and so far it hadn't been coached out of me.

I still idolised Muhammad Ali. As a heavyweight his speed was phenomenal, and he was the best in the world by a million miles. He had the brain and the speed and the strength to be the best the world had ever seen. You can have mega muscles but if you don't have speed and mobility you're nowhere. You only had to look at David Haye beating Valuev in 2010 to see that without speed you can get beat by someone half your size. It was billed as David and Goliath and Haye looked like a midget next the giant but he picked him off with ease.

Boxers with big muscles and strength but inferior speed eventually get tired chasing you, then all you have to do is to stay tight and go *'whack, got you mate'*. I'd already learnt that I could run and run and keep running. I could run around the ring and a scrapper would chase me, but they didn't have the athleticism they needed, and sooner or later you can just hit them.

Mick said to me that he'd be knackered running around like that all the time – but that's the point. You have to have the speed and the energy to keep going. I was already doing as much speed training as I did strength. I wouldn't have survived if I hadn't worked so hard on my endurance, but I did. And whoever was in the ring with me had to keep up, and if they didn't have it in them – whack! If you're moving around well enough you can make the other guy go where you want, and then you can do what you want.

Brendan tried to use me as an example when I was sparring. He'd draw lines in blue chalk on the canvas around me where I'd been. He hadn't yet come up with an original idea, but he had decided that maybe the others could copy me. So he watched what I was doing and he drew the circles and lines, so that everyone else could match my movements. I guess it was worth a try.

♦

It wasn't long before Brendan started to talk to me about how far I could go. He said that if I listened to him I could be World

Champion some day. I couldn't believe it at first. I had big confidence but not that big. But then again I was only seventeen and Brendan was a wily old businessman. Maybe he was right.

Up to now he had concentrated on Mick and when I arrived I had challenged his position as the main man in the gym. But the way Mick saw it, it wasn't really a fair challenge. He was a street fighter who hits you hard and I wasn't, I was playing a different game. When he did manage to catch me I didn't like it, so I made sure he didn't catch me again. And he was a straight talking straight forward lad. Eventually he got so frustrated with me that he told me and Brendan quite succinctly that he hated sparring with me:

*"I'm not fucking sparring wi you again you bastad, unless you stop fucking moving!"*

Brendan liked Mick's style and that was understandable, as that was the type of boxing around in the UK at the time. Ali was so far away in terms of his stratospheric talent, and Brendan didn't aspire to emulate that…. it was just too far away for him I think. He saw Mick as a good solid fighter and that's what he understood at the time.

But he gave me lots of attention and made sure that I got as much exposure as I could. And I liked that.

One Saturday after a sparring session Brendan came over to me and said:

*"Hey Herol we have an exhibition tomorrow, so we need to set off from here at twelve. Make sure you get to bed good and early tonight."*

An exhibition… wow! This was going to be great. I was going on an exhibition and I'd only been in Sheffield for a year. I did what Brendan said and got to bed early. I was really excited when I got up in the morning and I certainly wasn't disappointed.

Exhibitions got to be a way of life for me over the next few years and they were great fun. We went to working men's clubs all over the place in towns like Batley and Wakefield and some little mining communities. It was a right laugh.

The exhibitions were mainly on a Sunday and they were a good day out for the Yorkshire sport loving lads. We never had any hassle and I met a lot of coal miners, who were big physical men who just wanted to let off steam after spending a week doing one of the most courageous and ultimately thankless jobs in the world.

They were always full and popular events, partly because at that time there was not much Sunday sport on television. So guys might go to a football match on Saturday, out for a few pints on Saturday night, and then down the club on Sunday for a few more and a boxing exhibition. Great weekend.

But don't be fooled by the term exhibition. There were no flashy venues, no polished presentations, no music, well that's not strictly true. There was usually some old music, often Elvis banging out on a crackly record player and accompanied by one or more drunken blokes.

The first one I did was at a club somewhere near Hillsborough. As we arrived in the car park on a rainy Sunday afternoon I could hear the shouting and laughing from inside. On the door was a hand written poster which said:

## Boxing Exhibition

## Sunday 15<sup>th</sup> October

## Sheffield's Own World Class Fighter

## Errol the Bomb Graham.

The poster was soggy so I tried to smudge an 'H' onto the front as Brendan gave me a hoik and said:
*"Come on".*

Inside, there must have been almost a hundred blokes there, all with a pint of bitter or mild in their hands, and most with a cigarette. A cloud of smoke hung about three foot above the ring, which was a square on the dance floor made out of four rows of about ten chairs, turned the wrong way round. As I smiled at one bloke who was looking at me, I coughed and Brendan said:

*"Don't do that Herol, it makes you look sickly".*

I coughed again.

We sat down at a table next to the gents' toilets and Brendan handed me my bag. So I got my gloves out, and started to get ready.

At this, the blokes at the bar and around it started to gather, and within five minutes the two rows of seats around the makeshift ring were full, and there were a few rows of people standing up behind that. At the edge of the room there were some kids standing on a table, and next to them a bloke in a wheel chair balanced on another table. I whispered to Brendan:

*"Does that thing have brakes on it?"*

He just pulled me forward.

The guys who had set it up hadn't put a gap in the chairs, so we had to push our way through with *'Excuse me's'* and then climb over the last chair and into the ring. I'd probably had nearly a hundred amateur fights by the time I started doing exhibitions, so I wasn't nervous. I didn't expect a cheer, but there was a kind of pissed moan of appreciation as Brendan slipped on some spilled beer on his way to the middle of the ring.

*"Gentlemen, gentlemen."* He started.

*"Oi have here Bomber Graham the Nottingham champion boxer. He's now training in Sheffield and ranked in the top ten amateur fighters in Yorkshire. Is anybody brave enough to come up and have a spar with him? He can't hit you but you can hit him, do anything you want."*

All the blokes were looking at me and I heard a voice say:

*"He looks black!"*

Then this other guy put his hand up and shouted:

*"He can't hit me?"*

Brendan shouted back that I couldn't and the big man stepped forward. Brendan went over to him and whispered something to him as he put his gloves and head guard on, and then walked back into the middle of the ring and announced:

*"Over here we have the challenger, what's your name?*
*"Martin.*

*"We have Martin from....where you from? Okay it's Martin all the way from down the road, and originally from......where? Okay...down the road."*

Then, as there wasn't a bell, Brendan shouted:

*"DING DING, ROUND ONE."*

And I started to move around on my toes. Immediately Martin waded in towards me swinging wildly. He was a big guy; about six foot four so he had a long reach and he was throwing punches everywhere. But none of them hit me. After ten seconds of this he started to speed up and was thrashing around at thin air. It did cross my mind that if any of these caught me I could be on my way out of here on a stretcher. But thankfully Martin had been in the club for two hours already so his aim wasn't that good.

After a minute of thrashing and swinging he started to slow down again, and I realised that he wasn't going to hit me, so I started to do my thing. I spun him around and tapped him on the shoulder. Then I did it again and slapped him on the arse and a big cheer went up in the club. This was a right laugh. So I did it again, tapped him on the backside and said:

*"You naughty boy you can't do that to me!"*

And the audience was going mad. The third time I did it the guys on the front row stood up and were laughing and cheering. I was having a great time and Martin, to his credit, had a rueful smile as we shook hands, and he went off in search of his much needed pint.

Brendan saw that the lads were enjoying this so he upped the ante:

*"There's a tenner for anyone who can knock the Bomber down!"*

Ten pounds was a lot of cash in those days, in the terms that these lads understood, about twenty pints and four pie and peas – so that would be a couple of hours taken care of for four mates.

One group of lads pushed their mate forward and we went through it all again. He swung at me like a whirling dervish for about thirty seconds then I tapped him on his left shoulder, then his right, then his left again. The audience couldn't get enough of this.

After this bout, Brendan shouted for volunteers again and a short stocky guy stood up, sat down, then stood up again and lurched forward.

*'I'll have a do'.*

He must have put a few pints back by this stage because he couldn't get his first glove on, and Brendan whispered to me to be a little bit careful, before shouting:

*"DING DING"'.*

I stood on my toes and waited for the guy to lunge at me. And I waited. And I waited. He just stood, red faced, staring at me and swaying gently backwards and forwards. He was breathing heavily and looked like he was preparing for his onslaught as I jumped up and down on my toes. I waited a little longer.

Eventually I thought I'd better coax him out so I skipped over towards him and moved about in front of him, keeping my head moving just in case he sent out a shot. He looked like he was winding up for a big one, as he stared at me, trying to follow my movements and burping beer fumes generally in my direction. Still nothing, so I tapped him on the shoulder at which point he leapt into action, took an almighty swing and spun, without me touching him, a full 180 degrees. So I slapped him on the backside and .........

*"BLOOOAAAARRGH!"*

A flood of vomit shot out of his mouth as he emptied the contents of his stomach all over the floor and splashing the front row as a mighty cheer went up.

So the exhibition had come to a natural end and all in all I thought it had been a roaring success. I'd had a great time in any case.

These boys who went to the exhibitions were great fun, and really friendly and warm to me. Whenever I did the exhibitions there was never a hint of hostility and I always felt welcome. No one ever came after me outside, there was never even a hint of anyone getting proper pissed off, even though there was a lot of beer around. It was just a sporting, friendly atmosphere and I always looked forward to them.

Whenever anyone came to challenge me they invariably ended up sat on the floor exhausted, but they all wanted the challenge. It was a fitness thing, no one wanted to hurt me, but they were desperate to land just one shot, and beat all their mates.

I carried on doing these exhibitions after I turned professional. I was more than happy to carry on and Brendan had been quite smart in that. That's how we built up a friendly but passionate fan base in the early days, I wanted to go out and have fun with them in any case. And if they liked me they decided that they would support me. It was really good. It started to build up more interest in boxing around Sheffield and Brendan had people asking if they could come down to the gym to watch. Some even started training and sparring down there. I enjoyed sparring with them just as much when they were sober and tried to teach them a bit about the sport, the way I saw it.

As time went on the other guys, Mick Mills, one of the other lads called Glyn Rhodes and later Johnny Nelson, when he started to come down, sparred with the audience as well. We had a really good togetherness feeling and a support for the gym. I think Brendan had used me to up the profile of his gym but I didn't mind that at all. It was nice.

We even started going out to schools in Sheffield to talk to the kids about fighting, not to hurt, but to stay fit. We were a bit ahead of our time when it came to wider participation and healthy lifestyles. I was really enjoying myself making friends with everyone, just as much as the boxing. These were good times.

# 5

# <u>Root of Some Evil</u>

*"Money, money, money*
*Always sunny,*
*In a rich man's world."*

## ABBA

The opportunity to carry on doing exhibitions always gave me something to do on Sundays, which had the knock on effect of making sure I was in bed at a reasonable time on a Saturday night. I liked going out to the clubs, but this discipline of frequently working on a Sunday kept all that in reasonable check. That, in turn, must have helped me to work my way up the amateur rankings.

Over the first couple of years in Sheffield I had another twenty or so amateur fights. They weren't always easy to get, and I was just starting to see the first signs of the problem I came up against in Nottingham, where, as my reputation started to get around a bit, the fights were harder to come by. But if I had stayed in Nottingham I may well have dwindled out altogether. Brendan had to work hard at it, but he was good at getting me fights and picking opponents that would test me a little bit more each time.

In 1976, shortly after I arrived in Sheffield, I had won the Junior ABA Championship, and the following year I lost in the final of the Senior Amateur Boxing Association Championship. I was getting ever closer to my hope of becoming a professional fighter, because I was still only eighteen and after the ABA senior title, there isn't really anywhere left to go in the amateur game. By the beginning of 1978 I felt ready to have a proper tilt at the ABA Championships.

The way the ABA worked was on a knockout basis but before the final stages there were smaller regional groups to get through. It was a bit like the football Champions League is now. You progressed through the early rounds locally and then when you reached the semis and final you were on a national stage. It made sense to do it that way so that we didn't have to travel far unless we were genuine contenders.

My regional group was probably the hardest in the country. Sheffield and the Midlands was probably the strongest area outside London, partly because there were some tough areas around here, where fighting was the only way out for some people, and partly because there was quite a big black population in places like Leicester. But I knew everyone around Yorkshire and I'd boxed most of the best lads and beaten them, so I knew I didn't have anyone to worry about close by. And when I was down in the Midlands the only guy who had beaten me was Tony Sibson, but he was older than me and had already turned professional. And I had fought plenty down there before my move north. I never expected a walkover but I had every reason to be confident. And in the event I was right to be. I made the final without losing a round.

Sometimes the national ABA final was held in Blackpool, as it was the previous year but in 1978 it was at Wembley Arena in London. I travelled down to London for the final with Brendan and my friends from the gym; Robert, Glyn and Mick were all there. Mum and Dad didn't come down. I only told them I had made the final again the week before, but I don't think they would have come anyway. They still wanted to know how I was getting on of course, and they had followed my amateur career, even after I had left Nottingham. But they'd made it quite clear that boxing just wasn't their thing, and I didn't mind that. They always said *'well done'* when I went to see them and told them what I'd been doing. But they still tried to talk me into furthering my education at every opportunity, which was what they were really interested in. They probably knew that wasn't for me when I left home at sixteen, but they hadn't entirely given up hope. And to be fair to them, Mum and Dad let me make my own decisions and never tried to stop me going to Sheffield. Dad briefly carried on telling me that boxing wasn't a great career choice, but he was fighting a losing battle on that one. But he put his money where his mouth was and went back to university himself, while I carried on boxing. He ended up getting a better degree than my sister Leonie, and she is very bright! But then he studied theology, and if you work at something you love you always have a better chance of success.

It was the biggest fight of my life so far, but I didn't want my parents to be there watching me fight just because they loved me, and not to enjoy it. I guess it would have been nice to see Dad there, but in my heart I knew they wanted the best for me; they didn't have to say anything.

Wembley arena was enormous, it was by far the biggest place I'd boxed in, and when I walked around in the afternoon I was just amazed by the massive space around me. I felt a buzz of excitement and had a sudden realisation that this was quite some step if I succeeded. Winning the Juniors two years ago was good but this was the real thing in the amateur world.

I was fighting a guy named Delroy Park. And Brendan told me that this was a fight that I should win. On the way down in the car he was talking about a lad called Terry Marsh, a Royal Navy bloke who was always in and around the ABA's at that time. He usually made the late stages, but I hadn't come across him but Brendan told me what a tough lad he was. So it was probably a good thing that I was up against Delroy but I didn't really care, I had to beat whoever was in front of me, and as I didn't know either of them, it made no difference to me.

Everybody wanted to fight at Wembley – it was a real status thing, particularly in the amateur world. And we all knew that to win at Wembley in the ABA would usually be a catapult into the professional game. It would enable you to get a good backer, someone like Micky Duff or Mike Barrett who were around and very active at the time. Boxing is a money game, although in all honesty that was a side of the sport that I never really got to grips with. But there were a few money men sniffing around whenever the ABA finals were in town.

Delroy was a short stocky boxer, with closely cropped hair, he was from the armed forces as well – I think it may have even been the Marines. He was very strong and clearly a decent fighter to have got this far. But as the fight eventually got under way I could see that he wasn't all that quick. He was a methodical, upright boxer, very sure footed but not really agile.

As we moved into the second round I started to pick more points up, and I soon realised that the only way he could beat me was to knock me out. Which he never got close enough to do, and so when the points were announced at the end, I'd won it all the way. I didn't have a scare throughout the fight and although Delroy was obviously no mug, in some ways it was almost surprisingly easy. Everything had gone exactly to plan, I'd done what Brendan had told me, I'd also done my own thing, and the result was that I was now the ABA Middleweight Champion. Bloody Hell! That was me. I looked over to see Brendan grinning from ear to ear and with a bright twinkle in his eye.

♦

On the journey back up the M1 it all started to sink in. We stopped at a service station near Leicester and got a cup of tea. We didn't have mobile phones in those days so I couldn't ring my Mum to tell her, so I told the middle aged lady on the till:

*"I've just won the ABA Middleweight Championships."*

*"Ooh that's lovely, well done."* She smiled, clearly clueless of what I was talking about. But it's always nice to have someone say *'well done'* anyway.

Brendan was like a dog with two dicks and he had been talking about our future all the way up the road. I wanted to turn pro, Brendan wanted me to turn pro and so there was a lot to talk about, so he said. But in all honesty I thought it would all be pretty straight forward. I'd carry on boxing but the fighters would be better, so I'd get paid. Simple. I was exactly the sort of sportsman that promoters and managers love. In short – naïve.

In the autumn Brendan took me to meet two friends of his, Mick Cowan and Tony McKenna. They were business men of some sort or other, and dressed the part. It seemed to me that they'd obviously had some pretty big discussions with Brendan already, because when I met them they seemed to know exactly what they wanted to do. They said that they could take over the management side of things while Brendan did the day to day training. And there was a lot to talk about the financial side. Mick said:

*"Don't worry about the money side of things. That's where we can help. You'll get all your training gear and a percentage."*

That sounded good to me. The way I understood it I'd get all my training kit and lots of money. It was when they started talking about percentages and all that sort of business that I started to drift off.

I didn't really want to be bothered by all that. There wasn't any doubt in my own mind – I just wanted to turn pro. That was all I'd wanted for the last six years and now it was finally happening for me. And I was really excited because I was going to make money for myself. I had no idea how much and how it would all work, but I was going to make money anyhow.

I tried to listen to the discussions between Brendan and Mick and Tony, but, if I'm completely honest, I didn't really understand what they were talking about. I wasn't the businessman, I was the boxer. And I'm not the type of person to push hard for a deal. If I was offered twenty five per cent I wouldn't say, *'no I want fifty'*. I didn't want to have twenty grand in the bank, that wasn't the most important thing for me. Sure, I wanted to make loads of money but I didn't know what loads of money actually was, and more importantly than that I wanted to box. So I was happy to trust the people who seemed to know what they were talking about. How many eighteen year olds would have the balls to take on some battle worn old business man if he was talking about financial matters? All I could do was to trust them to do the right thing. And that didn't worry me at that very moment. I was still on Cloud Nine and had the world, or at least Sheffield, at my feet.

I think they must have known that I wasn't that interested in the finer details of a contract when they said stuff like:

*"And you'll get twenty five per cent Herol."*

And I just replied:

*"Okay."*

That seemed absolutely fine to me. If we could get a fight and fill the Sheffield City Hall, that's all that I was concerned about. I just wanted to do my thing and I trusted the money people to make sure I was paid a fair amount for my efforts. An older business head may have asked:

*"Twenty five per cent of what?"*

But if you can remember when you were eighteen, would you have asked the right questions? And at that very moment, if they told me that I would get two thousand pounds in my hand when I fought then I would be delighted. I had no idea, and still don't for sure, exactly how much everyone else was sharing and how it was all worked out. Not my thing. These were very shrewd men and I had no reason not to trust them.

I never really had an awful lot of contact with Mick and Tony, they were there in the background for three years or so, but I just did all my work with Brendan. They were getting the fights and managing the finance and I was boxing. Square pegs in square holes.

At the time I turned pro nobody really put their arm around me and sat me down to tell me exactly what would happen. These days, or in fact not all that much later, sports people started to get agents to represent them, so they had more protection. But even the agents have their own priorities. They're in it for money. There's lots of money in sport for a legion of guys in suits, and nowadays there is more protection for the players. In football it's gone the other way, where player power has arrived to such an extent that players and agents can tell their owners that they'll leave to play for the team's biggest rivals unless they get their wages doubled, even if they have a contract. I feel a bit sorry for the fans when that happens.

Back in the seventies, sports players were more naïve in any number of ways, and there was still the employer and employee relationship, where the player got what he was given and was bloody well grateful. There must be a sensible middle ground somewhere. But finding people to handle big amounts of money fairly isn't always the easiest thing to do. Businessmen, by nature I guess, aren't often blessed with generosity of spirit.

I just needed someone to take care of my interests, to look after my money and give me my spending money when I needed it.

♦

So, happy in the knowledge that I didn't have to worry about the business side of things, I concentrated on getting myself prepared for my first professional fight. I didn't have to wait too long and I was billed to fight a guy from Wales, called Vivian Waite, on 28th November 1978. And the great thing was that it was on my own turf at the Sheffield City Hall.

I was very nervous, but there was no difference in the fact that I was now professional, because as an amateur I was always nervous. But that was a good thing. It brought me down and helped me to concentrate. Before a fight I always thought, *'what can he do? He might beat me. What will I do then?'* I always had nervous energy coursing through my veins and this time was no different. As those things went through my mind I worked out what I needed to do to make sure it didn't happen. I had to keep my hands up as much as possible, but then just do my thing.

Sheffield was a close community, like a village in many ways, everybody knew someone who could do this or that, and Mick and Tony did seem to open some doors for us. We had some fights later at Top Rank in Sheffield, and Mick and Tony had some interest in that, they either owned some of it or knew the guys who did.

Away from the business side of things, the strong and close community was a big boost to me too, because whenever I stepped into the ring when I was fighting at home I could see the familiar faces of boys that I'd met on exhibitions over the years. And this time on my first professional fight Martin from down the road, the guy in the wheelchair and Mr Vomit were all there.

The place was packed out, and I wouldn't be surprised if there were a thousand people in there watching. The Sheffield Star had given us a lot of coverage in the lead up. I already knew the boxing writers Tony Pritchett and Peter and Steve Hastings, the photographer, pretty well. They were good guys. I was always happy speaking to the press; they were easy people to talk to.

After six three minute rounds I managed a win on points, and now I was really on my way. Vivian made me work but it was more of the same, just professional instead of amateur. It wasn't a spectacular fight by any stretch. It built my confidence though, which by now was getting sky high. I was desperate to prove to myself that I could be a professional fighter. There is more pressure when you're a pro, and I guess it crosses everybody's mind that they might not be good enough when they first set out. I knew I had other fights coming up straight away, and so it was crucial for my self esteem to get off with a win.

Brendan was pleased with me and the following Tuesday he gave me my cheque. I can't remember exactly how much it was for; I think maybe about six hundred pounds. Most people can remember how much their first wage cheque was, but not me. I guess that tells you something, and it tells me something too.

But I do know that the cheque was enough for me to put a deposit down, to get a mortgage on a house on Newman Road which I bought for £11,950. It's funny how some figures stick in the mind and others don't. So that was quite a sensible thing to do. Possibly the most sensible thing I ever did.

I had left Brendan's house a while before. With five other kids there it was hard work for Mrs Ingle looking after us all the time. And the kids were all growing up, which brings other complications when you're all under the same roof, not least having to share a bathroom! I stayed briefly with some boxing friends called Dave and Rita Marriot. They were lovely people and they made me very welcome in their home but now it was time to stand on my own two feet and it felt brilliant.

I didn't move straight into the house full time – I kept flitting between mine and Rita and Paul's for a while. But at the age of eighteen I had somewhere I could call my own.

♦

The week after my first professional bout I had a second, down in Southend, to fight a guy called Curtis Marsh. I travelled down there with Brendan and Tony McKenna. I liked it there – Mick Mills used to box down in Southend quite regularly. It was a nice sort of place and close to the seaside, and very slightly warmer than Sheffield, so just about freezing!

I was particularly excited about this one because I had a new pair of bright turquoise shorts and gown that had been made for me by my friend Brenda. I had met her years ago when I worked on the market when she had a stall there. She started making my shorts for me and when I turned professional she really upped the ante. The shorts got more and more outrageous and were usually a combination of blue, black, turquoise and purple, with a bit of orange thrown in here and there. They were outstanding and I always had to give them to people for auctions after each fight. That said, they were often so garish that everyone thought I was gay!

So armed with my killer shorts we started the bout at Southend's 20th Century Cliff's Pavilion in front of a tight crowd, who, while they were rooting for Curtis, weren't particularly hostile. As soon as the bell went Curtis tried to bomb me out straight away, but he kept on missing, and soon enough I caught him and he went down. And didn't get up. So I had a first round knock out in my second professional fight. That hadn't been my style so far; I usually won on points by out boxing people rather than knocking them out with a haymaker. But whichever way it came I was happy to take it and my confidence continued to soar. So a four hundred mile round trip and one and a half minutes work later I was ready for a Christmas break.

In my first fight of 1979 I stopped Jimmy Roberts in the second round in Bradford, which came as a bit of a surprise to me. The guys in the north are normally tougher than boxers from the south, but this one was quite easy in that he seemed to run out of steam very early. So now I had a full set - points, knockout and technical knockout. Three out of three ain't bad.

Next I fought a guy called Dave Southwell at Top Rank in Reading and I beat him on points. Dave was an awkward fighter and it was a difficult match for me. He thought it was a bit close and so we got it on again two weeks later in Burslem in Staffordshire. Brendan assured me that the first fight was close enough for it not to be a waste of time. So I beat him again. I managed to show him that I was a bit better than he thought. That took me to five, albeit two of them were Dave!

I think everyone I fought was struggling partly because I was leading with my right. Southpaws in boxing are about as popular as left handed batters in cricket. I am right handed in everything else but when I boxed I led with my right, with the bigger shots coming from my left. Wrong way round but it worked for me.

Fights continued to come thick and fast, and I ended up having nine in the year. Sometimes it was hard to get the fights and Brendan told me that we had to pay boxers to come and take me on. I had built up a reputation straight away of not being hit so as we went on it carried on being a challenge to get fights. But they kept coming in dribs and drabs and all the boxers I came across were of a similar style. They were all pretty tough and dogged. I remember one boxer called Lloyd James who I fought at Sheffield City Hall. He didn't move very quickly but every time I moved him around and hit him, he'd just come back at me, slowly but relentlessly. It was like fighting a zombie; he just kept on coming back. He wasn't hurting me at all but I was worried that if I let him get too close he might start eating my flesh. Thankfully this was an eight round fight. We'd still have been there now if it needed a knockout. I'd be smacking him on the head with a chair, and he'd get up and stagger back towards me!

When we were in Sheffield at the City Hall or Top Rank we always sold out. Sheffield's a great sport city and people here are very knowledgeable. And Brendan's policy of getting me out to the working men's clubs good and early was paying off. Even when we went down south to London or Southend we got big crowds. I didn't have a following down there but as I was becoming well known in the north, the national press started to give me a mention now and then. And eastenders love their boxing. And in turn, fighting down south got me more national exposure and more people came to watch me all over the place after that.

I still didn't know what I was earning, not just for me, but for everyone else as well; the bosses told me what I was getting, and in all honesty I liked it that way. As time went on my cheque started to increase a little. And by the time I had been professional for a year, I was still undefeated, so I started to take a bit more of an interest and began asking what I was getting before I was told. We were selling out with big crowds and the cheques were creeping upwards from six to seven to eight hundred pounds.

♦

At this time, and to supplement my income, I had a job at the Mulberry Tavern in Sheffield. Sometimes I worked on the bar and sometimes on the door. I loved working on the bar because I was meeting people all the time; meeting, meeting, meeting and chatting, chatting, chatting. I loved meeting new people and where better to do it. I spent the whole evening just talking and talking, mainly to blokes of course! There were lots of nice people coming in and a great mix. In the afternoon all the middle aged and older guys used to come in and have their Guinness, and then at night, when the old guys had gone to bed, the place was bouncing with the young lot.

Going on the door was easy, but I didn't really like doing that. I didn't often have to hit anyone; I just stayed behind the door, but as the night went on and people got drunker there was often trouble. Every now and then a clown would recognise me and want a go, but almost always he was stopped by his mates because they were boxing fans. The bar was much more fun. They knew I didn't like it on the door but if they were short of hands they'd call over to me.

Back in the ring I carried on loving the fights I had, particularly in Sheffield. It was always better fighting at home, because as well as having the home crowd you're more likely to get a decision if it's a close fight. That's just the way of the world and it can work for you or against you. And the crowd was always fantastic to me. One guy told me he loved watching me because it looked like I was going to get hit, but they kept on missing me by inches. They might as well have been a mile away as two inches, it has just the same impact. None. He always worried that I'd get knocked out one day, but so far I never had. It was a big cat and mouse game. The longer I went on the crowd always wondered if I was going to get beat the next time.

When we fought away from home we had coaches going everywhere with us, and when it was as close as Barnsley I had a great following. I went there at the end of the year to fight a Manchester lad called Billy Ahearne. He was strong and busy. The fighters I was starting to come across were getting better by this stage. But Billy was so busy and worked so hard for two rounds that by the third he was gone and the ref stopped the fight. For the first two rounds I moved him around and he kept on going, but at the beginning of the third round I could see that he wasn't moving as freely as he was. I kept tipping and tapping him and then gave him a slap, at which point he woke up and exploded for thirty more seconds, then he was gone for good. When someone's so tired you can hit them once and it's all over. He'd tried so hard to stay with me that he had beaten himself.

I could tell the fighters that spent more time in the gym whacking the punch bags than running around, and there were a lot of them about in those days. It was quite easy for me to beat these lads, providing I stayed focussed, carried on picking up points and avoided getting hit. I knew if I kept moving, they'd have to keep moving too and soon enough they'd get knackered. It's a simple strategy really.

Even if they stayed for eight rounds, by the end they were so tired that I could score virtually at will. I knew that not everybody liked my style. A few fighters certainly didn't, and the fans who wanted to see a scrap and a bloodbath didn't. But I had more people on my side than against me.

Over the next year I started to take a bit more of an interest in what else was happening in the boxing world. Marvin Hagler was the most exciting world name in my weight, and in the UK Tony Sibson, another battling sort of fighter, was doing well. He was a big hitter, very much of the old school. He was rough and tough and always gave a good fight. I was never likely to fight him professionally as his profile was at its height while I was on the way up, and by the time I was ready he had retired. Although he had beaten me as an amateur I don't think he fancied it now. But if you're going to be the top fighter you have to beat the guys at the top, and they have to have a reason to fight you. A quick southpaw was never going to be the top of anybody's list. Somebody told me Tony put it a bit more bluntly when he said:

*"Why would I want to fight a limbo dancer?"*

# 6

## <u>Shiny Happy People</u>

### *"Everything exists, nothing has value."*

### E M Forster

The nineteen eighties were heralded by a new era in the United Kingdom. We had our first ever female prime minister, Mrs Thatcher. I thought that would be quite a good thing to get a more feminine and kinder approach to running the country after years of tough government. She had become known as 'Thatcher the Milk Snatcher' when free milk in schools disappeared during her time in the department of education. But that was just a blip and we were all looking forward to a caring administration.

Punk rock had almost fizzled out and was replaced by the New Romantic movement which allowed some blokes to wear make up and girl's clothes. The other white blokes' music was heavy metal. So with the alternatives all seeming a bit crap we just carried on listening to reggae and soul, which is why we always walked around with a smile on our faces. Wicked.

In the world of sport, the England football team was still struggling having missed the last two world cups, mainly because their shorts were now too tight. But Ian Botham, unperturbed by the tightness of his cricket flannels single handedly smashed the Aussies.

And me? I was having the time of my life just doing my thing, a professional boxer, king of the dance floor and all around good time guy. It was sweet.

Brendan was pleased as punch with the progress we'd made together, but he wanted to make sure I stayed on the straight and narrow, so he started looking around for someone who could look after me in the run up to fights. I'd left his house after I kind of outstayed my welcome a few years earlier and I'd bought my pad on Newman Road, but Brendan still wanted someone to keep an eye on me. He wasn't so worried about the training side of things because he knew I was a fitness nut, but he did worry about all the other sort of distractions, because I was a red blooded, black skinned guy in his early twenties, and I loved going to Josephines and Anabellas with Brian and the boys.

There was a young lad called Paul Marriott who used to spar with me at the gym. He was a good little boxer and we got on well together. Brendan and Alma Ingle knew Paul's mum and dad, Rita and Dave. And Brendan had been talking to them, to see if they would help to keep an eye on me. And they agreed. So from hereon it was arranged for me to go up to theirs for two or three weeks before each fight.

Rita and Dave were very welcoming and I had the best of times while I was there, though not in a partying sort of way. In fact, they were almost manic in the way they kept everyone away from me. I assumed that girlfriends would have been shot if they came within firing range, so I wasn't tempted to sneak them in, even though Rita and Dave gave me a key as soon as I arrived. It was a brilliant place for me to prepare in though. I could relax without any worries at all, and Brendan could relax in the knowledge that I wasn't in Josephines.

Everything in the Marriots' house was cut off for me. We were cut off from the rest of civilisation, and I often wondered how their own kids felt about the whole upheaval for two or three weeks every time I had a fight. When I had to eat, the whole family had to eat so they all trooped down and sat down at the table two hours before they were ready.

Without Rita and Dave I honestly don't know how I would have done, they were really that good. They provided the kind of food that I needed to eat and Rita was a great cook.

They were very welcoming in every way but made sure I behaved myself. Rita particularly was really strict with me. She always made sure I was in bed before she turned in for the night.

But now and then I just wasn't tired and so I'd get something to read. It was like being twelve again, but for all the right reasons.

One time I was so awake I just snuck down the stairs to get a glass of water and then I sat in the living room and turned the television on very quietly. It was about eleven o'clock and as it was a Saturday, Match of the Day had just finished and Halloween was just about to start. Perfect. I put my feet up and prepared for terror.

But rather than a maniac in a hockey mask wielding a big knife, to my horror the first entrant was Rita pointing at the clock:

*"Come on Herol. Early to bed, early to rise,"* she chirped as the screen disappeared into a small dot and my evening's plans were scuppered. If I had said 'no' I swear she would have booted me up the stairs.

But Rita always had the very best of intentions in her heart. Dave was fantastic as well. He said he'd already brought up three kids so one more wouldn't be a problem. And he coped brilliantly with my mood swings in the few days before each fight as I became tenser. It was almost like having Brendan with me in a way. He could calm me down or lift me up if he saw that I needed it, and between them, Rita and Dave should take a lot of credit for some of my wins at that time.

They came to support me as well and while I was staying with them over the next few years, they saw me win the Commonwealth and European light middleweight titles. They always made things right for me and I remember the part they played when I had my first professional title fight. By the end of 1981 I'd made my way up to being the contender for the British light middleweight title and Brendan had got me a fight with the holder Pat Thomas at the Sheffield City Hall. He was a black Welsh guy and a really good fighter and everyone expected him to beat me quite easily. This was the biggest fight of my life in more ways than one. It was the first fight that I had which was scheduled for fifteen rounds and so I knew that I had to be physically at the top of my game. Rita was looking after the nutrition and sleep side of things and I was running ten miles every morning and doing all my speed and strength work in the gym, where Brendan was feeding me with his endless pearls of Irish wisdom.

I always got nervous before fights but, since the ABA finals, this was the most important bout of my life. I still wasn't well known outside Sheffield and no one gave me much of a hope. I wouldn't go so far as to say I was starting to doubt my ability in any way, but I was right on edge. My laughs were less natural and Dave could see me having quieter times, more often than usual. So one evening, as we sat watching the news, he leaned across and quietly said to me:

*"You know what to do, don't you Herol?"*

*"What?"*

*"Just do what you always do. And you'll be fine."*

Just as I'd found an uncle in Brendan, I'd found another in Dave. And the way these guys can fill you with self belief just with the simplest of words makes all the difference. If someone else believes in you then you have no reason at all not to believe in yourself.

I beat Pat Thomas in every single round, he hardly touched me and everybody, not least Rita and Dave, played their part.

♦

I had the best of both worlds in those days, a great place to stay when I was in the intense run up to a fight, and my own house on Newman Road when I wasn't. That house was fairly small, but perfect for me and it was special because it was the first one that I had bought for myself. But being the upwardly mobile type (without the red braces and massive mobile phone) I decided to move to a new house on Bentley Road, which I could do up and turn into a really cool place. I had bought the house on Newman Road when I was still staying at Brendan's now and then and spent a lot of time up at Rita and Dave's. But now I thought that I needed somewhere a bit bigger that maybe I could settle into. And, who knows, maybe I'd soon enough have someone settling in with me.

And it wasn't long before that thought came to fruition, but not exactly in the way that I'd expected, or even hoped. I had just finished sparring in the gym one day, when Johnny Nelson wandered over and said:

*"Hey Herol, can I crash at yours tonight man?"*

*"Sure."*

I was always happy to help a mate out and Johnny was an okay guy. He was a good looking lad and a bit of a player, he was a real character and knew how to get what he wanted, and he had plenty of girls following him around. As a boxer he was pretty average at first, but over the years he worked hard and he did get a lot better, but at this particular time, his talent was not in his gloves, it was a bit lower down.

I guessed that he wanted a bit more freedom than he had at his Mum's house and so I said it was fine for him to stay over. But he never left. Over the next few years he lived between my place and his Mum's and he became part of the furniture. We trained together, went home and ate together, watched telly together, but we didn't sleep together! I was the cook in the house (that's cook) and he never complained about the chicken and rice and peas. I guess that's probably what he'd grown up on too.

Johnny was happy to stay with me in the early days because he didn't have enough money for his own place. He didn't pay me any rent, but I didn't mind that because I hadn't paid Brendan any when I stayed at his house. And I always worked on the principle that if you help someone, then if you need some help in the future then they'll help you if they can. And at the beginning of his career Johnny was always understandably skint. He never had his own money, he often thought that he had some but couldn't find it. So I lent him money when he needed it and I didn't ask for it back.

I didn't mind Johnny bringing 'friends' back to the house at all, as long as they didn't make a mess. It used to make me laugh though because sometimes he pretended he didn't have anyone with him when he did. He must have done that at home.

One night I went to bed early while Johnny was still out, because I was training for a fight and due to go to Dave and Rita's at the weekend. As I drifted off to sleep I could hear him fumbling at the front door, and then it opened. I counted to myself 'one, two, three, four, five, six, seven, eight,' then I heard the door close. So I shouted:

*"Who've you got in Johnny?"*

I knew someone had followed him in because it took so long to shut the door.

*"No one."*

Brilliant.


A couple of weeks later when I came back from Rita's after the fight I noticed one of the pictures of me, that I had hanging on the wall was tilted at an angle. It was the one that the Sheffield Star had given to me after the Pat Thomas fight and it had pride of place in the living room. So I went over and put it straight and thought, 'shit, Johnny must have had an acrobatic guest in last week!' Then I thought no more about it.

When Johnny came back I just asked if everything had been okay, and he said it was all cool. I bet it was.

Later that week, Johnny came up to me in the gym and said:

*"You're going away this weekend aren't you?"*

*"Yes, why?"*

*"Well just make sure you enjoy yourself."*

*"Why, what's happening?"* My suspicions were aroused.

*"Oh nothing, nothing,"* he smiled his reassuring, truthful smile.


On the Friday when I got home he asked me what time I was leaving, and an hour later he virtually helped me out of the door, before waving me off and disappearing back into the house.

But unbeknown to Johnny during the weekend, my brother Noel, who was back from the army, planned a surprise visit to my house. And he himself was a little surprised when Johnny opened the door.

*"Hi, is Herol in?"*

*"Herol, no."* Johnny looked a bit flustered as Noel let himself into the living room, to be met by a rather glamorous looking blonde lady with legs up to her armpits. He said 'hi', left a message for me and made his way out before noticing that

the picture of me on the wall had been replaced by a picture of Marilyn Monroe. In fact all my pictures had gone. There was no evidence at all that I even lived there.

*"When's Herol back?"* asked Noel.

*"Oh I don't see him from one week to the next,"* bluffed Johnny.

It turned out that every time I was out, good old Johnny had been pretending it was his house for weeks. What a guy!

♦

The gym on Newman Road was buzzing in those days and one afternoon we had a new small addition to the team. A little Asian lad of about ten years old turned up. Brendan had seen him the week before when he was on a bus going through Sheffield. He had looked out of his window to see this little guy fighting off four or five kids in the playground with some gusto. Brendan hopped off the bus, called the boy over and within a week his older brother had brought him down to the gym. He was fantastic on the bags at the very first chance he got, and he even wanted to spar with some of the fully grown lads.

He was introduced to us as Naseem, although we all called him Naz. And over the next few years he followed me around everywhere. I didn't mind at all and it was actually good fun. I have always liked working with kids and that was my first real opportunity. I taught him every thing that I had worked out for myself in the ring and although the other lads tried to copy what I was doing, he was the first kid who took it on properly. He could imitate the way I moved and soon enough it came naturally to him. He tried and tried and when it clicked he never looked back.

Naz had the right attitude. He was hard working and ever so determined, and he had that little arrogant streak that started to make him look more dangerous. He had a way of smiling, and sometimes sneering when he hit someone and it hurt. I had a feeling, and I know Brendan did, that this lad could make it to the top.

So when I gave everyone a lift up to the swimming centre or up to Upperthorpe to get some cooked chicken from our favourite chicken man, Naz was always with us. He was good to have around, but he was a little monkey and you had to be on your toes. You couldn't leave your bag around because he'd be in it, then he'd swap stuff around with someone else's bag. The young lads, Naz in particularly, were tearaways. There was lots of banter, 'who's got this or that.' I don't think they ever really wanted to nick stuff but they just liked playing.

Naz's brothers were never far away. They couldn't box anything like him, but they wanted to look after him nevertheless. But they were happy for me to look after him while he was at the gym. I showed him the ropes and continued to do that for a long time.

I always enjoyed having friends around me; in fact I needed people around me. I'd grown up in a big family and then when I moved to Sheffield I went to live with another big family, and when I got my own house I either stayed with someone else or someone else stayed with me. I didn't mind being on my own, but as far as I knew, I didn't want to live alone. So Johnny being in the house was cool. And I didn't need too much encouragement to get out and about. Talking to people is what I do best!

But I didn't look after my money very well, to put it mildly. When I started earning people advised me to put it in the bank but it wasn't long before I worked out that you can take it out of the bank just as easily. I had some advice to put some money away in a five year bond of some sort to get more interest. But I kind of ignored that sort of advice and just kept putting it in the bank – where I knew I could get it out whenever I wanted. I was a bit shallow in a way and I often went out with my friends spending money like it was going out of fashion.

And I was always looking for the next thing to do. I was a regular down at the market where there were lots of boxing fans and I became friends with many of them, including a guy called Graham Longdon, who ran a jewellery shop with his wife. He was a big boxing enthusiast and he knew everything about sport;

boxing and Sheffield United in particular. And I had an eye for jewellery. I told Graham that I had always wanted to be in the jewellery business, which was a bit of an exaggeration, but I certainly liked it. He liked boxing and I liked jewellery so we got on well together. I started to go down to his shop and as people came in to talk to me, Graham soon realised that I could bring more business in for him, not only through the people who I knew in boxing, but also just who I was.

Before long we got to talking about me buying shares in the business. And with the ability to take money out of the bank, I emptied it, gave it to Graham and in return I received some shares, half of the business I think. I didn't see the need for a meeting at solicitors, because it seemed a simple enough process to me and Graham seemed like a decent bloke so I was happy to part with my cash.

From the moment I became a partner in the business I didn't know what was happening on the money side, but business was booming and I had a hobby that I enjoyed and that I might even make some money out of. People used to come in or walk past and shout:

*"Alright Bomber!"*

I loved it. It was a real feel good adventure. And they were great fun times in the shop. I only had to be in there for a few hours and we'd do a bomb. And some of the boys from the gym came down – they liked their jewellery too. Not Glyn though. He was much too sensible for all that stuff.

I wasn't getting much money out of the business though; I suppose it was reinvested in stock. But I'd put a lot of my money in it and sometimes I actually ran out and had to go and ask my Mum and Dad for a sub. I didn't feel right doing that because they'd worked so hard for their money and I felt bad. I hated it but I did it nevertheless. Parents will always help out, even when you're earning well. And I was definitely earning well, but they didn't question me.

Mum and Dad always helped me but I wasn't really helping myself. Some of my friends at the time took liberties with my money, and I was happy to let them. I was naïve in many ways but I always thought that a friend in need should be helped. You might say I've been stupid at times, I prefer to say trusting. But I think maybe I gave too much to some of the wrong people. I lent one guy twenty five thousand pounds and I didn't get it back. I can't even remember his name. But at the time I didn't mind it because the money was coming in and I couldn't see an end to that. But it was all going out as quickly as it was coming in, and on what?

And now I ask myself, 'What have I given to my parents?'

At the time I took them out for meals and did buy them stuff, but in later life it became a preoccupation for me. Mum and Dad had done so much for me and worked so hard to do that – I kept on asking myself the same question all the time, 'What have I given to Mum and Dad?'

But in the heady days of the early eighties it didn't concern me too much. It was a time to spend, spend, spend. And if I could carry on climbing the world boxing ladder then there was no reason why I'd ever need to stop.

# 7

## <u>Calm Down</u>

*"In sleepy London town there's just no place for a street fighting man!"*

## Mick Jagger

From time to time life can be going so well that you wonder whether you're actually in a dream. And sometimes you know you are in a dream and you simply don't want it to end. At the ripe old age of twenty six, and with the British, European and Commonwealth light middleweight titles under my belt, life couldn't really get much better. I had filled out and bulked up enough to move up to middleweight class and that looked like opening some pretty smart doors for me. I had been watching Marvin Hagler's career from across the water, and was in awe of the way he just took people apart. That was what I was aspiring to. And I was still unbeaten after thirty one professional fights. Brendan had his way of making me believe that I could go all the way to the top, but also he had his way of keeping my feet on the ground, as did the city that had become home to me.

As Hagler prepared for his biggest test to date, defending his world title against Tommy 'The Hitman' Hearns in sun drenched Las Vegas, I set out for my morning run in Sheffield, wrapped up against the cold and ready to get pissed wet through. But then again, no amount of sunshine can beat the wave and cheer of someone you know as you pound the streets. On a ten mile run I'd have at least twenty people shouting, 'Hi' or 'come on Herol' and it was always a massive lift.

And this particular day I was especially chipper because I'd just had my new house fitted out with new furniture and carpets, exactly to my exquisite taste. My favourites were the bright white carpet I had leading from the entrance and into my lounge where my brand new pink leather settee took pride of place. I'd come a long way from the days in Nottingham when Lilian and I cuddled on the settee adorned by a huge crocheted blanket, and surrounded by doilies. No such old fashioned chintz here, this pink leather beast was the ultimate weapon of sophistication and seduction. Barry White, the Love Walrus himself would have been mightily impressed. But oddly, Glyn wasn't.

*"What the fuck is that?!"*

He had the creased grimace of someone watching one of those red arsed baboons doing a shit.

*"Get your shoes off. You're dragging mud all over my carpet."* I protested as I reached for a brush. Glyn looked down and then hopped up as if he had just realised he was standing on hot coals:

*"Jesus Christ Herol!"*

*"What? You have no fucking class. This stuff is mega."* I was torn between being genuinely offended and highly amused by Glyn's disgust.

*"Just you wait until the ladies see this?"*

*"They'll be out of the fucking door before you can get your leather polish out mate. That's if they haven't gone blind!"*

So we had to agree to differ on that one, and Glyn moved away from Fen Chui and onto the altogether more comfortable area of boxing:

*"Hagler's going to get a whack next week."*

I wasn't sure about that.


There was a huge amount of circus hype surrounding the Hearns and Hagler match, which was being billed as the richest fight in history at over 40 million dollars. Each of the fighters was going to pocket over five million. The fight had been sold out in 24 hours with the cheapest of the 15,000 tickets at three hundred dollars.

Hearns was stoking up the fight and getting mouthy. He had a sign put up in his training gym at Caesars Palace which read:

## "TOMMY SEZ, I'M IN GREAT SHAPE. I WILL KO HAGLER IN THREE. I STILL DISLIKE MARVIN."

No particularly impressive words, but if it worked for Tommy fair enough.

It was a tough fight to call and Hearns had actually become the bookies marginal favourite, mainly because a group of wealthy gamblers from his home town of Detroit had been piling in. But Hagler was his usual cool self and the smarter money was backing him. He'd already defended his title ten times since he took it off Alan Minter in 1980.

During the build up Hearns started banging on about 'greatness' which seemed a little premature given that he was about to meet someone who already had that. And things took a turn for the sillier at the pre fight press conference when Hearns called Hagler a midget, not the best description for someone only three inches shorter. Hagler then called the Hitman a freak.

I watched all this with great interest. I'd never gone in for pre fight hulabaloo. I loved the attention but I could never be bothered with all that, 'I'm going to make mincemeat out of him, by the time I've finished he won't even know his own name,' sort of crap. I think it would have looked daft if I came out with that sort of stuff while I had to put all my effort into trying not to laugh when I was supposed to be looking mean. I'd look a right dick, and I thought that some of the guys who did it looked just that.

But then again, Hagler was the man I dreamed about meeting and Brendan kept telling me that if I bided my time then one day it would come. So there was a serious side when it came to watching what they were doing, and watching particularly how Hagler handled himself. Hearns was doing all the talking, saying that he would knock Hagler out in three, and Hagler was generally letting everybody else do the talking. Some pretty respected characters like Ali's old trainer Angelo Dundee said that if Hearns didn't knock Hagler out in three then he'd end up on the floor himself.

Dundee was nearer the mark than Hearn's backers as it turned out. Hearns was right about the third round but that was about the only thing that he was right about. He came out like a crazy bull from the start but soon Hagler was showering him with accurate punches. Hearns continued to have a go and in the third round he had drawn some blood from Hagler's forehead, but that just seemed to annoy the champion who immediately caught him with a vicious right hook that sent him crashing to the canvas on his face. Hearns struggled to his feet, then wobbled around for a couple of seconds, before looking drunk enough to convince the ref to stop the fight.

I had delayed my Tuesday morning run so that I could listen to the fight, and in the event I didn't have to delay it for too long. And as I took my first breaths of the early morning Yorkshire air and gazed ahead into the drizzle I missed Hagler's victory interviews, but I had plenty to think about.

My first thought was how Hagler had dismantled another dangerous fighter, and then as I ran along I mused what Hearns must be feeling like. He had been cocky to say the least and he'd been given a lesson. I never wanted to do that. I'd rather look cocky in the ring and get a lesson than shoot my mouth off and fall flat on my face, quite literally. And I wouldn't have come out at Hagler like a bull in a china shop and walk straight into a pile of punches. I worked though in my mind what I would have done and the more I thought about it, the more I thought that my dream could come true. Right then, I would have given myself a forty per cent chance of winning a fight against Marvin Hagler. That in itself probably sounded a bit too self confident, but what did I have to convince me that I wouldn't deserve a chance? Thirty one fights and I'd never been beaten. I resolved to get a fight with the top man within two years.

While I dreamt of battling it out with the best fighter in the world in Vegas, Brendan continued to keep my feet on the ground;

*"He's from fucking Liverpool, and believe me, they breed hard bastards over there."*

He was talking about Jimmy Price, the bloke I was going to meet the following week for the vacant British Middleweight title. And it was a serious fight. While Hagler was picking up his few million, I think it was eight in the end, if I won I would pick up the biggest cheque of my seven year professional career. Nineteen thousand pounds. Not bad at all. Not eight million, but it was more than most people in the UK earned in a year in the mid eighties.

And apart from the cash side of things, this was an important step on the ladder for me. If I was ever going to meet Marvin Hagler in the ring I couldn't afford to lose a domestic scrap with a Liverpudlian, no matter how hard he was. In any case, Brendan always seemed to have a big opinion of people in Liverpool, probably because a lot of them are Irish.

So I stepped up my training. I had plenty of speed work under my belt and so I worked more on my strength and punching. I spent hours punching the shit out of a sixteen stone bag and sparring with the lads in the gym. And Brendan was even keener than usual, as Jimmy Price's manager, Frank Warren had got under his skin. Warren was saying that I didn't have a big punch and that I'd been fed a long line of easy victories in my thirty one match run. I'd already been frustrated as Tony Sibson, Mark Kaylor and Errol Christie had all ducked fights with me and I could only beat what was in front of me. And some of them had been good. I had beaten Jose Seys, who turned Christie over easily enough and for all Warren's jibes I had stopped my previous nine opponents within the distance.

But I always trained for a twelve round fight, knowing that I was fitter and quicker than most. So if I was hitting hard, I felt I had more than enough to beat Price. He had won fourteen out of his fifteen fights, but the one he lost was against Ayub Kalule, a classy south paw who had flattened him in less than two minutes. I think that was why Frank Warren was spouting, because he knew that Price wouldn't fancy me. And Brendan drummed that deeper into my consciousness as we drove down to London.

Over the past week we had spent hours watching videos of Price and in the fight against Kalule we noticed that when he punched he opened his hand and so he left a gap. So I worked on my right hand uppercuts all week, while intermittently watching the videos. The other thing I noticed was that Jimmy seemed to be a slow starter. And he had that brilliant comedy

Scouse haircut, with the tight perm and moustache. I just hoped he didn't resort to saying, 'Calm down, calm down,' to me in the ring. That would have finished me off!

But all in all, as we arrived in London I felt mentally, tactically and physically prepared and I just wanted to relax in the hotel in the evening, but Brendan kept on at me:

*"This is a big chance for you son. Jimmy Price isn't in your class, you know where you can hurt him. But keep your eye on him. No slip ups."*

I sensed he was keen to make Frank Warren eat some humble pie.

How often does a plan go perfectly? Not often enough, but I felt that I had everything in my favour for this one. The tremendous Sheffield fans were there in their hoards, and when we arrived at the Britannia Centre in London's east end there must have been five coaches and fifty cars from Yorkshire outside which made me burst with pride and more determined than ever to do them proud.

The Britannia Centre was quite new, but from my point of view the architects had made a glaring omission if they planned for this to be a showcase boxing arena. I was shown to my dressing room, or a space more frequently used as the ladies toilets. Bloody great. They had gone to the lengths of advising all the ladies in the crowd to relieve themselves at least half an hour before the fight started. I didn't really want some desperate woman banging on the door as Brendan gave me my last instructions and I put on my shiny shorts. 'I bet Marvin Hagler doesn't get changed in the ladies' bog' I thought to myself. Having said that, I must admit that it was much nicer than most of the men's toilets I'd ever been in to. It smelled more of soap than piss and there were plenty of coat hooks to hang my stuff on. So I shouldn't complain I guess. This was the British Middleweight title fight and there's something brilliantly British about getting changed next to a machine that dispenses sanitary towels.

But all thoughts of ladies' poo quickly disappeared from my mind as I stepped out into the arena to be met by a fantastic cheer. I would guess the place held just over a thousand, and at least half of those were from Yorkshire, I could recognise so many faces. And as I climbed in to the ring I saw Tony Sibson and John H Stracey. I wasn't sure why Tony was there, other than for a night out. I didn't imagine that he wanted to fight me.

The bell went and Jimmy came at me in a blur of frizzy hair and whirling fists, much like Kevin Keegan going for Billy Bremner in the 1974 Charity Shield, but more dangerous. I moved about and watched, took a couple of shots and gave two back. And low and behold he was boxing just as he did against Kalule. I saw the gap and ripped an uppercut right through the hole and he went down. The crowd roared and the excited atmosphere suddenly reached a new height. Jimmy got up, took a count and then came at me again. And I got him again. Same thing – right hand right up through the gap and he staggered back again, before falling over.

The fight couldn't have been a minute old, and the Sheffield fans were going crazy. The cries of 'come on Bomber' that I heard on every run as I trained in the streets of Sheffield were now all united in an incredible passion that almost lifted me up off the canvas. They were a hundred times as loud. Jimmy came at me again and I jabbed, moved and ripped another right through the gap and he was down. The arena exploded as the ref signalled the end and called Jimmy's training and medical people in.

As the fans carried on cheering I was handed the Lonsdale Belt and I looked around the arena bursting with pride. Lilian had brought Natasha down to watch and she came in the ring to see me. As I lifted her up and the cameras flashed I felt like the luckiest man in the world.

Brendan came over with more than a twinkle in his eye. He knew that Frank Warren would have been gutted, but he was gracious enough to say that I'd done the job brilliantly. This was the best yet.

Tony Sibson wasn't quite so magnanimous. He said:

*"He won't want me even now,"* with all the conviction of a fat man who'd just been invited to take part in the World Limbo Dancing Championships.

♦

The Sheffield Star ran a big piece after the British Title fight which gave the fans a deserved pat on the back. They meant the world to me and I wanted to thank every one of them. The Star interviewed a few of them who all said that they'd take out loans to come to support me if I got a fight in America. One bloke called Barry came down to London to watch the fight the week after his house in Midhill had burned down, and he said he'd follow me to the US. And my oldest fan, Harry Crump, who was eighty four at the time, said I was 'the best thing since sliced bread'. The sporting passion of Sheffield had been there for all to see in London and was watched by millions on TV, and they deserved every bit of credit for opening eyes in the world south of Watford, as we did for working out Jimmy Price.

But while the Sheffield superstars made their way back up the M1, Brendan and I stayed in London. We'd been asked to meet with Barney Eastwood's people, and this was the first time that we had been noticed by more than the odd spectator on a world stage. It had been my biggest purse so far, and now Eastwood wanted me to be the top support turn on the undercard for Barry McGuigan's World Featherweight fight against Eusebio Pedroza at Queens Park Rangers in June. That was massive, and the plan was to line up a big American for me to have a shot at in front of the eyes of the world.

Brendan was delighted:

*"It's been a grind son, trying to convince everybody. But they've seen it for themselves now. You can do whatever you want to do; it's in your hands."*

We both had Hagler in mind.

But there were other doors opening as well. Even Tony Sibson's camp started making some noises that they wanted to get a fight on, going so far as to say that they would only stage a fight in his Leicester stamping ground. I didn't take much notice of that for too long, and a couple of weeks later he was stripped of his European title. He had injury and illness problems I was told, and he did look to me like he was carrying a bit of weight. He was threatening to quit the game after asking for a postponement and then being stripped of his title, so he was feeling a little sore I guess.

So the silver lining to that little Leicestershire cloud, was that I was named as the top contender for the European Middleweight title and was lined up to meet Ayub Kalule, the former World Champion. I couldn't do the date that he was due to fight Sibson, because it was only a week after I was due on the McGuigan card at QPR.

♦

I travelled down to London with Brendan on the sunny Friday evening in June, ready to fight at Loftus Road, on a card that would surely give me even bigger exposure. Barry McGuigan's fight with Pedroza was going to be screened world wide and I had been lined up, as the second billed fight, to meet the former middleweight challenger Wilford Skypion. Brendan had been reading boxing news and read out to me their opinion of Skypion:

*"There's no science about him; he's a strong brawler who likes to be the aggressor and take control of the ring."*

He'd had a World Title shot and done pretty well until Hagler picked him off in the fourth round. And Brendan told me that although he was the most dangerous fighter I'd met to date, he was easily disheartened. So I figured that if I moved him around quickly enough and caught him while he swung at me, I'd soon enough get the better of him.

The world class Sheffield boxing fans were confident too, and the following morning, some of them had even set off at five in the morning to make the ten o' clock weigh in. I was pleased to see them there because Skypion looked like one mean bastard, scowling at me as I smiled back at him – I needed all the support I could get but I knew I could rely on it. And when we arrived at the stadium in the evening there were hundreds there, many faces I knew, all cheering and shouting their 'good lucks'. The stadium itself looked spectacular with the floodlights on, stands full and the ring brightly shining in the middle. And no changing in the ladies for this one, we had a smart area sectioned off for us in the club gym. I was bouncing, right up for this and determined to do my friends proud.

As the time got closer, Brendan was called out by some officials and he left me in the changing area with Glyn. We didn't think anything of it, but when Brendan returned he had a furrowed brow:

*"There may be a problem with Skypion's skull.'*

*"What?"*

Before every fight there is a compulsory skull x-ray and for obvious reasons, but this time it seemed that the medics were having a closer look at something. Skypion looked hard enough to have been built artificially, but I'd never experienced a last minute check like this.

But we had to stay focussed and as we got within fifteen minutes of the fight I started to get my hands taped as Brendan gave his usual last minute bits of advice and encouragement. Then, as I took a swig from a bottle of water a guy in a suit came in and beckoned Brendan. After a minute of back and forward and hand waving on Brendan's part he came back over to me:

*"It's off."*

*"Fuck no. No way!"*

I couldn't believe it. How the fuck could they call a fight off ten minutes before it was due to start. I was right on edge, nervous, excited and now absolutely devastated. Wilford's head x-ray had revealed something the medics weren't happy with. So how in God's name did he come to get so close to climbing in the bloody ring? This was the most ridiculous thing I'd ever heard. Apparently there was a delay in the medical report getting through to the doctors. But how could this happen?

I was gutted for myself, we'd turned down other opportunities, including a European fight with Kalule, but these chances would come again I guess. But I felt like we'd let down hundreds of fans who had come down from Sheffield. The most disgusting thing was that they only found that the fight was off by word of mouth, after one of them spotted me in the press box and came for a word. These lads and girls had spent hundreds of pounds coming to support me and they were treated like shit. They didn't get to see us at all and nobody told them why. Two of them had even come down in a chauffer driven Mercedes to make a special day of it. It always took a lot to stop me from smiling but at that very moment I was absolutely furious, and so was Brendan.

♦

While we were still getting over the Loftus Road farce, we had another setback. One of the consequences of going on the undercard for the McGuigan fight was that my European date with Kalule had to be put on hold. And before we could get it on, Tony Sibson announced his comeback in the autumn and so I went back a step. I now had to wait for Sibson to defend his title against Kalule before I had my chance, and this pissed me off even more.

We didn't have anything on until a fight with Roberto Ruiz at the Albert Hall in October, but the lead up to that turned out to be more entertaining than I could ever have imagined. Brendan and I had gone down to London to discuss the fight with Ruiz and we were invited to a press conference that was being held in the run up to a fight at Wembley between Errol Christie and Mark Kaylor, that was an eliminator to challenge me for the British title.

Someone had been revving this fight up something rotten and there was already a fair bit of bad blood between the two. Errol was a black guy from Coventry with a nice but arrogant way about him. Mark was from West Ham and had some fans from within the National Front that attached themselves to him.

As we arrived at the casino restaurant where the press conference was taking place this guy asked me to go outside to have some photographs taken with Errol and Mark. When I went outside it was so funny because as I walked across I could see the two of them pointing at each other and clearly mouthing off. One thing you never do is to leave two fighters on their own in the run up to the fight, particularly if one is a cocky black man and the other has a fan base containing a smattering of skinheads with big comical boots. Errol was winding Mark up big style and I could almost see smoke coming out of his nostrils. Then what happened next was beyond the photographer's wildest dreams.

I can't remember exactly what was said to spark things off, but all of a sudden Mark grabbed Errol and tried to push him into a fountain that we were standing next to. Then Errol turned Mark over and he ended up on the floor. I was almost wetting myself at this stage as they started to brawl on the cobbles with cameras flashing and TV cameras whirring. By now some other people had come running out of the casino and shouts were going up. Brendan and I looked at each other and he said:

*"You'd better do something Herol."*

Before I could say, 'why me?' I found myself standing in between the two of them. Mark through a punch and I just managed to swerve it and it hit Errol smack in the face. As Errol wobbled, Brendan got hold of him and I got hold of Mark before their managers came out and belatedly started to calm things down. But it was all too late. There was a good twenty seconds of footage winging its way to TV rooms around the world and this fight now reached new levels of animosity.

It certainly wasn't a stunt, there were some very nasty things being said by the fountain and the two of them genuinely hated each other as far as I could see.

I was caught a bit off guard when someone shoved a recorder in front of me and asked me what I thought of the whole thing. I was still laughing but managed to hold myself together enough to say:

*"There was a complete lack of discipline and temperament."*

Aware that he was unlikely to get anything more sensible from me the hack decided to try his luck with Brendan, and was treated to the full extent of his story telling Irish blarney:

*"It was like something from the Wild West,"* he began.

Possibly Laurel and Hardy in my opinion, but ignoring my chuckles Brendan continued unabated:

*"The whole place was absolutely stunned. Bomber and I grabbed hold of Christie and Kaylor and things calmed down a bit when their managers helped to pull them apart."*

So we were heroes. Brilliant!

But the Board of Boxing wasn't quite as amused and threatened to pull the fight. The chief of police also weighed in saying that he was worried that there would be race related fights between fans. He wrote to the Board condemning Mark and Errol's 'appalling' behaviour and 'the effect it could have on the current climate of unrest'. This scuffle was sandwiched between the Brixton and Toxteth riots of the early eighties and the Handsworth riots to come. And a section of socially limited West Ham fans never need a particular reason to run around like gangs in a playground shouting some political slogan before sticking the boot in to the nearest passer by. So there was certainly a serious side to the whole thing. Mark and Errol could have shaken hands, laughed it off and got on with it all I'm sure, but the knuckleheads who knew very little about boxing would struggle to do that.

I don't think the national media were trying to help, they kept printing headlines like:

## "BOXING ON TRIAL"

… either with a picture of Errol and Mark rolling around by a fountain, or a picture of Mark looking like a steely eyed and clean cut member of Hitler Youth next to a picture of Errol laughing.

After lots of coming and going, attempts at reconciliation and threats by the board to scrap the fight, they eventually got it on in November. I went to watch it with Brendan, and there was a massive police and security presence. But there wasn't any trouble at all, just the odd firework going off. And this time, without the distraction of a fountain to try to lob Errol into, Mark managed to knock him out in the eighth round.

So all in all things had settled down quietly and the sport had got back to normal. After the fight Brendan took the opportunity to tell the press that we weren't really bothered who won, because I'd knock them out in four or five rounds whoever they were. It's not the sort of thing I'd ever want to say myself, but in all honesty I didn't mind Brendan saying it.

Unfortunately that wasn't the end of it for Mark and Errol though, as they both got hit by a big fine – twenty grand between them. Ouch! I bet that hurt more than the fight itself.

# 8

# <u>Sticks and Stones</u>

*"Actions speak louder than words."*

# 17<sup>th</sup> Century Proverb

Brendan had been talking to Barry McGuigan's people ever since we met in the run up to the QPR event. At the time it was a real cock up for me, because I'd wasted my time and the Sheffield boxing fans had wasted theirs too, not to mention the cash. But it seems that Barney Eastwood fancied having me in his camp and he'd made an offer to Brendan that he couldn't refuse.

I think he paid him quite a lot of money, but I'm not too sure, and then Brendan would pick up a percentage of my earnings afterwards. He was also going to stay as my trainer while Barney managed the financial side of things.

I also hoped to receive some money from the deal, but more than that, I was excited that I had now been taken on by someone with real financial muscle. I thought that signing up with Barney would get me on the world stage quicker and bring my dream shot at fighting Marvin Hagler even closer. By this stage I was twenty six years old and I needed a title shot before too long. I was still unbeaten, some people were saying I was still untested, but I could only beat whatever had been put in front of me, and I'd stopped the last ten opponents within the distance. I really felt that this was going to take me all the way, or at least give me the best chance.

Brendan knew the fight game inside out though, and I was happy that he was part of all the deal. And I trusted him. He had always kept me in touch with what was happening on the money side of things. He explained to me that when we got paid, I got my percentage after all the costs had been paid. Sometimes I didn't quite understand where all the money had gone but that wasn't my strength. Whenever we went abroad there seemed to be loads of people coming along that we were paying, and when I asked Brendan about it he used to say to me:

*"You don't see where a lot of the money goes because there's this and that to pay...we have to cover this and that... "*

So I was happy that he had control of it all. I got what I was due after everybody else had been paid, which I guess is how business works. But I always seemed to be paying for something. I got my percentage of the percentage and that's how it was. I couldn't complain though because I was getting paid an awful lot more than most of the people who came to cheer me on, so I felt grateful for that. I had my own house and could buy what I wanted, when I wanted, as much chicken and as many leather settees as I needed – so that was fine.

Sometimes I was paid cash and sometimes I was paid by cheque. We had carried on doing loads of exhibitions even when I was an established pro fighter and we never charged for those events, they were all done for goodwill. And I enjoyed them anyway. Maybe some managers, especially these days, would have said that we wouldn't go if we didn't get paid, but at that time we did it all for free. Sometimes they did a collection at the working men's clubs and the money went towards the gym, so we got something I guess. I suppose my percentage of that was being able to use the gym.

I didn't want money ruling me so I just got on with it. That was my nature. And now, it seemed that neither Brendan nor I had to worry about it. It was all going to be taken care of by the expert and we could get on with training and boxing. The Sheffield Star made out that Brendan was a bit of a financial muppet, saying that all the bills at home were handled by Mrs Ingle, and that I had been baffled by his blarney and non stop talking. I admit that I had sometimes got frustrated that I was stuck in Sheffield when other fighters were getting bigger profile in London, but all in all we had struggled through and I was happy to be with Brendan.

But now this was a fantastically exciting time. Barney said that in me and Barry he had the best two fighters in the country and I felt honoured to be mentioned in the same sentence as such a tremendous boxer and such a great man. I thought that I had the best of both worlds. I could now move with the top boxers and still keep my links with Sheffield.

We had some great lads at the gym on Newman Road. I was big mates with Brian Anderson, and he was some fighter. He got to be number three contender in Britain by the end of 1985. Brendan managed to keep us both going with me looking towards Europe while Brian worked towards domestic titles. He's a great bloke and we never really wanted to fight against each other. Glyn Rhodes became a big mate too but he has never stopped telling me I was as mad as a box of frogs. He was a straight talking, tough fighting little guy – great to spar with and he helped me a lot with training over many years. Johnny Nelson was a good laugh too, he fancied himself as a bit of a ladies man and a singer – I used to wet myself every time he started to croon. But he got his own back whenever he could.

We used to go to the old Sheath Valley swimming baths in Sheffield on a Friday evening because they had a sauna in there that we could use. We had bets with each other as to who could lose the most weight. I was more than happy going in the sauna wrapped up in towels, it was just nice for me but then Johnny always insisted we went in the plunge pool. When I was in it wasn't cool. I hate the cold at the best of times but I screamed the house down whenever it was my time to go in the plunge pool and everybody pissed themselves. Johnny was usually still laughing as we got changed before disappearing off to the night clubs.

Brian and I especially liked to go to Isabella's night club, having a few drinks and then doing our thing on the dance floor. We went there virtually every Friday night for a few years and got our faces known. Glyn often took the piss out of us sharking on the dance floor and one time he could hardly speak he was laughing so much. He'd met a girl who he knew from school who he had taken to Isabella's some two years earlier. She'd been away, travelling or something and had come back to Sheffield to see her parents. When Glyn bumped into her this evening the first thing she said to him was:

*"I can't believe it. I came here two years ago and saw Herol and Brian Anderson on the dance floor. I come back two years later and they're still there on the floor in exactly the same spot!"*

Well, I always say if you stick to the same formula and put the practice in you'll more often than not reap the rewards. But that was ridiculous and, in the event disproved my theory.

But these were great times and I was glad that making a move with management meant I didn't have to break all my ties.

♦

So I went to my fight with the Argentinean, Roberto Ruiz, with new management. At this stage I didn't notice any difference. Brendan was still in my corner, we did have some conversations with Barney, but nothing that changed anything we were doing. And I prepared for the fight the way I always did. I'd always been on an hour and a half run every morning before I went to the gym, and I saw no reason to change that. Brian often came with me and he was happy getting up at five to run eight miles before everyone else had made it for breakfast. It's a good way to regulate weight for a start. Once you have been running for forty minutes or so you start to burn off any excess fat. At first some of my mates at the gym thought I was stupid and I didn't have to do that, but I did. I needed my heart ticking away while I kept moving, because when I eventually stepped into the ring for a fight I wanted to be able to keep moving. I didn't want to be one of those fighters who stood virtually still with their hands up and then when they got tired just slugged it out until one of them fell over. Sport has more art than that. At the time there was a tennis player called Roscoe Tanner who served the fastest that anyone had ever seen. And he started a trend of big guys serving at 140mph and slugging it out with one shot rallies. I didn't see that as the best type of entertainment, I used to love watching Ilie Nastase and then John McEnroe.

I wanted to be quick and agile but also to have a wicked punch. I was stopping virtually everyone I came across so I must have been doing something right. I had started to go running in the morning with two kilo weights in my hands, so that when I got back to the gym and started sparring, my hands were much lighter and much quicker. They were like lightning –bang, bang, bang. Eventually I could move as quickly with the weights in my hands as some lads could do without the weights.

I was getting quicker at seeing off opponents and Ruiz was no different. At the Albert Hall I had cut his eye so badly that the ref stopped the fight in the second round, and so that was my third victory of 1985, taking up a total of less than eight rounds for all three.

My confidence was soaring sky high again, and I had my eyes on a European title shot against Ayub Kalule which was scheduled for the beginning of 1986. Brendan told me that I was now ranked third in the world by the WBC and that was amazing. By my reckoning, I could only really be two fights away from a world title shot, but Barney thought it would be nearer four. So I guess I'd be fighting people I should beat before I got a really big test. I couldn't quite work out the logic and I tried not to get impatient.

So I just carried on. We had a fight booked against a six foot four American called Sanderline Williams to be staged in Belfast. This was at the height of the troubles over there but there's nothing better than sport to unite people and Barney was keen to show people in his own country the new fighter he had signed. Belfast has a fantastic boxing tradition and we got a great reception as we went down the Shankhill Road, and Brendan was charming people with his blarney wherever we went. The only slightly uneasy moment was when we went to a do at a club next door to the Crumlin jail and the master of ceremonies introduced me as 'the Bomber'. You could have heard a pin drop. Until they realised I was black and evidently wouldn't know the difference between semtex and blancmange.

Williams was a journeyman kind of fighter and pretty well unknown, and so when we stepped into the ring at the Ulster Hall I got a big cheer from the packed crowd, they were on my side. Barney and Brendan's PR work had done a treat. The Irish had accepted me as an adopted son. And as the fight began the cheers continued while I did my thing, moving and scoring. But Williams was stronger and more awkward than I had expected and by the fifth, while Brendan told me I was ahead in three rounds, I was no where near finishing the fight. The crowd had expected some fireworks, particularly those who had looked at my record, but they never came. Over the next five rounds we just slugged it out. I kept trying to move him around and speed things up, but something just wasn't there for me. Williams was the first fighter I'd met for a while that I couldn't work out. I could sense that he was about to go in the ninth round, but I just couldn't find that extra ten per cent I needed to finish him off.

There was some disappointment in the crowd as, at first they went quieter and then by the end of the ninth round there were some jeers coming through. This was a whole new experience for me and I couldn't afford to let the poor show for the audience affect the result. So, just as I did when there were big cheers for me, I had to shut out the jeers and keep focussed on the job. Which I did well enough to win the contest on points, an announcement that was met by a fairly loud boo from one section of the crowd.

So that was it. Job done, less fun and time to get out and work on the next fight. Inside I was a bit hurt though and it made me realise that I wanted to be liked. I always had people being friendly to me in Sheffield and I loved that. I couldn't play the villain – I just wanted to make people happy and pleased with me but this time I had failed.

Brendan told me not to worry about it and, with his magical Irish spin, said that a fight like that might tempt one or two of the fighters who had not been keen to fight me, to come out of hiding. So, in a strange way, a poor fight may have helped me. Brilliant stuff Brendan!

His mood went a bit darker though when Barney got on his case, saying that my preparation was poor and that I should have had more structured training and had some American sparring partners. I guess he was even more pissed off when he read the same thing in the papers. And I didn't like it either. Okay, we may not have lined up a string of American giants for me to spar with, but I would have liked to have seen Barney get in the ring with Glyn! And as always, I had worked bloody hard. I did my runs, did my speed work, did the strength work and never veered away from my strict diet. And the way Brendan trained me hadn't failed me so far. We'd won all thirty four of our professional fights and this was the first time I'd gone the distance since 1982. I liked the way Brendan trained me. He gave me plenty of guidance and encouragement but he also basically left me to get on with it. I kept winning because my opponents had no idea what I was going to do next, sometimes I didn't. But I was always fitter and quicker, so unless they got lucky or could keep up with me, more often than not they'd end up on their backsides.

Okay, against Sanderline Williams that didn't happen, but every great fighter in any sport needs to win ugly from time to time. It's just a shame that the ugly fight came on my first tour of Northern Ireland and maybe it made Barney look a bit of a dick in his own back yard after he'd said that Barry and I were the best two in the business. Anyhow, there was no need to start flinging mud at Brendan, particularly in the media.

♦

Christmas came and went and the new year brought with it our fight against the former World Champion Ayub Kalule. This was going to be a massive step for me. It was for the European title and I was getting nearer to an eliminator for the World title. Marvin Hagler was fighting John Mugabi (no relation) and once he'd seen him off I would be getting closer and closer, always assuming I did my thing.

Barney was still chipping away, saying that he insisted on bringing American fighters over for me to spar with. Why? Kalule wasn't American; in fact he lived in Scandinavia, so maybe we should have brought Abba over for me to spar with. They were admittedly past their best but I bet the one with the beard was pretty handy!

While we were putting up with that, Brendan showed me an interview that Tony Sibson had done after my fight with Sanderline Williams. He had said:

*"I think Graham has conned a lot of people. A lot of his opponents have been hand picked and made to measure. He has got where he is through the back alleys."* A bit unfair, but he carried on. *"I sparred with him once and it was like sparring with a limbo dancer. It would break my heart to give him a pay day."*

I thought he'd gone away. But, in any case, why in the world would it break poor Tony's heart to give me a pay day? What did he have against me? I did spar against him but we were sixteen, and it was just like boxing Mick Mills – rough and tough and like a nineteenth century hard as nails fist fighter. Mick couldn't hit me either but he never bad mouthed me. I thought it was kid's talk and Tony should just grow up. Maybe he was trying to explain himself because he had given up his British Title when I was nominated to fight him – but his explanation was coming out a bit muddled.

The Kalule fight was scheduled to be at Sheffield City Hall on the 5th February. Initially Barney had suggested we fight in Belfast, but maybe the less than happy reception there made him decide to steer clear for a while. But then Kalule's manager, who turned out to be a bit of an awkward sod, started moaning that we hadn't offered an increased purse to fight in Sheffield. Early in January Barney sent a warning by telex saying that unless they confirmed that the fight was on within twenty four hours, then he'd ask for Kalule to be stripped of his title and someone else be found for me to fight.

The Italian fighter Sumbu Kalambay was lined up as a replacement, in the event that Kalule's manager dug his heels in. And Frank Warren, in the knowledge that Sibson was safely down the pecking order started saying that he should be lined up ahead of Kalambay.

After lots of toing and froing and threats of legal action from all sides, by the middle of January we could get on and prepare. The fight on the 5th February in Sheffield had been confirmed once and for all. Brendan was delighted. He slapped me on the back and said:

*"This is it. This is what we've been working for Herol. This is the big one. It's not only the European title it's a world eliminator son."*

Kalule had fought the best of them all, including Sugar Ray Leonard. He had held the World light middleweight title so he was clearly no mug. In fact, once again, I was coming across the most dangerous fighter of my life. But Brendan was confident:

*"Once you have beaten Kalule, you can get that bastard Sibson in the ring."*

I think Brendan was still sore that despite all his efforts, with offers of money, Sibson wouldn't fight me when he held his titles a couple of years ago.

Meanwhile, Barney was over in Sheffield looking at Bramall Lane and Hillsborough as potential venues for the future. He knew that he wouldn't make a stack of cash from the Kalule fight at the City Hall and he had his sights on bigger pay days. But he also knew what an advantage it would be for me fighting in the same ring where I had won my British and Commonwealth titles, backed by a passionate crowd.

And true to his word, Barney had shipped in a group of American fighters for me to spar with. Up until then I had sparred with all the boys in the gym, but mostly with Brian. He was doing ever so well and was up to number twelve in the European rankings, so he was great to spar with. But I admit that we did know each other pretty well and we were big mates, so things may have been getting a bit comfortable. There were two blokes from New York, Cecil Pettegrew (great name for a fighter) and Kevin 'Kid' Johnson (better), they both talked like James Cagney but they were bigger. Not as big as this lump called Victor Codova though. He was an unbeaten light heavyweight Latin American, Rocky Balboa lookalike, who didn't speak any English. He just grunted at me and certainly didn't mess about in the gym. He was so big, Glyn was stood behind him when he was sitting down and I couldn't see him! But I don't think he had much of a sense of humour, and I didn't think it'd be worth trying to find out. When I grinned at him and put my hand out to shake his, he just walked past me. But these lads had all sparred with Hagler and Hearns and so maybe Barney had a point. And my idea to get Benny from Abba was clearly wide of the mark. Barney was upping the ante in all ways, we had press and TV cameras at the St Thomas's gym and there was a professional feel about the whole thing.

No one would question what he had done for Barry McGuigan and I just hoped that he could do the same for me. Along with Barry, Dennis Taylor and Pat Jennings, Barney was one of the most famous faces in Irish sport. And he had made millions out of it. The money he had paid to Brendan for my contract was petty cash. And he was super canny with his cash, having made a bundle as a bookmaker.

♦

I was as fit as ever and getting sharper all the time. Sparring with Cordova definitely kept me on my toes and with two weeks to go before the Kalule fight everything seemed to be going to plan. But then Sibbo's manager Frank Warren turned up again to try to stick a fly in the ointment. Sibson had been out for well over a year, but as he was trying to make a comeback Warren was making sure he stayed in everybody's minds. He began waving a contract that he had for Sibbo to fight Kalule on the 26th February, and insisting that he couldn't step in the ring with me three weeks earlier. I was starting to wish that these two would just go away, but Brendan told me it was just a cheap way of getting publicity while Sibson was trying to get back,

Another win, but it looks like Brenden may have spotted Barney coming

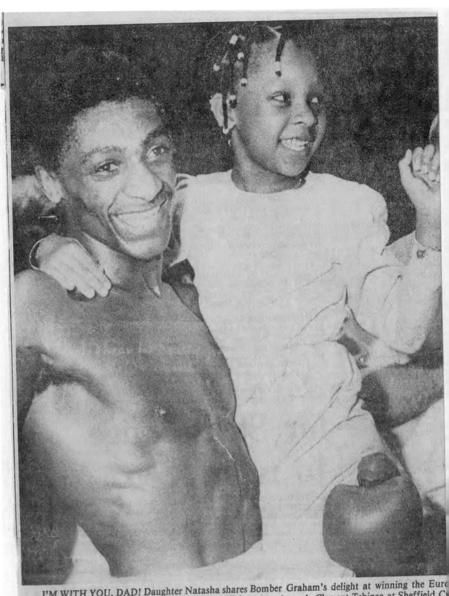

I'M WITH YOU, DAD! Daughter Natasha shares Bomber Graham's delight at winning the Euro weight championship in the second round against Luxembourg's Clement Tshinza at Sheffield C
Full story — Back Page.

A cheer for Daddy from my darling Natasha

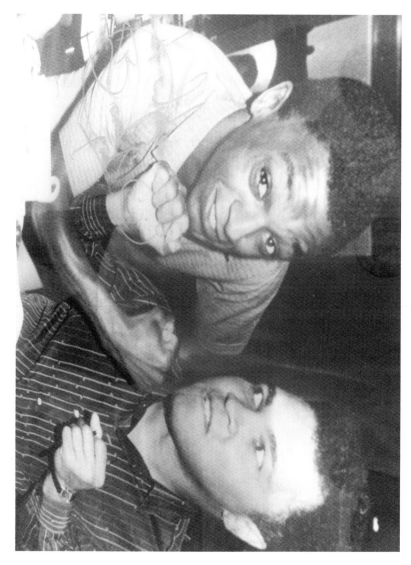

My Hero (the one on the right)

# I WON'T BOX MY PAL SAYS CHAMP

**BOXING champion Herol "Bomber" Graham is delivering a knockout blow to his own career—for the sake of friendship.**

He has vowed never to step into the professional ring with his best pal and fellow fighter Brian Anderson.

And he is refusing to break their amazing pact —even though it could mean losing his British light-middleweight title.

## Friendship

For Brian, 21, has been nominated as the man he must beat to hold onto his coveted Lonsdale Belt.

But 23-year-old Bomber says he will stand down and go for the vacant European title rather than trade punches with his closest friend.

"It's a small price to pay for our friendship," he said at their Sheffield training HQ yesterday.

"The only way we

BI PHILIP BRAUND

would square up in earnest is if we were both going for the world championship."

Brian, of Hillsborough, Sheffield, added: "We're great friends — Bomber was even best man at my wedding.

"There's no way we could fight for real. Each Punch would hurt me as much as him.

"Sparring is different. If someone gets cut you pack it in. But in a title match you go for the kill."

Sheffield boxing promoter Alma Ingle said: "bomber's gesture is typical of the lad.

"He's all heart— unless he's in the ring chasing honours."

**SPARRING PALS:** Champion Bomber and Brian yesterday.
**Picture: PHIL SPENCER**

Me and Brian

World Title - Mike McCallum preparing to snatch my body

Me at the birth of Natasha

Me with Glyn and Naz

 PANIX PROMOTIONS AND BANNER PROMOTIONS IN ASSOCIATION WITH JESS HARDING
**Proudly Present**

**12x3ₘᵢₙ rounds for the WBC SUPER MIDDLEWEIGHT International Title**

# The Taming of the Devil

## Good v Evil

# HEROL GRAHAM VINNIE PAZIENZA

**12X3MIN ROUNDS FOR THE WBC INTERNATIONAL SUPER BANTAMWEIGHT TITLE**

# PATRICK 'THE SCHOOLBOY' MULLINGS V HVIVHA HDRIAN

### PLUS FULL SUPPORTING BILL

 **6th December 1997**

**Ticket Prices VIP RINGSIDE £85, RINGSIDE £65, STALLS £40, £30, £20**

Doors Open 5.30pm                                    Boxing Commences 6.15pm

MATCHMAKER DEAN POWELL

WEMBLEY (CREDIT CARD BOOKINGS) 0181 900 1234 - JESS HARDING (CREDIT CARD BOOKINGS) 01707 642 982

PANIX PROMOTIONS 0171 247 1000 - MARTINI CARS 0181 667 0000

The pic that got me in a spot of bother

My beautiful kids

Karen and Me on the way to Michael Watson's tribute

and Barney said that he just didn't understand what Warren was trying to do.

As it seems is always the way, Warren threatened to sue, but the European Boxing Union then threatened to strip Kalule of his title if he didn't fight. Warren was trying everything he could for his fighter and I can understand that he was doing his job. But he seemed to be fighting a personal battle with Mike Barrett, the promoter of our fight. Apparently they had some history and on this occasion Barrett accused Warren of trying to sabotage our contest, so that he could get more publicity for his other client Pat Cowdell's comeback in Doncaster the following night. I'm not sure what Sibbo thought about all this. Just to add insult to Sibbo's injury, Mark Kaylor came out (not literally) in the papers and said that he was only interested in fighting boxers in the top ten in the world ( he was ninth). That ruled out Sibbo, who was still under the unfortunate impression that he was the best. He was a good fighter in his early years, and scrapped his way to a World title fight with Marvin Hagler in 1983. But that was a long time ago now and there were too many good European boxers around for him to have an easy route to bashing his way back up.

Eventually, just over a week before the fight was due to take place, Brendan got a telegram from the British Boxing Board of Control telling him that the European Boxing Union had confirmed that the fight would go ahead as planned. Thank God.

♦

Kalule flew in to Manchester Airport three days before the fight, bringing his impressive record with him. He'd lost only three of his forty eight fights, and all those were in World title fights. He was some boxer, a pressure fighter who liked to come forward all the time and he could hit hard with both hands. He had won the World light middleweight title in 1979 and defended it four times and no one beat him until Sugar Ray Leonard.

The mood in our gym was bouncing as always. The extra publicity had given us a lift, and the only downer was that Mick had to withdraw from the card when he injured his neck in training. We spent some time taking the piss out of Kalule's manager who, after trying to get more money for the fight when we moved it to Sheffield, kept saying that I wasn't good enough to fight his man. If he really thought that, then why didn't he just get someone else to fight him? Anyway, with his big glasses and comb over hair he looked like Bobby Charlton and Deidre Barlow's love child, so it was difficult to take him seriously, especially as when he spoke he sounded like the Swedish chef off the Muppets. But he kept saying I wasn't good enough anyway.

I knew Kalule was a good fighter and I had to be at my best to have a chance, but I didn't have to respect his manager. Having said that, Bobby and Deirdre's lad wasn't going to be in the ring, and Kalule, who was, had taken a lot of hammer over the years, he was very durable, so I thought I may have to go the full distance.

Brendan, as always, did his best to keep me focussed, which had been tricky at times when all the squabbling was going on over the past few weeks, but now we were both happy that the day had arrived and we could get on with it.

The evening had a special feel about it as we arrived in the dark, and snow fell thickly from the night sky. I hated the cold but it was one of the vital ingredients that always helped northerners to create a special, hostile atmosphere for visitors at any sporting event. How often do you see a London football club win on a Tuesday night in February in Lancashire or Yorkshire? We're tough up North and every bit of discomfort for the visitors is a bonus. Having said that, I wouldn't be surprised if Kalule's manager had arrived on skis.

Inside the hall the atmosphere was electric. It was packed to the rafters with the Sheffield and Rotherham fans, as well as forty commentators and TV technicians, and Harry Carpenter, who was introducing the fight on Sports Night, which was being screened live to twelve million viewers.

I could hear the chanting from the arena as Brendan taped my hands and passed on his last few words. He told me Alma, his wife, had predicted I'd take him down in the seventh and that made me smile. So that'd have to be it.

As I walked out towards the ring, lights flashed all around and the crowd went crazy, completely crazy. I tried not to look up too much, because I would have found it hard not to smile or laugh when I saw the faces of any of the guys I knew. So I just climbed into the ring, danced around a bit and just looked at the canvas.

When the bell went for the first round a roar went up and at last we were on the way. I was well pumped up and had the chance to get all the angst out that had been in me since the let down in Ireland, aggravated by legal farting about and Sibbo's camp winding me up. The tension worked for me and I went on the attack pretty early. I had Kalule staggering in the second and found it easy enough to get out of the way of his biggest shots. As I sat down at the end of the third I could hear the chants of 'Bomber Bomber' ringing around the place as Brendan grabbed my head from both sides and stared into my eyes. I can't remember what he said but I can remember the look of hunger and hope.

The runs I did in the mornings with the weights in my hands were paying off as I carried on hitting Kalule with fast two handed attacks. And in the sixth I really went for him. But just as I expected he was durable and as we neared the end of the fight he caught me a nick above my eye and for the first time in thirty five fights I had stitches. But I had won all but two rounds and so I just had to keep it going. If I couldn't get him down then I had to concentrate.

Finally, at the end of the tenth as I smashed Kalule with left and right time after time the ref jumped in to save him and the crowd went mad. Brendan threw his sweaty towel up in the air and it landed on a lady in a ball gown on the front row. It was pandemonium in the ring and when Harry Carpenter gave me the microphone I had my chance to tell my friends what I wanted to say:

*"Thank you for coming. Without you it would not have been a show."*

But it had been a show and the best one of my life so far. I had handed out an utter demolition in front of my own fans, a point that wasn't lost on Barney:

*"Why the fuck didn't you fight like that in Ireland? We could fill the City Hall ten times over for fuck's sake!"*

*"I don't know."*

The crowd definitely had something to do with it – they always did – I always felt unbeatable on my home turf. Maybe the sparring set up helped as well. Maybe Frank Warren and Kalule's manager had got far enough up my nose to ignite something in me. Who knows? But I hadn't fought like that in Ireland and that was now history. And more's the point I was the European Champion and one step closer to a World title shot.

But Kalule's manager carried on being a prick; he couldn't even accept with humility that I'd just ripped his boy to shreds. He said:

*"Graham is nothing. I have never rated him. He is a fair fighter but I do not think he has stamina."* WHAT?!

*"If this fight had been four years ago when Kalule was at his best it would have been no contest."*

Brendan said it would have been a better contest than this one. And if it had been eleven years ago when I was fifteen I would definitely have lost. Harry Carpenter agreed with Brendan and said that I was perhaps Britain's most skilful boxer and that was a very kind thing for him to say. I just hoped the Scandinavian moaner would get back to hassling chickens and leave us alone. Kalule didn't do himself any favours either by claiming that he thought he was ahead when the fight was ended. We stopped laughing about a week later.

But, undeterred, his manager carried on, saying that they had been forced into the fight, and hadn't been told that it was being screened live on television. I'd have thought that was a good thing for most managers. He even carried on moaning although Kalule took the majority of the £60,000 purse. Some people are never satisfied, and, other than what happened inside the ring, I couldn't really see what he had to be upset about. Hey ho.

Barney was happier and said that if I didn't go on to be a world champion he would eat his hat, and coming from a millionaire bookmaker, that was some pledge that I hoped he wouldn't have to keep to. And Brendan carried on with his blarney:

*"We've come a long way together. They laughed at us when we started but the paddy from Dublin is smiling now."*

For one horrific moment I thought he was about to break out into a rendition of 'When Irish Eyes are Smiling'.

To be sure.

♦

It was a good night all round for St Thomas's because Brian won the Central Area Crown and he was one step away from being a contender for the British Middleweight title. We'd become such good mates by this time that we made an agreement that if he was ever the next in line to challenge, then I'd hand the title in. I'd rather do that than fight him. I was the best man at his wedding and godfather to his child. No amount of money would persuade us to fight, and besides which, I don't think Brendan would have known which corner to go in.

On the flipside of that feel good discussion, an old grumpy debate was brewing again. And it was rather predictable. Sibbo's camp came out fighting, in the press of course. Brendan told me, after the Kalule fight, that a World title shot was at least a year away, because Hagler was already scheduled to meet Hearns again. So I thought that a fight with Sibson would be a good show that would fill the gap until then. And Sibbo, on the face of it, seemed keen. He was full of charm, as ever, saying that he wanted to play the piano on my ribs. I didn't know he was musical. But then he seemed to be trying to make things awkward by saying he'd only fight if he got a much bigger purse than me, when, as European Champion I was eligible for sixty per cent. That didn't bother me and Brendan and Barney agreed that an equal split would be fine. It was the fight that fans wanted to see, especially in South Yorkshire and Leicester.

While Sibbo huffed and puffed to the press, Barney played it a little cooler, saying that we were happy to talk to him and he knew where to contact us. But he seemed happier to go through the newspapers, saying that he wanted seventy five thousand pounds to fight, knowing that would price him out, and his ramblings started to get more bonkers and a bit distasteful. In one quote he said:

*"I watched the European fight and it gave me the hump. Graham won't get rid of me and will have to throw punches or die."*

Die?! Bloody hell. Sibbo had gone from playing a piano recital to killing me within a week. I started to wonder whether he had lost his grip. Meanwhile his manager Frank Warren had issued writs to the EBU, the British Boxing Board and Kalule's manager (he had stopped at the cleaner at the Sheffield City Hall) claiming damages in his contract wrangle with Kalule. So he may not have been on hand to advise Sibbo on what to say to the press to look sensible.

One morning as I ran through the streets of Sheffield with Brian, we were talking about Sibson and Brian thought that we'd never get the fight on, basically because Barney knew that I didn't need it, and Sibbo knew that losing to me so soon after his comeback would leave him in the wilderness:

*"He keeps saying he wants me."*

*"No he keeps talking about the money,"* said Brian.

Then I had an idea. As we wandered in to the gym I waved over at Brendan:

*"Hey Brendan, if Sibson really thinks he can beat me, and he wants more money, why don't we fight winner takes all?"*

*"You're joking!"* Brendan must have seen a flaw in the plan; maybe he thought the slim chance of me losing was not slim enough.

*"Why. He needs to put his money where his mouth is. I'm not bothered. But if he really wants me, he'd snap your hands off."*

Brendan was warming to the idea. It was certainly an exciting prospect. And it would be a fascinating fight for boxing fans. I was quite tall for the division with a long reach, and Sibbo was stocky with short arms. On the basis that I was difficult to hit at the best of times, you can see why trying it with short arms was not an enticing prospect for Sibbo. So after Brendan had spoken to Barney, my idea went out to the press. In the interview Brendan said again that Sibbo still hadn't explained why he gave up the British title as soon as I was nominated to challenge him. It was hardly the same circumstance as me and Brian. Sibson seemed to hate me for some reason, with hindsight I thought he'd relish the opportunity to play a symphony on my head or whatever. But, once again, Brendan asked that question. We thought that no one would be able to resist a fight when they were accused of constantly ducking it, and then saw a headline which read:

"WINNER TAKES ALL OFFER TO SIBSON"

I got a bit carried away when someone from the press rang me and I said:

*"I'll have him for breakfast, dinner or tea."*

I'd been watching too many Ali interviews I think!

Then, oddly, it all went a bit quiet again.

♦

After my European fight I got a civic reception at the Town Hall with the Mayor, a lady called Dorothy Walton. She was lovely, but she said that the smelling salts were out in her house when I got a cut eye, and she thought I might lose! Oh yea of little faith. I had my right hand strapped up because I'd damaged some tissue and had a fracture during the fight and it was pretty sore. So I had to shake everyone by the left hand. One old buffer, who looked and sounded like the Major in Fawlty Towers said:

*"Dear God. Are they letting darkies into the Scouting movement now?"*

The following week, the Rotherham Toyota garage gave me a spanking new black sports car; it said 'Bomber Graham Drives Toyota' on the side. Unfortunately I couldn't drive it away because of my hand, and Jane, my girlfriend of the time, had just failed her driving test.

While I was kicking around, I had an unexpected chance to hone my acting skills when the producer of a show called Carmen Jones, which was on at the Crucible, gave me a call. There were a few fight scenes and they wanted them to look as realistic as possible. It was a right laugh. The show featured an all black cast, so I asked the lady if I could have a part, but she said I'd have to stop giggling. The actors were great fun as well, but most of them would struggle to punch their way out of a paper bag. So I said if they want to make it realistic they should just insult each other, and then when one of them said, 'okay let's have a fight,' the other should say, 'only if you pay me a wheelbarrow of cash,' and then walk off. That didn't seem appropriate, nor did both of the fighters holding an upright tight guard and bumping in to each other. That would be bad theatre – they'd look like Tweedle Dum and Tweedle Dee having a barney. So I showed them how to jab and how to throw a hook, and how to evade it but look like you've been hit.

It was all going swimmingly until this big guy with staring eyes and a mean beard took a swing, aiming to miss, but connecting with his fellow pugilist, who went flying across the stage.

I half expected a flurry of, 'oh dear God, Luvvie, speak to me,' type comments. But the cast just fell about laughing until one of them recovered enough to go and see if their mate was still breathing. I still got free tickets for the show though. Top stuff.

While the star actor was knocking his mate out with one punch, Sibbo hit Abdul Sanda for twelve rounds and won on points to make him the number one contender for my European title. So hopefully the fight was getting closer. All that needed to happen was for Barney and Frank Warren to settle on a contract.

Negotiations seemed to be moving along, or so we thought, until a week later when Brendan came in to the gym to tell us that Sibson had withdrawn from the fight, apparently because Frank Warren thought it would be much more valuable in 1987.What? Glyn fell about laughing:

*"He won't still be fighting in 1987 for fuck's sake!"*

We were having a laugh and making chicken jokes, but it had started to seem like this was a dead duck and Barney would have to find someone else for me to fight while I waited for a title shot. Mike Barrett, the London promoter, was trying to get a fight on quickly between me and Mark Kaylor, but I was still out injured with my hand and, in any case, Barney was trying to get me a fight in America. He knew that I needed to get well known in the States to be able to attract a big US television company to finance my fights.

But then, all of a sudden, old Sibbo seemed to have taken the bait. He said that although Warren had different ideas for him, he managed himself (did Warren know that?) and he was willing to fight.

Was this more piss and wind, or was Sibbo really up for it? It seemed to be genuine interest this time. He was trying hard to make his way up the rankings and fighting regularly and he knew that he needed me to push him back up there.

But then in a fight with a guy called Rivera, in what looked like a bread and butter ten round fight, he got a nasty cut over his left eye and he needed seven stitches. He had a second cut on his eyelid so it wasn't a great night for Sibbo. But I guess he would have said, 'you should have seen the other bloke', who in fairness had probably taken quite a rib smacking.

So, undeterred, he carried on saying that he couldn't wait to get at me, and Frank Warren eventually won the bidding to stage the fight between us at a hundred and forty thousand pounds.

I thought that I'd hit the jackpot. Sibbo's people had ignored my 'winner takes all' offer and now seemed willing to take a smaller percentage of the purse than us. That sort of made me wonder what they were up to, but it seemed now that there was nothing much left to get in the way of us getting a fight.

In the meantime Barney had been working on getting me on the bill at Barry McGuigan's World title defence in America. Tommy Hearns and Roberto Duran were on the card too, and when he pulled it off, I knew it would be just the chance to lift me off in the States.

# 9

## <u>Viva Las Vegas</u>

*"America is a nation created by all the hopeful
wanderers of Europe."*

## Theodore H White (an American)

I love travelling. I'm like a big kid at the airport, and on this occasion I was like a big kid who had just stumbled across an unattended chocolate superstore. Could life get any better? I wandered around Terminal Two at Manchester Airport and watched the holiday makers and business people scurry about making their last minute buys for their trips and I felt so lucky. I wasn't off to Spain with the in-laws, or going to a life assurance conference in Oslo. I was heading for La La La La La L'America! Off to meet my stablemate (stablemate!) Barry McGuigan to train at Palm Springs for three weeks before preparing for the big US show.

It was the middle of May and I had over a month to spend in the US before the fight night on 23rd June. Barney had set up an opponent called Eddy Hall, who, as ever, I knew the square route of nothing about. But my right hand had fully recovered from the fracture and I was more than ready to fight again.

So as the aeroplane taxied around the runway, I settled back in my business class seat with my bottle of water, copy of the Beano and the world at my feet.

♦

California is the most incredible place I had ever been to. Some of the locals in Palm Springs actually drive around in Cadillacs (not all pink), the golf courses were neater than Sheffield's bowling greens and I'd never seen so many models. And if that wasn't enough to get things steamy, the sun beat down to lift the temperature consistently above a hundred degrees.

It was fantastic to feel the sun on my back at last, and to enjoy the sort of heat that I was designed to live in. And as immaculately presented hotel staff glided around the entrance lobby, it really felt like I was on some big American movie set.

And my room, apartment, suite, whatever you want to call it was enormous. It was bigger than my house on Newman Road and it had everything you'd ever want and plenty of things you wouldn't even consider that you needed. It was the first time I'd seen a b-day and having briefly attempted to squat over it, I decided it wasn't the place to dump.

I switched on the air conditioning, stripped off, put on the Palm Springs Bath robe, turned the gigantic telly on, and then turned the air conditioning off. Then on again. Then off.

After a while I poured myself a glass of iced water and went out on to the balcony which overlooked acres of the beautifully manicured hotel lawns, swimming pools and bars. This was surely paradise. My daydream was interrupted by the sharp trill of a phone. I didn't have my mobile phone with me, this being 1986 it would have taken me way over my luggage allowance, so I picked up the phone at the side of my king sized bed.

"Hello?"

"Hello Mr Graham, my name is Charlene and I want to welcome you to Palm Springs."

What? Literally?

*"If there is anything at all you want that will make your stay perfect then please call reception twenty four seven."*

What? Literally? And what the hell is twenty four seven? Was that the number to call?

The lovely Charlene insisted that I should have a nice day before hanging up and leaving me to ponder my next move. Within minutes I had plucked up the courage to test Charlene's promise and so I dived across the bed and picked up the phone. I rang 247. And soon enough it was answered:

*"Yeah?"* someone boomed.

*"Hello..."* I whispered.

*"Who's that?"* came the reply, before I heard the guy shout at someone, *"Did you order room service Bernice? No? There's some kind of God damned crank on the end of the line. Jesus H Christ!"*

I hurriedly slammed the phone down. Then the trill started and I looked at the phone and waited for it to stop. So 247 wasn't reception then.

I put the telly back on and flicked through twenty or so channels, half of them with beaming Dallas extras selling nasal hair trimmers, and then I spotted a book on the coffee table. It was the hotel guide. Brilliant. And I found the number I wanted. Restaurant – Dial 5.

I rang 5 and the phone was immediately answered.

*"Good afternoon."*

*"Hello, is that the restaurant?"*

*"Yes Sir it is. Will you be requiring a reservation or room service?"*

*"Room service please."*

*"Very good Sir, can I take your order?"*

Here goes:

*"Can I have chicken and rice and peas please?"*

*"Chicken and rice and peas Sir?"*

*"Yes."*

*"Very good Sir."*

And he hung up.

Ten minutes later there was a knock on the door, and I opened it to be met by a young lad in a white dinner suit carrying a silver tray, which he put down on the dining table. He then lifted the big silver lid off a plate to reveal half a chicken, a neat mound of rice and a spoonful of peas. Fantastic! Then he went to the door and said:

*"Will that be all Mr Graham?"*

*"Ooh can you get me a Crunchie?"* But then I offered, *"Only joking,"* as he looked a bit confused, before repeating:

*"Will that be all Sir?"*

*"Yes thanks."*

Then he coughed. And I looked at him. He looked at me, nodded his head very slightly towards me and coughed again.

*"That's a nasty tickle, you want to get something for that mate,"* I said before he beat a slightly disgruntled retreat. Strange lad.

♦

I was living in a dream. As I sat down in the restaurant at breakfast time and watched two guys in white dinner suits squeezing oranges, I remembered that Barney had set up some sparring sessions for me to break things up while I trained. Someone was going to contact me to say when and where, but in the meantime I was free to use the gym and pool at the hotel before the trainers arrived.

After breakfast I wandered around the gym and the training pool area and carefully around the plunge pool before deciding to go for a run. It was a far cry for running up Ecclesall Road in Sheffield, sunny green and endless, but very hot. And when I got back to the gym, one of the trainers was there to meet me.

*"Hi Herol. I've got your sparring arrangements here. You're starting tomorrow morning at Duran's gym."*

Duran? Roberto Duran? Former World Champion Roberto Duran? Fucking hell!

I think Duran was fighting against Sugar Ray Leonard, who was a skilful boxer and he thought I was the nearest available thing to spar with. And, even better, I'd get paid for it.

That night I could hardly sleep I was so excited. And in the morning I gulped down my orange juice and eggs something or other before getting my kit together and being driven over to Roberto Duran's place. It was apparently just around the corner, which I discovered in America could mean a hundred miles away. But thankfully, in this case, after driving past about ten golf courses and hotels we pulled up in the forecourt, which was about the size of Barnsley, of another hotel.

We made our way over to the gym and then through three sets of double doors before getting stopped by two six foot seven officials, one holding a clip board. Once we'd convinced them who we were we were led in to a huge gym, with a ring in the centre of it. Then I saw Roberto Duran, but only just, because he was surrounded by the biggest entourage of trainers, minders and people to make the tea that I had ever seen. It all looked a bit over the top for a sparring session to me, but then I saw that there were two or three press guys there with photographers.

Duran had a massive reputation, but he didn't look all that frightening when I met him. He was shorter than me, but muscular, and he had a stern look frozen on his face. He was very sure of himself and didn't have a lot to say, he just kind of sneered at me like some sort of pantomime villain. I smiled back.

We got in the ring and as I went to touch his gloves he just took a step back, so I thought 'this could be fun'. He didn't seem to have warmed to me, but maybe he was like that with everyone, or maybe he was in his zone. But as we got going, for normal sparring he was coming on a bit strong. He caught me twice and pretty hard, so I started moving myself about. I moved my shoulders and started switching back which made him miss me a couple of times. We kept moving about for another thirty seconds and he couldn't hit me. Then all of a sudden he stopped, glared at me, and pushed me in the chest with both hands saying:

*"Who do you think you are? My name is Roberto Duran!"*

I knew that already. I only managed to say:

*"My name is...."* when he turned his back on me.

We carried on sparring and he kept on swinging, missing and then beckoning me. After two rounds he'd had enough.

*"No, no."* He kept on saying *"I'm Duran - Duran"*. It probably didn't help my cause when I said, *"well I'm Spandau Ballet."*

So I was sacked. I have to say that before I'd met the famous Roberto Duran I was really excited about sparring with him but after I met him I thought he was a bit of an arsehole. He was so rude. Just my opinion of course, and he probably didn't like me for making him look silly in front of his people and a couple of press guys. I can understand if he didn't. He probably thought I was messing around.

Over the whole two rounds he had only managed to tap me three or four times, while I kept on tipping him and tapping him to get him out of the way. If he had wanted me to stand still then he should have said so at the beginning, but then I wouldn't have been all that keen to get in the ring with him, even though the money was good.

After a week or so of training in the heat I went back to my room in the hotel one afternoon and sat down on the bed. I switched the telly on, flicked through the shopping channels, tried unsuccessfully to buy a camel hair pair of trousers and switched off again. I was bored. And I was a bit fed up that I'd been sacked by Roberto Duran on my first day. And strangely, although I was in such an amazing place and could ask for whatever I wanted, I was sort of lonely, and a bit homesick. So I went out on to the balcony and sat down to write a postcard addressed to the gym on Newman Road.

*Dear Brendan and all the boys,*

*Wish you were here! It's a fantastic place, you can get anything you want to eat, there's girls everywhere and it's lovely and hot and sunny. I'm getting quite a nice tan.*
*My hotel is quite near to a beach but I haven't been swimming there yet.*
*I met Roberto Duran last week and had a couple of rounds, I think it went okay, but he didn't seem too pleased. When are you coming out here? I'm dying to get back to Sheffield.*

*Love*

*Herol.*

♦

I was lying in the middle of my gigantic bed watching some golf on the telly when there was a knock at the door. This normally meant a message of some sort. I had long stopped worrying that the man from room 247 had tracked me down so I went to see what it was.

I opened the door to see the big beaming smile I'd been missing. It was Brian.

*"Hey Herol. How's it going?"*

I gave him a hug and pushed him into the room.

*"Hey man, look at this. It's fucking wicked! Do you want a sandwich?"* and I picked up the phone.

It was brilliant to see Brian after having been here for three weeks. The people in the hotel were great but I was really starting to miss home. Brian had flown out the week before the fight with Brendan and Alma Ingle to help me prepare. We went down to the hotel lobby where Brendan was blathering on to the receptionist as Mrs Ingle handed their bags over to the lift guy. They had arrived in time for a gala evening at Caesar's Palace where the great and the good were gathering in the build up to the show, and Brendan had to be there of course.

So that evening we headed off together, all smart and Mrs Ingle in her best dress to Caesar's Palace, which looked like Disneyland when we arrived. I half expected a horse and carriage to come to collect us from the drive, but instead, a group of Elvis impersonators pointed us the way into a glittering hall buzzing with superstars, waiters and hangers on. I wasn't sure which category we were in – but it wasn't waiters, so I helped myself to a canapé with a big shrimp on it as it whizzed past.

Then Brian spotted Marvin Hagler. Wow! This was only the second time we'd been so close to the great man. His bald head shone under the glare of a chandelier and he looked every bit as imposing as I remembered.

I desperately wanted to fight Hagler. He was the best of the best and the type of boxer who only comes around once in a generation. I had been nagging Brendan and Barney for months, asking them when I would get a chance to fight him and they always just said that they were working on it. As I was only a couple of steps away from being the contender I'm sure Hagler knew who I was. Brendan kept on saying to me, 'it'll come – bide your time.' But as I had struggled to get people to fight me all my career, Hagler also knew I was a southpaw and a tricky one at that, so I don't think he fancied me.

I had been patient because I was still young, but time was running out. The big man had started to talk about quitting and had said that he was not interested in defending his title against Hearns or Sugar Ray Leonard. He hadn't lost a fight in ten years and had knocked out fifty two of his sixty six opponents, so maybe he was thinking of going out at the top.

He is a lovely person and a great guy to speak to, but on this rare opportunity to meet I was a little wary as I purposefully walked across to him, narrowly missing a waitress carrying a tray full of champagne. I stuck my hand out towards him and said:

*"Hi Marvin, it's Herol Graham, I met you once when you were over in London at a show."*

He has this way of peering down at you, which he did to perfection, smiled at me and said:

*"Mmmm."*

I carried on:

*"I haven't fought you yet."*

He smiled again and said:

*"Mmmm."*

What a man.

I was in awe of him as a boxer and the way he simply took people apart. And despite his economic use of words I kind of knew where he was coming from.


After that excitement Brian and I carried on looking out for celebrities and grabbing whatever snacks went past us, when Brendan came up to me:

*"Barney's been on the phone, change of opponent. Eddy Hall's pulled out."*

*"Marvin Hagler?"* I asked, knowing the answer.

*"Ernie Rabotte."* came the reply.

*"Ernie Robot?"*

*"Never mind."*

My attention was distracted by a big group of sharp suited guys who swarmed slowly past us like a shoal of basking sharks.

*"You know who that is."* said Brian.

*"Who?"*

*"Ali."*

Bloody Hell. Muhammad Ali. This was the man who had captured my imagination on the black and white telly twenty years ago, when I was six. The greatest boxer of all time. The man who I tried so hard to emulate and had inspired my every move from the first time I had set foot in a boxing ring. I couldn't believe my eyes. It was him. Twenty yards away from me and surrounded by about fifteen security guys.

I looked across at Brian and said:

*"Quick, get me a photographer."*

Two minutes later Brian hurried back with a photographer in tow and I looked across to see if Ali was still there. He was, so I grabbed the photographer and said:

*"You've got to take this photograph of me and Ali."*

He seemed happy to go along with me; I guess it would have been good for him as well.

So I jumped over next to the great man. The protection surrounding him looked like they didn't really want me to. He was free to roam around, but the guys were always hovering around him like wasps. Somebody knew I was boxing so they let me in and I was lucky enough to get the picture.

If I had been impressed by Marvin Hagler then now I was completely star struck. I said to him:

*"I'm in awe of you man, you're the only reason I'm boxing".*

Then he mumbled something and I just started crying. I was in bits.

So all in all it had been a great night. Brian smiled and said to me:

*"Nice one Herol. You asked Hagler for a fight and then blubbed all over Muhammad Ali. Brilliant work man."*

♦

When the fight night eventually came around, I had got over my meeting with my hero and had refocused on the job in hand. I was well used to working in this heat now, as I would need to be, I was first on the card in my fight with Ernie Rabotte. But meeting Ali had been by far the biggest highlight of my trip to California and it made me want to emulate the great man and try my hardest to achieve even a tenth of what he had.

Brendan managed to get hold of some English newspapers and in the sports sections there was a lot of build up to the 1986 World Cup and England's chances. Diego Maradona was all over every paper and most of the football writers thought that the little genius may ultimately have a hand in the outcome. But before a ball has been kicked there is always hope. Barry's

World title fight had lots of coverage as well, especially in the Belfast editions. And there were a few smaller pieces on my trip to the States. Alan Minter was quoted somewhere and he said that I was awkward. Coming from one of the best southpaws in recent boxing history I kind of took that as a complement although I'm not absolutely sure it was.

I met Ernie Rabotte at the weigh in and there was the same amount of hulabaloo there as everywhere else. When he stripped off I thought, 'Jeez.' He was built like a tank. I hadn't seen any pictures of him before but I'd never seen anything so rock solid. He looked like he was made out of granite. It didn't shake me up at all, but I was pretty uptight and nervous as I always was in the close build up to a fight. Anyhow, when we shook hands and the photo flashes went off I tried to look serious (I could never carry off the really mean look), then I farted.

Rabotte looked kind of stunned, and then a little disturbed. For my part I was just embarrassed and could only manage a weak smile. And as his entourage gathered their stuff and made the way for the exit, he looked over at me and as I tried to avoid his stare I thought, 'shit….shit – why did I do that?'

*"You did what?"* said Brian before he lost control for at least ten minutes.

Well, if things got tricky in the ring I could always guff and then smack him while he recovered.

I love the way the ringmasters really overdo it in the States and where better than Caesars Palace to put on a proper show. As I climbed into the ring to the sound of an Ozzy Osborne song I looked around at the seemingly endless black expanse showered by flashes of photography, and a bead of sweat trickled down my back:

*"LAYDEEEEEZ AND GENTLEMEEEEEEN. IN THE BLUE CORNER, FROM SHEFFIELD ENGLAND …… HEROL BOMBEEEEEEEER GRAHAAAAAAAAAAAAAAAAAAAAAAAAAAAAAAAM!"*

Come on! The bell went and Ernie the tank moved quickly over to me as I hopped out of my corner and he immediately caught me with a left jab which stung like hell. More flashes of light. Then he came again and I hit him with a right jab which hurt him, so I threw a left quickly and he went over. It was a good punch but I couldn't believe my eyes, he had gone over within thirty seconds. The count started:

*"One –a, two, - a, three-a, four-a, five-a, six-a……………. seven-a…………eight-a"* come on Ernie.

Finally, on the ninth count, which was in itself about ten seconds, Ernie got to his feet. He came over to me again to attack and quickly caught me again. He'd hit me as many times in a minute as Duran had in two rounds of sparring. I hit back straight away and caught him a beauty and over he went again. This time there was no need for a count, there was no way he was getting up and I walked over to my corner to get a hug from Brendan before the ref called the fight. It was a quick one but the American fans were appreciative and I got a good cheer. Brendan grabbed hold of me and said:

*"They know when they see natural talent. It's taken us eight years to get you here son. But now we're here"*

♦

It was absolutely fantastic to get back to Sheffield. Bloody cold but absolutely fantastic. The evening we landed back, Brian and I went straight down to Isabellas. I had one or two brandies and soon I was surrounded by lads and lasses chatting and laughing. It was a longer and more expensive night than expected, and my morning run was put on hold as I nursed a sore head.

I went down to the paper shop to get some milk and I picked up a copy of the Sheffield Star to see what I'd been missing while I was away. Not a huge amount so it seemed. And I kicked my heels for most of the rest of the morning, I had recently split up with my girlfriend Jane, that relationship cost me a few quid, and I wasn't in any hurry to get hooked up again.

So when Brendan suggested we went down to see Frank Bruno fight Tim Witherspoon in London I readily agreed.

I always enjoyed going to other people's fights, I didn't have all the nerves and could enjoy the occasion. I wasn't all that bothered about watching the fight, as I've never really been a boxing fan as such, but I loved seeing who was there and generally wandering around and having a good laugh.

This time down at Wembley I was strolling around the VIP area, trying to look like a superstar when I noticed this girl looking at me – she was very attractive, dark hair, lovely eyes and I said to myself 'Aha – nice girl'. So, being newly available, I went to sit down at a table just a few feet away and soon enough she came over to me and said:

*"Is anybody sitting there?"*

*"Can you see anybody sitting there?"* I asked, like a right dick. She rolled her eyes and let out a jet of smoke from her barely opened lips. I decided, with supreme and misplaced arrogance, that sarcasm was indeed the best approach. And as this girl was smoking, sarcasm was completely appropriate the way I saw it. I hated smoking. I hated, hated, hated it.

The girl introduced herself as Karen, sat down and started talking to me, and I took the fag out of her mouth and stubbed it out.

*"What the hell are you doing?"*

I just smiled.

Anyhow, miraculously, from that point onwards we seemed to get on – so well that, after the fight, I took her home to her London apartment, and went back to see her again the next day. We stayed in touch and soon enough we were meeting every week either in Sheffield or London. It was a long trip but worth it.

♦

1986 was going to be a big year for me, with my trip out to Las Vegas and then the planned clash with Sibbo in the autumn. That was going to be my biggest pay day so far, some reports said I was going to get over eighty thousand pounds. I knew that was before all my percentages had been applied but it would still be pretty good. Sibbo's camp had declined to take my 'winner takes all' offer, thinking it better to take a smaller percentage of the purse, even though in the early stages of negotiations he was insisting that he should get paid more than me to try to take my European Title.

Anyhow, I had to kiss that cheque goodbye when it turned out that Sibbo had put twelve pounds on over the summer and had moved in to the light heavyweight bracket. I'd have had to spend the next month eating pizzas and cakes to get anywhere near him so I just had to accept that was that.

Brendan said that it just proved what he always knew. Sibbo had never had any intention of fighting me, let alone using my ribcage as a piano at this year's Proms.

So I had an alternative fight set up with an American called Tony Harrison due in October. But, as nothing on the fight scene seemed to be going to plan since I made it back to the UK, I had another setback.

I was on my way home after a sparring session at St Thomas's when I felt a bit groggy. So when I got home, I had a glass of water and went to bed, hoping that I'd feel better in the morning.

I awoke with a blinding headache. I could see flashes of white light and they were searing through my head. I sat on the side of my bed with my head in my hands and then threw up. This was pain that I had never known. I struggled into my living room and sat down. Johnny Nelson was staying with me at the time and he heard me moving about and came to see what I was up to. I was so dizzy that I had to stay sat down and could hardly speak. He could see that it was not a mild headache or hangover and so he rang for an ambulance and by two o' clock in the morning I was in the Royal Hallamshire Hospital.

The nurses gave me something and I briefly went to sleep but then awoke again with the same blinding headache. This carried on for the next twenty four hours and I was almost crying with pain. I couldn't really take in what the doctor and nurses were saying to me. I just wanted to get to sleep somehow. Brian came to see me later in the afternoon and told me that they were going to do some tests for brain damage. Then all sorts of shit started going through my mind. It was only a month or so ago that I had seen my hero Ali, but he was struggling to speak clearly and that had made me fall to pieces. Was the same thing about to happen to me? I hadn't even had a World title shot and I could be near the end.

Over the next twenty four hours they poked around with me and did all sorts of things I didn't like. At one stage they shoved a curled needle up my spine and I screamed the place down. I wasn't sure they knew what they were looking for.

Brendan came to visit as well and he spent more time talking to the doctor than he did with me. I had been through a few brain scans and eventually Brendan came over to me and told me that I'd be okay. He said that everything from the tests was pretty clear and that the only reason I hadn't had headaches before was because I wasn't often hit. For reasons known to him, Barney told the press I had some kind of a virus and I'd be okay to fight Harrison, but I wasn't so sure.

Over the next four days the headaches subsided and the nurse told me I'd had a pretty big migraine, but there was no reason to think that it would be regular. But they were keeping me in for another two days as a precaution. As I felt a lot better I thought, 'sod that.' So when the lights were dimmed in the evening, I got up, put on my pants and t-shirt and snuck out, pretending to go to the toilet. I hailed a taxi back to my place and then had an idea. While everyone thought I was in hospital I could drive down to see Karen for a couple of days - which I did.

After a lovely three day break at Karen's, watching telly, drinking hot chocolate in trendy London Café's and just chilling out I thought I'd better ring Brendan. He wasn't pleased:

*"Where the fuck have you been? We've been looking all over for you – you stupid bastard."*

Poor old Brendan had been worried sick. I don't think he'd have minded if I said I was off to London, but I he did mind that I hadn't bothered to tell him. I just wanted to get away for a few days without anyone knowing. But all the time Brendan had been bullshitting every time he had a call from the press, and panicking about where I might be.

So I made my way back up the M1 with my tail between my legs. And I kept my head down and tried to prepare for the fight with Harrison. But, unsurprisingly, the British Board of Boxing Control wanted to see the medical reports before they let the fight go on and there wasn't enough time to get clearance before the date. So I lost out on that one too.

But I didn't have to wait too long before my next big match. Mark Kaylor had worked his way up to number three in the WBC Middleweight rankings and Mike Barrett was already working on a get together which would be an eliminator for a World title shot. And an opportunity to meet Mark at a press conference again, which was never dull.

# 10

# The People We Hurt the Most

*"It's sad, so sad, why can't we talk it over?*
*Always seems to me that sorry seems to be the*
*hardest word."*

## Elton John

After the panic of my brain scan Brendan decided that a bit of a rest for the next few weeks or so wouldn't do me any harm. The Harrison fight had been called off and while the promoter, Mike Barrett, was working on an upcoming fight with Mark Kaylor I had the chance to do a bit of charity and TV work. As my profile was building up, particularly after Harry Carpenter's very kind words on Sports Night, one or two opportunities started coming my way. The persona of Bomber Graham was building up; in the public eye I was always laughing and joking. I was invited to do Question of Sport and was on Billy Beaumont's side. He was a great laugh and he didn't mind at all when we lost. I got my two boxing questions wrong but I got the rugby, golf and cricket ones right! No real surprise there. Billy asked me if I knew anything about boxing at all.

If he'd have asked Glyn Rhodes he'd have got a straight answer. One evening Glyn and a couple of the lads from the gym had come round to my house to watch a big fight. I think it was a Hearns fight on in the early hours, and that day at the gym everyone was talking about it. I was the only one who had Sky which is why they piled round to mine. As we sat in my lounge watching the build up, all with our shoes off of course, the lads were buzzing but I was getting a bit bored, so I picked up a copy of What Car from my magazine rack, and started to read it. I was quite happy and didn't realise that the fight had started, and when Glyn looked round at me at the end of the first round he couldn't believe his eyes:

*"Fucking Hell Herol! Are you not interested?"*

*"A bit."*

I also got the chance to do some charity stuff, and I was delighted when I was asked along to help at the Yorkshire TV broadcast for Children in Need. I love doing anything for kids. Not knowing how serious I could be on a training camp, and just seeing my smiling face here and there, they thought I'd be okay to fool around. So that's why I was splattered in the face with a custard pie by Bertie Bassett the giant liquorice allsorts man. I looked a complete cock in the full page newspaper picture!

And while I recuperated and tried to keep my fitness going I agreed to do a charity run in Barnsley. It was on a bright and crisp Sunday morning so I thought I'd take Glyn along with me. He wasn't convinced:

*"What is it?"*

*"A charity event."*

*"What sort of charity event."*

*"I've forgotten. Anyway it'll be fun. Come on Glyn, I'll pick you up in ten minutes."*

Then I hung up.

As we drove across the moors to Barnsley Glyn was still grumpy. I'd got him out of bed and he'd missed his breakfast:

*"I'm sure there'll be stuff to eat there,"* I reassured.

But as we got nearer to Barnsley Glyn's mood took a turn for the worse when he saw a bright yellow sign at a junction with an arrow on it:

*"What the fuck's that?"*

*"Dunno."*

When we arrived on the edge of Barnsley it was getting busier; there were cars parked and people walking past us with shorts and t-shirts with numbers on. And then I saw the starting banner:

## BARNSLEY HALF MARATHON

*"Herol, it's a fucking half marathon!"* Glyn was almost shouting.

*"That's what I said isn't it?"*

*"I wouldn't have come if you had told me it was a fucking half marathon!"*

*"Well, you'll get a bottle of water and a cereal bar,"* I said.

Glyn didn't reply. He just had his head in his hands. I think he might have been crying.

A bit over an hour and a half later Glyn came over the finish line, five minutes after me, red faced and still swearing, and the car journey back was a bit quiet. Some nice lady had given me a bacon sandwich and a cup of tea, so I let Glyn eat his cereal bar in peace.

♦

Down in London, Karen had started taking an interest in the boxing world and she rang me one day to tell me that Barry McGuigan had split up with Barney and was taking a legal action to void their contract. So Barney only had me to manage. I didn't think too much of it and didn't speak to Barry to get his side. A couple of days later Brendan took a call at the gym and it was from Barney. Then he called me over and said:

*"Kaylor wants the fight, it looks like it's going to be on."*

And sure enough I was called down to a press conference at the beginning of October to meet Mark and talk about the fight, which was scheduled for the 4th of November, giving the headline writers plenty of scope for 'Fireworks' puns.

This was the first time I'd met Mark since he'd had the scrap with Errol Christie at his last big press conference. And the press started to build this up, saying that we were both determined to avoid a recurrence, when in reality there was more chance of Brendan having a crack at the doorman.

I liked Mark, he was okay, but he was a bit gobby. Once the fight had been confirmed he started saying what he was going to do to me and what he wasn't going to do to me. I just laughed at him, I just laughed at everybody actually. I knew we'd find out soon enough what was going to happen.

Everybody outside the press was talking about Kaylor's supporters and saying that a few of them were racists. There were a lot of black boxers around so some of the more violent West Ham fans attached themselves to Mark and tried to build him up as an Aryan elitist. This was all a bit sleazy and it was at the height of tension as well, being not long after the Handsworth Riots. And all the National Front people were muttering 'fuck 'im – we can't have him beating Mark.'

But behind it all we were pretty friendly, I never felt victimised and I was happy to talk to everybody. Mark was okay with me and always civil.

When we arrived at the press conference Mark turned up wearing a pair of handcuffs. His publicity people suggested he do it as a stunt to remind everybody of the scuffle with Errol and to stir things up here. For my part I had to say in the press that I was determined not to get involved in an ugly scene, which was never going to happen, but it built things up anyway. Mark actually felt like a bit of a prat. And low and behold, the press conference went off without a bang. Everybody heaved a collective sigh of boredom.

Tony Harrison, the American fighter I had missed out on, came to spar with me after he had knocked Kaylor out in the fight that was set up instead, so he was the obvious choice. At the same time, down in London, Alan Minter was helping in Kaylor's camp because he was a southpaw and Mark didn't have much experience there.

I think I surprised Harrison a bit when we sparred. After a couple of sessions he did an interview on the radio and said:

*"Man, this guy is good; he ain't nothin' like I've ever come across before. He punches from any stance and misses punches the other guy throws like nothin' I ain't ever seen."*

Nice. But Harrison didn't stick around for long, he had to go back to the US, so I had to go back to Brian and Glyn, which was never an easy ride. Glyn was great. He didn't really respect anybody. Well he did, but in his own way. When we sparred we could go full on at each other, but if he was sparring with someone else and they touched him he'd go wild.

As the fight drew nearer I was on edge with anticipation and couldn't wait for it to happen. I was getting up even earlier, at half past four in the morning to go running and Brian was getting a bit pissed off with that. Then I went in the gym for a morning and an evening session. It was full on all the time. The whole gym was up for it but if anybody came to talk to me Brendan just ushered them away. He was watching me closely and he said that he'd never seen me punch so hard.

I went, as usual, to stay with Rita and Dave, which kept me away from the spotlight and gave me time to think. I knew how important this fight was as it was an eliminator that could lead to a fight with Hagler or Hearns. Mike Barrett had said that we could get a fight with Hearns in Sheffield and I couldn't stop thinking about that. I was becoming more desperate to get it on as the days passed.

The week before the fight we all got a great lift when Brian beat Tony Burke to take the British middleweight title that I had left. I was ecstatic for my mate and now I just wanted to do my thing.

Meanwhile, Mark started getting a bit more gobby in the press saying:

*"If Graham lasts the distance I can assure you he'll be a loser suffering a lot of pain."*

He was talking it up, but he knew that I was 3-1 favourite with the bookies and they don't often get it that wrong. And it was a great chance to get myself in front of the Londoners again to show what I could do. I was getting a bit sick of all the *'Herol who?'* stuff coming out of there, and I was starting to think that I'd have done better if I'd been in the capital.

The day before the fight all the press stuff was going bananas with headlines like 'The Big Bang' and 'Capital Punishment'. I had to do a photo call in my trunks waving two sparklers around, which wasn't so easy wearing boxing gloves. Then one clever dick suggested I put one in my mouth (the non sparkly end) to look like I was smoking a sparkly cigar. With hindsight I would have said 'no' but, strangely, it didn't seem such a bad idea at the time. It was only when the sparkles started to shoot into my eyes and I had to spit it out did I realise. Good job Brendan wasn't there!

My old mate Sibbo got in on the act, saying that my ranking was false and Mark had lost a few fights because he was fighting world class opponents all the time. So he said he was putting some money on Mark to win at 3-1. Sibbo and Minter kept going on about Mark's 'bottle'. It was like listening to an early episode of Eastenders, I gave up listening to all the bloody cockney rhyming slang when someone said I'd get an Andy Capp in the Bull and Bush……. or something like that.

♦

Lilian brought Natasha down to the fight. She was nine by this time and growing up into a lovely little girl. She had a real sparkle about her and was very clever. I was ever so proud, but a little bit worried what she might see and hear in the Wembley crowd. I was sure I would win, but I was worried that I might get some pretty nasty stick from the West Ham element in the crowd, and I was right. On the evening, about half an hour before the fight, the police moved a group of my supporters that had been surrounded by people making monkey noises and shouting anti Sheffield stuff. Arseholes.

And as Brendan gave me his last words of wisdom in the changing room I could hear some pretty rough football chanting. I thought to myself, 'Bloody Hell. Wait 'til they see my shorts.' I was very proud of them. Brenda had done them as always and they were a great light blue satin, almost powder blue, but not I'm sure, to the taste of the diamond geezers who had packed the stadium. Then I heard, quietly but definitely, a chant of:

*"Yorkshire, Yorkshire…"*

It was very quickly drowned by a loud and obscene rendition of Knees up Mother Brown, but enough to tell me I wasn't on my own. As I walked in to the arena I could see about a thousand of my fans in one corner but then I knew I had to shut out all the noise and concentrate. It wasn't easy. On the other side of the stadium there was a pretty big group of skinheads making their noise and when my name was announced I couldn't hear our lot cheering. But I knew they were. And so I was going to do it, for them and for Natasha.

As the fight began the noise was deafening. Mark came out quickly as we all expected, but I went straight in to meet him and I had a lot of success right away catching him with right jabs and left hooks. By the end of the round there was already blood on his face and the crowd was hurling some pretty vile abuse at me. As I sat down in the corner I could see Lilian taking Natasha out. I didn't know it at the time but she was crying her heart out.

In the third round I cut Mark a bad one above the eye and the ref stopped the fight for it to be looked at. But Mark being Mark, he came out again in the fourth and had a real go. I hit him a lot more than he hit me, but at the end of the round neither of us heard the bell and we carried on trading whacks until the ref jumped in.

In the fifth we clashed heads and that cut me just above the eye but I was still well on top. I threw him around, spun him and threw punches that he never even knew existed. But I hadn't found the big punch to finish him. He was cut all over the place. And in the sixth round I started to rile him a bit when I dropped my hands and began chatting at him. So he hit me a few times.

By the beginning of the eighth I think Mark realised he was so far behind that he had to do something. So he starting taunting me and beckoning me, and I went in. All the hard punching I'd done in the gym, all the desire to get nearer to a world title and all the angst about the abuse that I'd been getting came out in a flurry of attacks which I think Mark hadn't fully expected. And so at the end of the round his manager, Terry Lawless threw the towel in and that was that.

There wasn't the bedlam I had expected, there was actually some applause and the Sheffield fans were jubilant. Mark took it all in good heart too. At the end of the fight I did wonder whether he was going to hug me, but he did and said:

*"Good fight".*

A security guard had found Lilian and Natasha outside having an orange juice and told them it was all over, and so my little girl came running up to me and her tears were all dried. Then, to top it all, Dad showed up!

He'd never seen me fight before and as a devout Christian didn't really agree with boxing as a living but I think he'd quite enjoyed it. Noel was there as well and he later told me he hadn't seen Dad so chuffed since he'd left home to join the army.

I was happier than I'd ever been. I'd won a tough fight and was next in line for a world title shot. The people I loved most in the world had been there, only Mum was missing. And to add to that Sibbo's credentials as a professional gambler and financial advisor had been questioned. Shame.

And my love life was in good shape. I was happy and settled with Karen, and as we sat down on our bed in the hotel I knew that I wouldn't be able to sleep. So we ended up window shopping on Oxford Street 'till four, stopping now and then outside the jewellery shops!

♦

Thoughts of settling down aside, I hoped that my time had come. But the following day my prospects of a quick tilt at the World title disappeared when the WBA announced that Hagler was to fight Sugar Ray Leonard in April, so there would be nothing doing for me until after the summer. We thought that Hagler was going to be stripped of the title but the WBA decided to leave things until after April. I rang Brendan and he just said to bide my time. I knew I was getting nearer but how long would I have to be patient? I was now the official number one world contender.

But as time went on we realised that I needed another fight to keep me moving. And so Barney set up a match with the

American Charles Boston, and he wanted me to go back to the Kings Hall in Belfast, where I'd had a tricky time the year before.

This was frustrating. I really thought I deserved a title shot now and didn't need to fight again. But I just had to carry on I guess, training, sparring and I was still able to do the best bit – a few exhibitions.

At the beginning of December we had a ring set up in a big pub in Sheffield and invited anyone to come in and have a crack at me. I had my hands clasped behind my back and if they could hit me they won a fiver. It was a great laugh. A few boys had a go, swinging wildly and reminding me of the days in the working mens clubs, and it was decent training for me too making sure I was moving quickly enough. Then a girl climbed into the ring and the announcer shouted:

*"This is Debbie from Hillsborough. How old are you Love? Twenty four."*

Debbie didn't look twenty four, and she didn't look big enough to fight her way through a trifle, but she was willing to have a go. What I didn't know was that Debbie was a copper. It had been fairly easy for me with all the blokes who came at me with solid stances and threw punches from where I expected. But Debbie matched me with her hands down approach. And then she slapped me with a massive back hander that nearly knocked my teeth out. The audience roared with approval and laughter as Debbie took her fiver, winked at me and walked off.

♦

I didn't need to be hit by a girl to encourage more goading though. No sooner did I think that Sibbo had lost interest in insulting me, Charles Boston's people started. His managers, Kenny Bogner and Angelo Taverna were telling anyone that would listen that I would be better off on a running track than in a boxing ring. I just wished that these people would give up. What the hell is the point of getting hit? I had beaten fourteen of my last fifteen opponents inside the distance and recently it seemed that each one was saying I'd never fought anyone tough before them. How long would this go on? I'd have to end up fighting Sylvester Stallone to shut some of these idiots up. Bogner said:

*"Tell Graham to fight and not run. He talks about a world title but you don't win belts backing off. You have to go in and take them."*

To be fair to Boston, he had just stopped Errol Christie in December, and he was a hard man. His career was stalled in 1984 for a while because he had been shot in the leg. So he certainly wasn't scared of me, but there was no need for all the insults.

Brendan wasn't too concerned. I think he was happy that I was starting to get a little angry and I was hitting harder than ever. On one session in the ring I was hitting the pads and I knocked him flying. I thought he was kidding. But he just got up, smiled and said:

*"Jesus Son, that was one of the hardest punches I've ever felt."*

Boston's managers kept on right up to the fight on the 17th January, saying that I was a runner and Boston himself joined in saying that he was coming to Ireland to 'lick me' – unpleasant. He said that he was going to take my place as the number one contender.

So I stopped him in the seventh round.

The best thing of the night, apart from taking Charles Boston apart, was that the Irish crowd really gave me a good backing. They were singing, 'Here we go, here we go....' and shouting my name, so it all felt good and Barney was pleased. He needed a bit of cheering up because Barry McGuigan had gone and wasn't for returning, and he wasn't even at the fight. It was a bit embarrassing because the only personalities the MC could introduce were three blokes called 'The Antrim Coasters' who had won a quiz show on television. Classic.

♦

The legacy of my fight in Belfast was not only a better relationship with fight fans over there, but also a fractured hand. God it was sore, and the medics told me that I'd be out of action for at least six weeks.

While I was spending my days running and sitting on my backside I had plenty of time to think about things. We'd come a long way since I arrived in Sheffield, and I was grateful to the lift up that Brendan had given me. But more and more, especially since Barney had arrived, we were arguing, and the atmosphere in the gym was taking a dive. Everybody knew that things were not as they should be, and the laughs that usually helped us through the work were fewer by the day. By early 1987 Brendan knew that he was losing his control over me, and at the same time I had to watch Hagler get beaten by Sugar Ray Leonard when I thought it would have been me. So we were both pissed off. We argued about the usual sort of stuff but, for the first time I can remember, I asked about money. I had been due to receive a percentage of the money Barney had paid Brendan for my contract, but it had never materialised. I didn't push it too hard. After everything I'd been through with Brendan it didn't seem right. He was like an uncle to me.

I think Barney was keen to get Brendan out of the way, not only because of the northern and southern Ireland divide, but maybe they had also got to the stage where they could see that they both wanted to take control and a power struggle had started. The tension had been there right from the start. Barney had money coming out of his ears and it seemed to me that Brendan wanted some of that, but didn't want Barney. And Barney was getting more and more critical of Brendan's training. I used to get dragged into it all the time when one or the other would say:

*"Isn't that so Herol?"*

*"Yes, yes."*

They'd carried on using me like a kid when they were warring parents. Not very good parenting. They never really had any major bust ups but just niggles, and Barney knew that as well as his financial muscle, he'd made progress with me in Ireland, just as Barry McGuigan had left him, so maybe he needed me.

Eventually, like many rowing parents they decided to split up and the custody battle began. I think Brendan thought I'd go with him, because he'd looked after me since I was a kid. I didn't know what to do at first, and I was getting advice from all over the place but Johnny told me that it was my own decision and only I could make it.

My heart was telling me to stay with Brendan, but my head said that I should go with the man who could open doors and take me to the very top. And that seemed more likely to be Barney. I needed someone who could guide me. Brendan could train me but Barney could guide me, although Barney couldn't train me. I trained myself a lot of the time anyway, even when I was with Brendan. The guys in Nottingham had helped and so had Brendan, of course, but it was always my way of boxing, and I kept myself super fit, so I needed someone to hone the technical side and guide me.

After a lot of soul searching I made my decision to go with Barney.

I talked a lot to Karen about it all. She thought that the Ingles didn't like her. The Ingles thought she didn't like them, but she didn't mind them at all. They thought she had too much influence over me, and Karen said that if I went to join Barney's camp they would maybe even blame her. But I had made my own decision. Karen wasn't bothered either way as long as I was happy and getting the right deal for my future.

I rang Brendan to tell him that I was leaving and it was a short conversation to say the least. I think he was very upset and we didn't speak for a few days, and I felt really awkward about it all. It came out in the local and national press. The guy at the Sheffield Star asked me whether it was about the money and I said it was financial and personal. Brendan said that he thought the money Barney had paid was a personal award for him and his family, but my view was that Barney was paying for the special partnership that had come so far.

Maybe Brendan thought that I'd taken a few liberties when I lived with him. I didn't pay any rent, or not much, as far as I can remember. But then I'd helped other people as much as I could. Brendan and I went to see a solicitor together, and we decided to let things lie. At that time I was doing okay financially anyway.

◆

I'd had a lot of sleepless nights but Barney was just 'business as usual' when I spoke to him. He didn't seem to care much about my split with Brendan, but then why should he? Guys who have made so much money have to be single minded I guess. So I left my mates at Newman Road to set up a new gym in Savile Street, on my own.

Stepping in to the big, empty gym was one of the loneliest things I'd ever done in my life, and for the first time since I'd been in Sheffield I felt a little bit vulnerable. I still talked to Brian and Glyn and Johnny, but I was out of the team now, and I didn't have Brendan's reassuring hand on my shoulder. I knew I had made the right decision but I kind of missed his constant, stupid blarney.

As there was no world title shot in the offing, Barney had set up a fight at Wembley with the African Italian Sumbu Kalambay. It was a dangerous kind of fight for me to get in to. Kalambay was a good fighter and had won thirty seven out of forty one fights, but he was maybe past his best. No doubt there'd be the usual knockers if I beat him.

Unbeknown to me, Barney had been preparing for me to split with Brendan and had been speaking to a Panamanian guy called Frederico Plummer, and as soon as I left Brendan, Plummer was recruited to train me.

He came over to Sheffield to meet me and I didn't feel that much either way about him. He seemed an okay kind of person but I didn't know as much about him as I knew about boxing. Boxing is boxing to me. He was as different to Brendan as you could imagine, black for a start, and neat and tidy and quiet. I knew he was in a difficult situation coming in to replace

Brendan. There were loads of comments flying around in the press saying that Brendan understood me and no one could replace him. And we definitely wouldn't be able to get as close, because he was based in Los Angeles and would be travelling over for fights. The more I though about that, the more I thought it was maybe a stop gap. I didn't really know what Barney was doing to be honest.

But as we got in to the preparation for the Kalambay fight I soon realised that Frederico was going to try to change my style. Brendan had always just let me do my thing, but Frederico wanted to make me more of a fighter and less of a boxer. He wanted me to be more orthodox and started working on that straight away. And he also did an interview with the Sun that pissed me off no end, when he said:

*"Graham is a good boxer but he makes some basic mistakes. The most dangerous is when he moves back with his head high in the air. So far he has been able to get away with it. When he's in the ring he does everything wrong but he's highly successful at it."*

Thanks a fucking heap Frederico. Brendan had never criticised me like that. I thought the idea was to talk up your own man and try to break the confidence of the other guy. Just a thought.

As the drills in the gym went on Frederico was watching me like a hawk and I couldn't get away with anything. I wondered if this was how Sibbo and Duran felt and whether Frederico actually wanted me to get into a scrap. But I knew that if I tried to get into a fight like ninety nine per cent of other boxers did, then I'd lose the edge that I had on them, my speed would no longer be an advantage.

We were doing more strength work and less speed work. And that was different to me. I had always been very good at moving quickly in the ring and getting points at the same time. But standing still and trying to trade shots was just not my thing. Frederico's view was that the bigger the shots the better. It was all about hustle and bustle and not really boxing. I wanted to be relaxed and be able to move easily but Frederico wanted me to have my hands up and stand firm. I should have stood up for myself but I never had to before, so I guess I just didn't know how to.

I was due to go over to Bangor to prepare for the fight. Barney had been nagging me to go over to Ireland permanently but I couldn't see myself being over there all the time. It would have been a hell of a commitment and I had family and friends over here as well. I still needed my mates around me.

But I did go over to Bangor to train for the Kalambay fight and even this was new to me. When I was with Brendan, I usually went to stay with Rita, out in the country at Stannington, where it was better for my runs, quieter and with fewer distractions. Even Karen used to stay in my house on Newman Road.

So on this occasion I left Karen in Sheffield two weeks before the fight and headed over to Ireland. One of the younger boxers would be there to chaperone Karen while I was away, make sure she was okay, take her shopping, that sort of thing. I didn't see much of her in the fortnight before I left as I prepared for the fight.

♦

When I arrived in Ireland I was met by Frederico and Eddie Shaw, Barry McGuigan's old trainer was there as well. I was well on course weight wise. I had been sparring and sparring and sparring and thought that my speed work was okay. As the final week arrived I was completely in the zone, but I hadn't been for the previous couple of weeks. In all honesty I had still been thinking about how it would have been if I was still with Brendan, and you always think about family and girlfriends as well until the final few days when you shut everything else out of your mind. You have to be a hundred per cent focussed, and emotional stuff from the rest of your life has to take a back seat for those last few crucial days. But I had said something in the press that was still on my mind. After Fredercio had arrived I said to a reporter:

*"Now I know what it feels like to be fit."*

I was just trying to say the right things, because I couldn't say that I was pleased with the training, I was actually struggling to take on his ideas, so fitness is what I focussed on. But as soon as I'd said it I regretted it. I worried what Brendan might think of it, and Karen said she thought he would actually be quite hurt.

We were staying in a very nice guest house near the sea shore that was run by a lovely lady called Jean. It was really homely and we had everything we needed. Most importantly of all we were out of the way of any distractions. I had done a couple of interviews at the local gym in Bangor but nobody apart from Barney knew where we were, not even Karen. It was relaxing and absolutely the right environment to get fully prepared. Jean was fantastic, always checking that I had everything that I wanted. I couldn't understand much of what she said but she kept giving me this stuff called soda bread and was keen for me to try some brown lemonade, but it looked like diarrhoea so I politely declined.

Everything was cool, I was relaxed, in the zone and prepared as well as I thought I could be in the circumstances. Then, the day before we were due to travel to London, I received a telephone call. It had to be Barney. Jean put it through to me in my bedroom:

*"Hello Barney?"*

There was nothing.

*"Hello?"*

Then there was a woman's voice on the other end that I didn't recognise. To this day I still have no idea who it was, but the voice quietly and coldly said to me:

*"I think you deserve to know Herol, that Karen is having an affair."*

*"Who the fuck is this?"*

*"A friend."*

And then the woman hung up.

I went ballistic; I shouted, kicked the wall and then stared out of the window. I didn't know what to think. Maybe it was just a malicious hoax, but maybe it wasn't. It had to be. Karen wouldn't do that to me. I was suddenly scared and wondering what was happening. What the fuck was happening? Who would want to upset me like that two days before the biggest fight of my life? Who had it in for me? I had always tried never to upset anyone, to be good to everyone, so who would try to hurt me? Somebody, and I still don't know who, wanted me to wobble at this very moment.

I rang home to speak to Karen but she wasn't there. Fucking hell. Where was she? I started to panic and rang again and again. Eventually Karen answered the phone and I blurted out:

*"I've just had a message from a woman who says you're having an affair."*

*"What?"*

*"I said.... I've had a woman on the phone saying you're having an affair."*

*"You don't believe it do you?"*

*"I don't know Karen."*

*"Oh bloody hell Herol. It's not true. They're just trying to get to you."*

*"So you're not?"*

*"No, I'm not. Get it out of your head."*

But I went over and over it. Who knew I was there at Jean's guest house in Bangor? Who was watching Karen? It started to drive me mad and I didn't know whether to believe the woman on the phone or whether to believe Karen.

Frederico heard the commotion and came to see what I was getting upset about. Then he told me to calm down and rang Barney to let him know what had happened.

I never found out for sure one way or the other whether Karen had been unfaithful, but in my mind the damage had been done. From that day on Barney insisted that I never take phone calls in the week before a fight, but in this case my head was well and truly fucked. I had been putting all my energy in to trying to box in a way that I knew wasn't right for me and I'd just taken a phone call telling me that my girlfriend was messing around. And in that state of truly shit turmoil we headed off to London.

I had two days to get my head clear and I just had to concentrate on the fight. I was putting my life on the line to follow the dream that I was so near to achieving, but somehow, somehow I had to get my head right. I tried. But all this stuff was going round in my head..... Karen..... Brendan..... Karen. Girlfriend.....trainer......oh shit. The more I tried to focus, the more the little voices kept talking to me, '*Is Karen cheating Herol? Brendan would let you fight the way you can win. Come on Herol, you know the truth.*'

I felt like I was going insane but I was desperately trying to hold it all together. It was really starting to piss me off and so I kept on telling myself that I was good enough to win this fight, and moreover, I had to win it. Everybody wanted me to win it, well everyone apart from maybe one or two who knew how to get to me. Shit.

I was quiet all the way to London. And Brendan wasn't there to ask me why. I didn't want to fight and I told Frederico. But it was too late to pull out. When we arrived in the hotel in London, Glyn rang me to tell me that he would drive Karen down to the fight so I knew she'd be there.

♦

On fight day there was all the usual hype around the match, the weigh in, the TV stuff and that took my mind off everything else for a while. I was ninety per cent focussed. I needed to be a hundred, but I still had the day to get it absolutely right.

As always, I didn't know a whole lot about my opponent, other than he was a strong Italian and this was a European Championship fight, one step away from a World title fight. This was an eliminator and I simply had to win.

Over the last few weeks of training my mind was Frederico's but my body was constantly going back to what it wanted to do.

I'd start as Frederico wanted me to but soon enough revert back to what I knew. Frederico had changed it all and I was in conflict as to what I should do.

So when I stepped into the ring I felt under pressure to take shots when I didn't really have to. But there was no real doubt that I'd win. I was 7-1 on favourite and a lot of money was on me to finish it within five rounds. And I started okay, scoring plenty of hits but Kalambay was a strong fighter and I quickly started to take too many silly shots.

By the sixth round he was still on his feet and I was thinking, 'if I was with Brendan I wouldn't be doing this – I'd be doing it my own way.' My head was all over the place, not just on the boxing front. But I kept asking myself why I didn't do it my own way. If I did that I would have got in trouble and got some smacked hands! But Brendan knew that I was a free spirit and he let me do what he knew I could do the best.

I was still ahead in the fight but by the eighth round Kalambay's wicked right hand was doing too much. He kept hitting me in the face, thump, thump, thump and I got a cut eye and my nose was bleeding. He started to look like he was tiring but the bugger stayed on his feet as we traded punches. I couldn't work out what to do not to be caught. I knew in my heart that all I had to do was move him around quicker, but that wasn't what I'd been told to do. I just had to try and fight like everybody else and no longer like my hero, Ali.

It just wasn't working and as I sat in my corner before the start of the final round I knew that it was much too close. I heard someone say:

*"You'd better do something this round or you've blown it."*

Any suggestions?

The bell went and I came out fighting. But even though I wasn't moving around as much as I normally did, I was getting more and more tired and was taking more and more shots. I was in with the rest and I couldn't do my thing any more. And in my heart I didn't really believe I was rough and tough enough to win that way. When Kalambay caught me and I slid across the ropes, the world could see me saying, *'Oh shit.'*

And as the bell went I threw my hands in the air as I always did, but I knew that I had lost.

I'd have won that fight if Brendan had still been in my corner.

This was the first fight I'd lost and I didn't understand it. It was an entirely new feeling. How did I lose it? I struggled to get my head around it. I didn't know whether it was the training, the phone call or whether I just wasn't good enough. I think I was good enough, and maybe, all in all I lost it because of immaturity. I didn't have the maturity to stand up for what I believed and I couldn't cope with all the things that were happening around me. Not accepting the girlfriend situation was bad. If that's the reason I lost then I should have coped better. It hurt me more than it should have done.

And it was a bitter blow. I was seamlessly on my way to the World title and all of a sudden it had been taken away from me. So I didn't much care about anything else. I split up with Karen as soon as I got back to Sheffield and she was distraught. I didn't know what had happened while I was away and at that very moment I didn't care any more.

Karen went straight back to London but she ended up in a very low place. She had threats every day because lots of boxing fans blamed her because the News of the World ran an article headlined:

"CHEATING LOVER COST ME WORLD TITLE FIGHT"

It took Karen years to recover. She was spat at in the street and was always looking over her shoulder. To this day I have never said those words. I spoke to a reporter and he wrote what he wanted.

Everybody had an opinion as to why I lost. Brendan took the chance to say the tactics were wrong and I couldn't blame him for that. Barney said someone might have slipped me a Mickey

Finn in my tea, whatever that meant. He said I seemed like I was hypnotised on the stool in the corner.

Brendan spoke to me in the weeks after the fight but I can't remember exactly what he said. Lots of people were speaking to me telling me I should have done this or I should have done that. It was all *'should've, should've'* and now and then I thought, *'Why didn't you get in the fucking ring then?'* But I never said that. I always wondered how the experts who were criticising me now would have coped with taking that phone call, changing my style, running an hour and a half every morning carrying weights. I don't tell them what to do.

For the first time in my adult life I was battling with myself, and not just trying to beat someone else. I doubted myself for the first time, and for a brief moment I felt as vulnerable as I did when I was eight and couldn't recognise a very bad man. The memory of what had happened to me as a child was never far away, but it sometimes faded. But for the first time in ages I remembered it, thought about it long and hard and cried.

Self doubt can eat you up.

To this day I never found out the truth about Karen and I never really wanted to. What was done was done, and I had to learn a hard lesson a very hard way. But something had been spoilt.

Karen, or a hoax, had hurt me. Then I hurt Karen. And I think I had already hurt Brendan. It's always sad when a loving relationship ends, but two at the same time. That's really sad.

# 11

# Holy Grail

*"We must learn to live together as brothers or perish together as fools."*

## Martin Luther King

I hadn't felt so alone for twenty years. Getting my head round my first professional defeat was too hard for me to do on my own. But I couldn't go back to the Newman Road gym, and I didn't have a girlfriend. I thought about contacting Karen but whenever I picked up the phone I just put it down again. Brian took me down to Josephines now and then and we had a laugh, but for the first time in my adult life the laugh wasn't real. There was something behind it, eating away at me.

Losing is one of the worst feelings in the world. I thought that I had let people down, particularly the fans in Sheffield. And everybody starts blaming each other. Even though I had split up with Brendan, he was still arguing with Barney and at one stage Barney lodged an official complaint to the British Board of Boxing Control. I think he was upset about something Brendan said after the fight. They'd never got on and Barney was somehow blaming Brendan for my defeat, saying that there was something wrong before I fought Kalambay that had distracted me. That wasn't the case at all. I had been distracted, but it was all to do with my training and my personal life, and at the last minute. Either way it was a fuck up of someone's making, and I didn't see any point in going over it again and again. I didn't speak much to Barney over the next few weeks, he didn't seem to be that bothered with me, and I kind of got the impression that I'd somehow set him back. We all wanted to win of course, and no one more so than me, so I didn't feel I'd let Barney down, just the fans.

I did speak to Brendan though and we talked about stuff in general, as well as the fight. He said that he could see that I was trying to do something unnatural and he feared for me as early as the first round.

I wished that Brendan had been in my corner, but he wasn't, and now it was all history. But I wanted to start fixing things somehow, and I didn't know where to start. Going out with Brian and Johnny was okay but I wanted to decide what to do next with my career.

Then out of the blue I got a call from Brendan. He started off by asking how I was and I did the same. It was a bit awkward at first and then he said:

*"Why don't I come down and see you?"*

We met down at the jewellery shop and stayed there for about three hours. Both of us wanted to make up I think, both of us knew in our heart of hearts that we needed each other. Eventually Brendan suggested I come back up to the gym and I didn't need a second invitation. It was like a weight off my shoulders. I thought I might have a second chance to fight how I wanted to and it felt immediately like the right thing to do. It turned out that it was his 26th wedding anniversary and Mrs Ingle still hadn't got her card by the time he went home at seven o'clock.

Neither of us had to back down or eat any humble pie, but on my part I just wanted to speak to someone who really knew me and I wanted to have a look at the old place before I made a solid commitment. Nothing wrong with that.

But when I walked into the gym and saw Glyn and Mick sparring, nothing seemed to have changed. And I felt homesick. And Brendan knew how to play me:

*"You're not going to get back on your feet unless you get all these upsets behind you and get back in the ring and concentrate on what you do the best."*

*"What can I do?"*

*"Well that's just up to you Son."*

So what could I do? There's no way I could stay on my own, but then I didn't want to risk getting a new girlfriend to move in. I loved the companionship of living with someone, but not the hassles, and I thought I'd had my fair share of hassles with Jane and then Karen over the past couple of years. And all things considered, getting back with Brendan would solve at least one thing. I could fight how we both wanted me to. I needed to get at least one worry out of my mind. I'd never had worries as an adult before, and I didn't like it one bit. Getting rid of a big one was very attractive to me.

So less than three months after we split up I was back with Brendan. I thought that maybe Barney wouldn't be happy but I didn't much care about that. I wasn't absolutely sure what influence Barney was having in my life. I knew what Brendan had done for me, but I wasn't sure what Barney had done to move me up. Since he joined me I had been to the US but then I had lost my first fight, so it wasn't a major change. With Brendan I'd had thirty seven wins, without him I'd had one defeat. It was a no brainer and I didn't much care that Barney and Brendan looked like getting into a legal battle. It had taken me a few weeks but I realised that I just wanted to box, and I wanted to train with my mates, and I wanted Brendan in my corner. Simple.

The conversation with Barney was pretty short and sweet. And at that very moment I suspect my relationship with Barney had taken a turn for the worst. When I beat Ernie Rabotte in Vegas I thought I was on my way, but I felt that if Barney had my interests at heart he wouldn't have put me in the ring against Kalambay. That might have been unfair of me, because from

Barney's point of view it would have been a nightmare to pull the fight so late. But I wasn't sure that it was working financially for me either. Before that fight I had signed something around the TV money on the basis that I'd get a better basic rate, but I'm not sure how it worked.

But at least I had Brendan back in my corner and I could start to get my fighting back on the right track.

And it was great to be back in the gym. The lads were just the same and it was good to see them all. Johnny was honing his craft and getting a bigger reputation locally and Naz was making a lot of headlines too with his classy and arrogant style. We knew there were big times ahead for him.

Slowly, as the year went on, I started to get my mojo back and I was ready to get back in the ring. Barney had been quiet though. Barry McGuigan had left him some time ago, so I'm not sure what he was doing. I know he was always busy. I had to sit and watch Kalambay take the IBF World title while I was waiting, until eventually I had a fight lined up against Ricky 'the Brickhouse' Stackhouse – good nickname!

The fight was set up in Doncaster and it was live on television, and Barney told me that I needed to put on a good show to impress the TV audience and get myself back in the frame. I didn't think the fight would be a big earner, but being on TV it might be okay.

I was more concerned about winning the fight than the money side of it. And for the first time I had a real fear of losing. I always asked myself what was going to happen if I lost, but now I actually knew the reality of it. And I didn't like it one bit. I couldn't afford to lose again and I was terrified of letting myself down.

I went to stay at Rita and Dave's as usual. That was another added benefit of getting back with Brendan, because they were such good friends of his. By making up, I'd not only got my mates around me and my trainer back, but I'd got the last two weeks routine back that had been so successful up until this year. When I sat down at Rita's to watch telly after we'd eaten our tea I realised that I was safe again. The doubts and fears that had haunted me for the last six months were all but gone. I was just the usual focussed, moody guy in the run up to a fight.

And it worked. In the ring at Doncaster I felt like I had my freedom again. I moved around as I'd always done and I didn't take any shots that I didn't need to. After three rounds of this I could use Ricky as a punch bag, and I cut him in the fourth round before knocking him over in the fifth. The referee stopped it a couple of rounds later and I was back on the way again.

But I was on the way back more slowly than I wanted. I had to wait another six months before I could fight again. I found this difficult. When I was just with Brendan, even though we found it hard to get fights from time to time, I usually had one every month or two, and we were always busy. That way I had made progress. Now it seemed like I was only going to fight twice a year and not only did that put a lot more pressure on each fight, it was bloody frustrating. I spent a lot of the time just running, sparring, coaching Naz, eating chicken and going to Josephine's. It was okay I guess, but since I'd been beaten I was inwardly taking it a lot more seriously. I desperately wanted to get myself up there for a title shot again, and quickly. While I sat on my arse, I watched Tommy Hearns lose the WBC World title to Iran Barkley and thought that could have been me as well. The other problem was that although I hadn't had a serious challenger in Britain since I fought Mark Kaylor, there were one or two others emerging, including Nigel Benn, the aptly named Dark Destroyer who had done just that to all eighteen of his opponents inside the distance and who held the Commonwealth title.

It was getting to the stage where I'd have to fight Benn before I could get a World title shot at this rate, and so I was a bit impatient when Barney set up a fight in Sheffield for me to contest the vacant British middleweight title with a guy called James Cook from London. Cook's manager, the comically named Darkie Smith got pissed off because I wasn't giving his boy much respect. To be fair, with his fantastic afro and big moustache he did look like Shaft, but I'd made the mistake of saying to a reporter that I'd have to get Cook out of the way before getting to Nigel Benn. That was stirred up in the Evening Standard on Cook's home turf and Darkie Smith had a pot at me saying that they weren't just coming up to Sheffield for the money. I didn't mean him any disrespect at all, I was just getting impatient. But the British Board of Boxing had him at number two behind me so he deserved the fight. He had already beaten Michael Watson, who was up and coming, and I sparred with him before the Kalambay fight so I knew he was a fair boxer.

Darkie said in the press that I had problems and woman trouble and that Cook would be going back down to London as the number one. But I was back on my home turf where I'd never been close to being beaten. So I was confident. And bursting to get in the ring.

It was good to be home, in front of the Sheffield fans and they were in good voice. And one of my favourite referees, Sid Nathan was reffing his last fight. I think he'd been in the ring over thirteen hundred times.

Everything was right for me, I was hungry, the fans were excited and Brendan was in the corner. So I came out in the first round like a train (with a big punch) and floored Cook with a right and left combination. In the second round I battered him into his corner and when he fought back I moved backwards, dropped my guard and picked him off on his head and body. I was back and loving my boxing, but I think I went a bit far in the third round when I dropped my hands and stuck my tongue out at him. Naughty.

Cook's eye was closing so in the fifth round he had a real go and launched himself at me, at which point the crowd noise became deafening as they shouted me on, and I dropped him with a big right to his head. When Sid stepped in to stop the fight, the crowd were singing:

*"ARE YOU WATCHING NIGEL BENN?"*

And Natasha was in the ring to give me a big hug.

Old Darkie Smith was quite kind after the fight. He said that Nigel Benn probably wouldn't be able to find me let alone hit me (I think that was a compliment) and that I'd get a World title shot if I could defend my British title against Johnny Melfah, a fight that was on the cards before the result of this one. Things were going in the right direction again for me.

One year on, the pain of Kalambay and Karen, and the split with Brendan seemed like a distant memory, although in truth it was not all that long ago.

I was fighting as I wanted to again, but over the previous nine months, while I was back with the team, it wasn't quite the same as before. Something had changed but I couldn't really put my finger on it. Brendan no longer seemed to be like an uncle and was more of a trainer. I guess he may still have been a bit sore when I'd chosen to go with Barney the year before, but to me that was all water under the bridge now.

And it seemed that Barney was cheering up a bit, not least because he could see the benefits of a potential fight with Nigel Benn. Boxing fans from all over the place wanted to see that fight, and Barney was talking about getting it on in a football stadium. He knew that if he could do that the live gate receipts alone would be over a million pounds. I wouldn't sneeze at the money either, as well as being a final eliminator. I was already contracted to defend my British title against Melfah, so that wasn't up for grabs but it all made sense anyway.

But I'd missed my chance to ever fight Marvin Hagler as he had quit almost as soon as I'd beaten James Cook.

I started to do a bit more sparring with Glyn because he was the nearest thing we had to a maniac in the gym. And I also started to watch what Benn was doing more. He had quickly gained a reputation as the hardest hitting middleweight in the country. Like Mark Kaylor he was from West Ham, so he had a tough background, and I doubt many of the National Front window lickers would have said to his face what they thought. And he was impatient, like me. He was in the middle of a legal action to get rid of Warren as his manager, because he wanted higher profile fights, saying he wanted Michael Watson, me and Melfah. I knew where he was coming from as I was getting more frustrated by my slow progress over the past two years, and starting to wonder whether Barney really liked me.

I had been careless with my money for a couple of years now, I guess because I had what I wanted, a nice house and a sponsored car, but it was starting to eat at me, just exactly what I was giving away and what I was getting. I could see other fighters becoming millionaires, but years of taking things for granted and being easy with my money had got me into a sloppy habit. But there was a little part of me telling me that I should take it more seriously now.

I asked some of the lads what they thought about it and I spoke to my Dad now and then. I even plucked up the courage to ask Barney about it but I didn't really understand his answer. I didn't get the whole TV situation, and he'd told me that some seats had been unsold for my last fight.

But Barney got to hear some rumours that I was unhappy, and that I thought that he'd made a killing out of me. These things do go around pretty quickly, and maybe some other people thought that maybe I had been taken for a ride. The truth of it is, as always, I don't really know. But the upshot was that it looked like Barney had got fed up and he didn't bid to promote my next fight with Melfah, leaving that to Frank Warren, and he said in the paper that sometimes he makes a profit and sometimes he doesn't and that he was hurt by the rumours.

But it was eating me up. Really eating me up and we started to have rows, more often on the phone because Barney was over in Ireland most of the time. But they got pretty nasty. I got to accusing him of ripping me off. Having big rows was out of my character but I could do the shouting on this. But I was also way out of my depth financially. So then I made a big mistake.

Because I was taking the finance side more seriously I was getting myself angry, partly because I didn't know what was happening and partly because I didn't understand it. But when I got a call from someone at The News of the World I spilled my guts out to them. I told them that I had been promised more than I received when I fought Cook and that Plummer had changed my style before I fought Kalambay. They ran a massive exclusive and did it again the following week and wrote it as if I had written it, in language that I would never have used. The one thing they said that did come out of my mouth was that I never wanted Brendan out of my corner again.

Barney was fucking furious and he let me know. This was a worse row than I'd ever had with Brendan, sure we had our spats, but we never got to this stage.

Johnny Melfah added a bit of fuel to the fire by saying in an interview that I was past my best. I was good enough to win a World title two years ago, but for some reason my handlers had kept me away from it. That didn't cheer Barney up one bit.

I wanted to break my contract with him at this stage because it seemed that everything had broken down between us. But Barney was a good businessman and he had the ability to put big rows behind him if he thought that there was a good deal to be had. And he arranged for me to get a fight with the winner of a World title clash between Kalambay and Doug De Witt. So despite all our disagreements Barney seemed to have done the business for me at last. And then I started to think. When he had declined to promote my upcoming fight with Melfah, maybe he was being completely straight with me after all. I thought that maybe there could be a conflict between managing and promoting but a lot of the successful guys seemed to be able to do both.

While my row with Barney simmered on in the background Brendan was taking the front seat again and had started to talk like he used to:

*"You've wasted some time Son, if you'd been a better listener you'd have had a title shot long ago."*

I knew he was right. I wasn't the best listener in the world, and maybe I'd listened to the wrong people from time to time, and I was easily bored. But he encouraged me as well by telling me that I was a lot younger than Sugar Ray Leonard, and I'd taken very little punishment in seven years, so I had my time ahead of me. And I had learned something. I was steelier in my determination, whereas before I was just impatient, and I think I allowed that to make me hit out at people.

So Barney had let Frank Warren promote the fight with Johnny Melfah in Bethnal Green, but he was there and we shook hands before the fight. The fight itself was a bit of a mismatch in the end. Johnny wasn't really in the right class and the ref stopped it in five rounds. I'd done my job professionally and now I just wanted to get my World title shot.

But first I wanted to take some time to get my head completely clear on what I was going to do next. This year I'd had a major bust up with Brendan and then made up, I think. Then I'd had a major bust up with Barney. I started to wonder if it was me.

So I set off to Tenerife for a week in the sun. On my own.

♦

When I returned from my beach break I felt a million times better. The week away had given me the chance to get my head straight, as well as some much needed recuperation and sun on my back. Running on the beach in the morning was a long way from Newman Road, but by the end of the week I'd met enough people to get some waves and shouts as I ran along. It was like home from home! The sea was a bit cold though so I stayed out of that.

The thinking time was a real bonus. 1987 had been one hell of a year for me, and not the best in more ways than one. I'd lost three things, my trainer, my girlfriend and my unbeaten record, four if you count my temper. Maybe I had got a bit too big for my boots. The whole problem started when I decided to leave Brendan and go with Barney. Then, within a month I had been smashed by Kalambay and split up with Karen. That can't all have been a coincidence surely.

It had preyed on my mind all year. Maybe I was so cut up about splitting with Brendan, that I lost my judgement and faith in Karen, and then lost my confidence in the ring. Who knows? Anyway – it was all history and we had to move on. I knew that I wouldn't be happy without Brendan in my corner and my mates around me, so I'd sorted that out and was back at

Newman Road. Everything was alright again on the face of it, but there was always a little bit of an undercurrent. I think Brendan resented the earlier split but he realised that I was the goose that had laid the golden egg. He had put a lot of effort and time in me and wanted a return, and I was happy for him to get that. We still had laughs in the gym, but there was a more businesslike feel about the whole thing. It wasn't quite the same but life went on. On both sides there was still a lot of trust but maybe one per cent of it had gone, and if all else failed that would keep us on our toes.

And then there was Barney. I'd had a furious bust up with him over the Kalambay fight and in the heat of battle I was convinced I was in the right. But then, lying on a beach in the Canaries isn't such a tense place to be. So as I became more relaxed as the week had gone on, I started to think that maybe he could be good for me after all. You can't make all that money without being a clever businessman and he had guided Barry to a World title. So I decided maybe it would be best to let things lie on that one and see what happened.

I returned to the Newman Road gym refreshed and ready to go. Sparring and running, bag work and skipping, all the same stuff but I had more energy again and a smile on my face. And it wasn't long before Barney came up trumps for me. My tentatively rebuilt faith was justified when he got on the phone to me one day:

*"Mike McCallum. In May at the Albert Hall. So you'd better get yourself ready. And get your head right."*

Fuck me. I put the phone down and sat quietly for a moment, and then hopped across to the ring where Brian and Glyn were sparring and started singing:

*"Get up, get on up, get up get on up, like a sex machine, get on up..."*

Glyn gave me his weary look:

*"What the fuck's up with you- you daft bastard!"*

Brian looked like he knew, but I left them in no doubt:

*"THE WBA MIDDLEWEIGHT CHAMPIONSHIP OF THE WOOORRRRLD. MIKE McCALLUM VERSUS HEROL GRAHAAAAAAM!!"*

*"Yes!"* shouted Brian.

Glyn mumbled:

*"Jesus Christ. You'd better stop fucking around then."*

♦

Finally. Finally I'd got my shot at a world title. And what a fight. Mike McCallum was from Jamaica and he was a brilliant boxer. Brilliant. He'd been a world champion at light middleweight for three years and had recently moved up to middleweight, where he was beaten for the first time by Kalambay of all people. I think he'd been unlucky in that one, because he arrived in Italy only a few days before the fight so he must still have been suffering the effects of jet lag. And he also said that his head wasn't right, because he was thinking too far ahead to a proposed fight with Duran. Kalambay was on a happy run of meeting fighters with messed up heads!

I knew a bit about McCallum. He was tall and quick, a skilful fighter and a body shot man. He was known as 'The Bodysnatcher.' The moment I found out that I was fighting him I knew it would be a hard fight but I wanted to beat the best in the world. And I knew that if Kalambay could beat him then so could I.

The training schedule kicked in straight away and I started increasing my runs. There was no danger of over training and Brendan made sure that I had my rest days, but then again there was no messing about and it was pure training, much to Glyn's delight. I knew, in fact we all knew, that this was the fight that would make me if I could win. And it was bound to be a good fight.

The intensity of my training built up gradually and within a month, just two months before the fight, I was sparring for an hour and a half at a time in the gym. The lads who were sparring with me took it in turns. As soon as one got out the next came straight in and we just carried on. I just had thirty seconds rest between rounds. And then after the sparring I went for another run. It was hard work and I was absolutely shattered.

I had some sparring sessions arranged with an American guy called Ron Essett. Barney had picked him out as he was like McCallum and was ranked seven in the world by the IBF. He was a good guy, and he told me that the feeling in America was that McCallum was past his best and that I'd probably beat him.

And then about a month before the fight Barney set up a public sparring session for me at the gym with Chris Eubank. He'd invited the press and public to come in and watch. It was the first time we'd sparred, in fact the first time I'd met Chris. He was an up and coming fighter from Brighton, with a powerful crouching style and a funny lisp when he spoke. As he became better known he started to play on that and developed a camp, sort of upper class style. He even started wearing a monocle and carrying a cane. Funny guy.

We had two sessions set up and the first was attended by about ten press guys and fifty or so boxing fans. It was a good laugh. I think Chris had under estimated me because I spent the first few minutes boxing his head off and then I had the audience to begin messing around. I dropped my hands, skipped around him and picked him off here and there. Then I drew him in and tapped him at will. I think I annoyed him because he caught me off balance and floored me with a vicious hook. But I got up smiling and battered him.

He was very good about it, and went out in the press to say that I'd beat McCallum and that Nigel Benn shouldn't get in the ring with me. But I don't think it necessarily helped me in the future when Chris became a big star, because he stayed out of my way. He went onto Look North on the telly and said with his trademark lisp:

*"I will never, ever....ever.....ever.... fight Herol Graham."*

Barney was on the phone more and more as the fight approached and he was trying to persuade me to go and train in Ireland or even at Terry Lawless's gym in London. I know there was still a simmering disagreement between him and Brendan, and maybe he just wanted Brendan to have less influence on me. We still argued about the Kalambay fight, I thought that Plummer's coaching had been no good for me but Barney was having none of it. And when he came to watch the sparring with Chris and Ron Essett he wasn't best pleased. He told me that I was up to my old tricks, just dancing around and basically fucking about:

*"Herol, judges aren't awarding points for fancy footwork these days. WBA judges reward aggression, even if it's foolhardy. Runners they do not like – however elegant! You've got a good punch if you can be bothered to find it."*

I kind of resented the idea that was still hanging over me that all I did was run around. Some things never change, and my sparring sessions had done little to convince Barney that my way of fighting was right. Up until the Kalambay fight I was beating people up but in my own way. There's absolutely no point in getting hit, as far as I could see.

Barney just kept on telling me I needed to get to a proper training camp, in Ireland or London and apparently McCallum was spending fifteen thousand pounds on his preparation. I knew that I'd get a decent purse out of the fight, but the truth of it was that I just didn't have the money in my bank account to shell out five figures on training. I'd only spent a few hundred on my holiday at the end of 1987.

All in all, apart from not having the cash, I think it was a case of once bitten, twice shy for me. I wanted to stay with Brendan and Rita and Dave. So Barney had to put up with that, but he wasn't happy.

Mike McCallum jetted in to London a couple of weeks before the fight and so the media sparring began, spearheaded by McCallum's trainer, a seventy seven year old guy called Eddie Futch. He had trained Joe Frazier and Larry Holmes so he knew his stuff, but he didn't have such a big opinion of me. Funny that. To be fair, the only trainer I'd come across that had a go at his own man rather than the opponent was Plummer, so this sort of thing was par for the course.

Futch said that they'd watched videos of me and knew that I was quick and clever but had spotted my weaknesses that they could exploit. I'd been doing my own preparation by watching a video of McCallum where he demolished Don Curry with a single shot. Barney threatened to burn it because he didn't want me having too much respect for him. But it was important for me to know what he could do.

Brendan was talking to me as usual saying how I could beat McCallum. I don't know if he was speaking much to Barney at the time but, as usual, I seemed to be getting a different message from each of them. Barney wanted me to be more aggressive and he didn't tire of telling me that.

The first time I met Mike McCallum was at the pre fight press conference. He looked in great condition; he'd been training for the last eight weeks in Vegas before arriving in Britain. I thought he was a nice guy actually although he didn't say all that much. Eddie Futch did his talking and all McCallum said in the whole conference was:

*"I've got no excuses. I'm over the jet lag and I'm ready."*

Short and sweet. I think he was still sore about his defeat to Kalambay, as he was still talking about jet lag. But he had a proud record with only the one defeat just like me, and to the same man.

Barney made it absolutely clear to me that Mike wasn't coming over for nothing. He wouldn't be coming if he didn't think that he'd beat me. This was my opportunity and I had to get out there and do it - otherwise get out there and do it! There was no other option.

♦

When we arrived at the Albert Hall everything was right. At the check weigh in I was aiming to be eleven stone six. I was eleven, five and a half so I had a drink of water and it put me right on my weight. By the time we had the actual weigh in I was smack on my weight and so was he.

As we got ready in the changing rooms Brendan didn't need to say anything else to me. But he did. It was the last minute instructions and advice. I was listening but I wasn't listening if that makes sense. He'd told me what to do a thousand times already and it was in there. But I guess he couldn't stand a bit of silence at that very moment, and then again neither could I.

The hall was packed and there was a big crowd from Sheffield there. The official ticket allocation to Sheffield was two and a half thousand but there must have been double that number in the arena transforming one side of the Albert Hall into a passionate corner of Yorkshire. I could hear them chanting:

*"WE LOVE YOU BOMBER, WE DO!"*

I managed to cut myself off. The crowd chanting was great but I knew it could give me false confidence so, as always, I tried to bring myself back down to earth. That way I could concentrate and do my thing. The crowd shouting was good because they wanted me to win, but I couldn't afford to listen to what they shouted, particularly if they were shouting at me what to do. I had to do my own thing and do what was right for me. Sometimes the crowd could be right of course but I always had to concentrate.

And I concentrated well. As the first round started I was in my rhythm straight away. I won the first two rounds without a touch on me, moving him around and catching him with the left and constant jabs as Brendan had told me. Every time I landed a flurry of punches the fans went wild and the chanting started again.

I was back at my happiest in the ring. No problems with style and moving at the pace that I wanted. But in the third round Mike came back at me with a pretty fierce assault and that was the last time in the evening that I dropped my hands and chatted at him. This was a serious fight. I'd cleared out of my mind what was at stake but I knew that I was in a contest.

As the match wore on it came down to a gruesome, gruesome battle. It was a very tactical fight from the off and Mike was clever, but he could fight as well as box. At the end of the third Brendan looked worried, and told me to start dictating the pace again, and to get more jabs in, and over the next three rounds I did that and I felt like I was nicely in control. In the fifth round Mike went down but it was a bit untidy and although he took a standing count the ref warned me.

I had won five of the first six rounds, but as the rounds passed by he started to come after me and was scoring punches, but I was meeting him punch for punch. I started to feel that the referee was leaning more for Mike, not because he was bent, but because Mike was the world champion and it was up to me to beat him clearly and by some margin. I had to prove to the ref and everybody else that I could be a worthy world champion without any doubt. World champions who are defending their title are always more likely to lose by knock out than on points. The challenger has to prove they've won. This was not just against me, but against every challenger and I accepted that. So as time ticked by I started to get more anxious, knowing that if Mike came back at me, then I might need a knock out. But he was showing his experience and starting to pick me off more and more and he was getting more slippery.

In the eighth round he went over again but it was because we had started wrestling and my growing anxiety had led me to push him to the ground, which got me a warning and a one point deduction. And then I lost the ninth when Mike had a run of success and my left eye started to close.

As I sat down after the eleventh I knew I was still ahead but Mike had been getting closer and closer. I thought I might be as much as a round and a half in front. But you can never be completely sure, so the way I saw it I just needed a strong finish and to stay on my feet to win the fight.

In the last round we traded punches and kept on moving and it was a session of pain and bravery for both of us. At the end of the round I thought it had been half and half and so I knew I was in with a good chance. But I also knew it was close and certainly too close for comfort. I could have picked it up more in the two previous rounds but then so could Mike.

As the bell rang a massive cheer went up and my corner rushed over to me, two of the lads picked me up and carried me around the ring shoulder high and there was bedlam in the crowd. As I plonked back down on the canvas to wait for the decision Brendan came over to me and put his arm around me as the announcer tried to make himself heard.

The first judge, a guy called Jesus, clearly with a divine inspiration, gave it to me 117 to 114. But then the second judge scored against me 115 to 117. So it was a split decision and my heart almost stopped. We waited. Until the third judge's score was announced:

*"One hundred and fifteen points, to one hundred and fourteen points to ...........MIKE McCALLUM."*

The auditorium went quiet. They thought I'd won but I wasn't quite so sure. I looked around and all I could see was people crying. Natasha was there and crying, the lads in the corner, crying, I think even Barney was shedding a tear.

I'd lost it on a split decision. We had the same points but I had lost. The point deducted in the eighth round was the point that lost me the World title. Or one of them at least.

Even though the Sheffield fans thought I had won there wasn't any booing, just a hush. It was an empty sort of feeling.

Oddly, I seemed to be coping okay. I didn't cry and it didn't seem like the end of the world. Mike was the World champion and I liked him. He was a good guy and I had enjoyed the fight. I thought I'd done myself justice and there was no shame in losing to a great fighter.

But what next?

# 12

# <u>More to Life</u>

*"Life is a gamble at terrible odds. If it was a bet,*
*you wouldn't take it."*

## Tom Stoppard

You know that feeling when one minute you're everybody's best mate and the next, they're kind of tip toeing around you and they don't want to have a laugh with you any more. Well that was what happened in the few days following my fight with McCallum. I read an article in the Sheffield Star that ran the headline:

### SOMBRE FINALE FOR FANS
**Bubbly supper goes flat on the way home**

What the hell's a bubbly supper? Anyhow, the article summed up how we all felt in the aftermath. Some of the most fanatical lads said I was robbed and should retire out of a sense of injustice; some said I threw it away after the sixth round and should retire; and the more balanced guys said it could have gone either way and I should have another go.

For my part I didn't once think of retiring and I didn't really share the sense of injustice of some of my biggest supporters. Okay I lost a point for spinning Mike which didn't look so bad when I watched the video and maybe, just maybe I shaded it. But that wasn't enough. Mike would have been well within his rights to say he won it fair and square and when the margins are so tight it just comes down to opinion.

I didn't feel anywhere near as down as I had when I lost to Kalambay. That was a disaster that I shouldn't have allowed to happen. But this was a good fight and I really believed that I was mentally prepared and I did my very best. That's all I could do and if it wasn't good enough then so be it. Mike was an exceptionally good boxer and in my mind this didn't mean I was at the end of the road – far from it.

And just like when people realise that the guy whose pet hamster has just croaked isn't suicidal about the whole thing, once my mates had realised I wasn't about to join the French Foreign Legion, they started to take the piss out of me again. And that's how it should be.

And over the next few weeks, as people saw me back on the streets running with Brian, or in Josephine's the shouts of 'Hey Bomber' were soon back again. In fact I had lots of adulation after that, people were constantly slapping me on the back and wanting to wine and dine me, and I just hoped that it would be like this all the time. It was a great feeling actually. I think the British love of a courageous loser together with the Yorkshire ethos of 'fuck 'em' combined to make me the perfect sporting celebrity at the time. And I didn't have too much competition in the city. Sebastian Coe was the other big name but neither football club was having a great time, Sheffield Wednesday were on the way back but United were still struggling and I think Jessica Ennis was about five. So I got the free lunches!

And this attention and love gave me just the lift I needed to give me the self belief to fight on. While I never considered retiring, even in the seconds after the end of the fight, I pretty soon recovered my faith that I could do it. I would get another shot at a world title and I could do it.

But not everyone was getting on with a smile on their face. Barney was really disappointed about the defeat and he said that it was my own fault for not shelling out for training camps in London. He also said that I didn't have my head together. Brendan didn't agree:

*"He's talking rubbish – a load of crap. You fought your heart out Son and you'll be back and get another shot and next time you'll win it."*

Brendan was pretty defensive about our preparation and I agreed with him. Okay McCallum had spent fifteen grand on training camps but he was in America for a lot of that time, and I didn't have the weight problems that maybe he had. And we had used the sparring partners that Barney had suggested, but Ron pissed off back to America after five days when he realised he couldn't hit me and Chris Eubank just said he'd never get in a ring with me again. Neither of them was as tough as Mick and Glyn in any case.

But Barney was relentless:

*"A few dollars more spent on training is always a good investment."*

That's all very well if you're not the one spending it and particularly if there isn't an adequate gym in place. I was starting to get smarter with my money, admittedly a bit late in the day, and Wincobank was where I was happiest doing my training.

To be fair Barney had every right to have a go at me for losing but he seemed to be punishing me in the press, saying that I was stuck in my ways and mean and that I didn't listen. Maybe I didn't always listen, even Brendan told me that. But mean? Bloody hell, stupid I could accept, but not mean. And I thought he should have just left his criticisms between us and not the whole world. Barney looked like he was blaming me and Brendan, but I have to say that at times, during the fight, there were disagreements going on in my corner. I didn't know who I was fighting at one point. But that was all in the past and I just wished that we could get on with life. That's what I wanted to do anyhow.

♦

While the post mortems were rumbling on I was determined to enjoy myself so I went to see Johnny fight for the British cruiserweight title at the Sheffield City Hall. It was high fives all around when people were coming up to me and that's what I loved. I'm always at peace when I have got people around me. And I was pleased to be able to support Johnny; he was becoming a better fighter and was hoping that he was going to be the next big thing. And despite him taking a few liberties when he stayed with me I sort of liked looking after him.

I was acting like an older brother to him at times, and in the autumn when I reached the grand old age of thirty I took stock of my own life again. I had a new girlfriend called Claire and things were going pretty well there. Johnny was staying less at mine and Claire was staying more. A much better balance. Claire was pretty cool for me at that time and it was a way of helping to get Karen out of my system. It had been a couple of years since that whole drama and it took me a good year to get over it, but finally I seemed to be getting my head together. Okay I'd lost a World title fight and was rowing with Barney. But on the other hand I'd run Mike close and I was still a strong contender. But at the age of thirty I had to start taking things pretty seriously.

On the boxing front Nigel Benn had just lost to Michael Watson, who was due to have a crack at McCallum. But I was taking my inspiration from an unlikely source. My old mate Roberto Duran still held a World title and he was thirty seven. If he couldn't lay a glove on me a few years ago I doubted whether he'd be able to even see me now!

I thought that my best chance of getting another quick go at a title was by meeting the winner of Watson and McCallum, who were due to fight in December. But in the meantime I had a fight set up to defend my British title against Rod Douglas at Wembley. Rod was a big punching cockney who saw this as his chance for a major breakthrough and so I anticipated a tricky sort of fight. He was an intelligent lad as well. He was actually on the bill when I was fighting McCallum at the Albert Hall, but he missed my fight because he was playing chess in his dressing room. That's the way he likes to relax and wind down.

Before our fight Rod went to Florida for a three week training spell and came back full of confidence. He had an American southpaw sparring partner over there and apparently he had some problems to start with but then he beat the living daylights out of him. He was only twenty five and had only had twelve professional fights, but he was unbeaten and his manager, Mickey Duff, said he was happy to put him in the ring with me because I hadn't fought for six months and because of my 'mental state'. I asked Brendan what he meant by that and he just explained that it was the long running row I had with Barney that Duff was going on about. Mental? Me? A little bit mad maybe, but not mental. I didn't need or want to say anything in the run up to the fight, I just wanted to get my preparation absolutely right and get back on the winning trail. And in any case I'd had enough of the press for one year.

On the fight night, as Brendan taped up my hands he said:
*"Oh and by the way, Douglas is twenty six today so don't be too hard on him."*
*"His birthday. Cool. Let's hope he's eaten too much cake."*

In the event the fight itself turned out to be a bit of a breeze. Rod's southpaw partner in the States clearly wasn't as hard to hit as I was if he leathered him as Mickey Duff had said. And the way he was rocking as early as the third round he obviously didn't hit as hard as I did. So I just carried on doing my job and scoring points at will. I started to tease him a bit, dropping my hands, asking him to come on and I started humming 'happy birthday' when I caught him with each hand.

By the end of the ninth round the ref had seen enough as Rod struggled to get to his feet and he was counted out. I'd battered him.

After the celebrations had died down I noticed that Rod was still sat in his corner so I went over to ask him if he was okay. He said 'yes' and wished me luck. Nice lad.

We stayed over in London, had a meal and I went to bed at about one in the morning. But then about an hour later my phone went and it was Glyn:

"Herol?"

"Who's that?"

"It's Glyn."

"What the fuck do you want? It's ........ Jesus it's two thirty."

"It's Douglas, Herol. He's having surgery for brain damage. He's got a blood clot."

Fucking hell. Brain surgery. Oh Christ. My heart started going ten to the dozen and my mind was all over the place. What had happened? I knew that I had hit him hard and a lot, but that was boxing. Apparently he had woken up a few hours after the fight feeling sick and with a headache so he was taken in. But then I thought of the time in the late seventies when Alan Minter battered the hell out of Angelo Jacopucci and then he died three days later. Then Johnny Owen died when he was knocked out in 1980. And he had a blood clot just like Rod. Oh fucking hell. I started to panic.

One neurosurgeon had described a violent punch as being like a blancmange being whisked around in a box, it scrambles the brains. But why did this happen to me and Rod? It could have been me in the hospital and Rod panicking. Whenever you step into the ring this could happen but you never ever think it will. Otherwise you wouldn't get in.

I didn't sleep another wink and just wandered around my room drinking water and sitting on my bed. At five o'clock I went out for a walk and just paced the streets, past people sleeping in doorways and some boarded up shop windows. All I could think of was Rod and whether I'd killed him. When it came light I went back to the hotel and went to find Glyn. But as I walked through the hotel lobby a receptionist guy came up to me and said:

"Sorry about last night Mr Graham, thank God he didn't die."

Thank God indeed. What a relief. He was alive. The surgeons had removed a blood clot on his brain in a two hour operation and thank God he survived. His wife had been at his bedside after the operation and couldn't tell their four year old son that his dad was still with him until the morning.

It looked like the end of Rod's career though. No boxer had ever recovered from this type of injury to fight again.

♦

For weeks after my fight with Rod and his battle for life I was devastated and for the first time in my life I thought about quitting. I didn't want anybody to do that to me, and I didn't want to do that to anybody else either – ever again. I nearly killed a man who had a four year old son. Where's the sport in that. The anti – boxing lobby made calls for it to be banned, as they did every time there was this type of accident. But Brendan said that boxing was the hardest sport in the world, and in any case lots more people were maimed or killed in motor racing and there were never calls for that to be banned. I kind of saw his point but it wasn't him who'd battered Rod.

I carried on training and doing lots of running but I really didn't know whether I wanted to step into the ring again. Christmas came and went and the new year brought us in to the nineties, along with a recession. But I didn't much care. I didn't much care about anything to be honest and I just seemed to drift along, training, eating, going to Josephine's and going to bed. I was still with Claire but as always I looked for solace from my mates. Johnny and Brian did their best to cheer me up and on Saturdays I went down to the jewellery shop and slowly I started to feel better about the world again.

But my heart still wasn't in my boxing and Brendan had to chivvy me along more than he used to. And he did that by telling me that I could get another shot at the World title. He knew that was the ambition in me that had been burning me up for the last five years, and it had only stopped when I had the tragedy with Rod. But somewhere deep in the depths of my soul the spark was still there and eventually Brendan and the boys managed to reignite it.

As always I was helped and brought around by my friends, not just in the gym, but those who cheered me on when I was running down the street. And by the middle of 1990 I was ready to fight again. The demons that had plagued me for the past six months or so were gone and I was ready to go.

I was spurred on by the fact that the WBC title had been left vacant by Roberto Duran, and when Brendan told me that I'd been nominated to contest it with Julian Jackson I was made up.

My training was back on track, and against the backdrop of Barney suggesting I should take a tiny offer from Don King to fight, I concentrated on getting my mind and body honed to perfection, to make sure that I took my chance the second time around.

Nigel Benn had already overtaken me in a way because he had won the WBO title earlier in the year and had started to mouth off that he wasn't going to fight in the UK again because he wasn't in it to make any money for anyone else other than himself. I thought that was stupid, because we were all trying to make money and so the only way we could help each other was by fighting each other. Otherwise, for us and for the sake of poor Rod Douglas what was the point of it all? Anyhow the WBO title was a Mickey Mouse title at that time and I put that out in the press. Nigel didn't much like that and called me, Michael Watson and Chris Eubank a bunch of cry babies. Strange man.

I just concentrated on my fight with Jackson. After all the toing and froing trying to get the bout on somewhere because of his dodgy eye I was more than ready.

So please don't ask me again why I didn't just skip around the ring for the last twenty seconds of round four. If I had a pound for every time someone has asked me that, and I've asked myself I would be a very comfortable man.

I'd taken so much verbal stick over the past five years about my style. Everybody from Tony Sibson to Kalule's trainer and even my own manager had called me everything from a limbo dancer to a runner to a head case. But I had no idea why these people kept on getting at me. Of my last twenty wins nineteen had been finished within the distance. They said I was a runner and not a fighter but I'd battered nineteen out of twenty so fucking hard that they couldn't stand up. I'd nearly killed one poor guy for Christ's sake. These people seemed to think that boxing was just about seeing who could get smacked in the head the most and still carry on. What's the fucking point in that? In my two defeats before Jackson I went the distance so I could take some punches and all the guys I boxed knew that I could give some too.

So why oh why oh why, when Jackson could barely see me and was so far behind, did I feel like I needed to hit him one more time? Was it all these comments from all these people saying that I was defensive? Was it watching Nigel Benn bludgeon his way to the WBO title? Had I finally backed down and decided to fight like everyone else rather than use my brain? It was probably none of those reasons. It was probably the fact that, no matter how professional and serious about my sport I could be, I was always an entertainer. Whether it was dropping my hands like Ali, sticking my tongue out, or moving so quickly my opponent started to spin. And knowing that I had won the fight I just went in for a spectacular finish and hit the blind man. But the blind man hit me. And I was unconscious for five minutes. Nobody's fault but mine. Nobody made me do it. But please don't ask me why I did it.

And, having done it I was royally fucked. Two world title losses in a year, in my thirties, still rowing with my manager and with a pretty dim view of the world. I'd shed a few tears over the past couple of years and none more so than after this fight. Was this how it was meant to be?

I felt emotionally drained again and started to fret about all the things that had been happening; Kalambay, Karen, Barney, McCallum, Rod Douglas and now Julian Jackson. The heady days of fighting Mark Kaylor and winning the European title seemed a million miles away. I still had all my mates with me, my true mates, and the ones that hung around to see if I had a lot of money. But I brooded over this defeat for a long time. In fact, it still preys on my mind right now. I just need to learn how to deal with it a little better.

My emotional state needed a pick me up, something to settle me down and thank God it came before too long. Claire gave birth to my son Oliver and I entered a new phase in my life. Oliver became a focal point for me and I was a dedicated father and took my responsibility seriously. Claire and I split up soon after and for a good few years it was just Oliver and me. He was living with me from a very young age and as I was still boxing at the time I relied on many friends to help me out with baby sitting. Johnny, Brian and Brenda all dug in for me and I am eternally grateful for that. While I had taken a couple of hefty knocks in my professional life Oliver and I did everything together and it was a very special time. He was the apple of my eye and, just as I was so proud of Natasha I worshipped Oliver. I briefly had a girlfriend called Cheryl who used to look after him from time to time but that didn't last.

After that relationship broke down I was sort of pleased that it was just me and Oliver again. Sweet.

# 13

## <u>The End - No Really</u>

*"God seems to have left the receiver off the hook, and time is running out."*

### Arthur Koestler

Life in the gym at Newman Road carried on pretty much as normal and I tried to keep myself at peak fitness, healthy body healthy mind and all that. And I needed that because no matter how hard I tried to focus on other things, the Jackson fight, and particularly the end of the fourth round were never far from my conscious thought. I must have played it over in my mind a thousand times, visualising a well controlled and concentrated end to the contest. But then the reality always hits and the utter madness of losing a fight that was well and truly in the bag by walking into a sledgehammer in the dying seconds returns. Fuck.

And there was a stark difference between the aftermath of this one and when I'd lost to Mike McCallum. On that occasion, once everyone realised I was okay the banter started almost immediately. But this time I think everybody felt as frustrated as me, and above all sorry for me.

I was okay. Okay, but quite often preoccupied. I was happy enough at home with just me and Oliver and the legion of baby sitters, and happy to be training. But there was a return to the state of limbo that I'd experienced from time to time. There was no clear direction for me to go in. If I had won the World title then that would have been sorted. Defend it; defend it again and so on until I could make it to a well earned retirement. The difference between winning and losing was huge, just as the margin of my lead was huge, as well as the mismatch between Jackson's right hand smash and my head had been. But I'd lost. Get over it. Easier said than done.

I looked at the rising stars in the gym, Johnny and Naz, and suddenly, for the first time in my life I started to feel old and I wished I was in Naz's shoes with the whole thing ahead of me. I didn't feel like it was the end of the road for me, but it certainly felt like the road was on the incline. I had definitely grown up as a result of what had happened to me inside and out of the ring. Losing makes you grow up, and in life your mistakes make you grow up, unless you are a complete muppet of course! I don't think Brendan thought that though. Whether we were seventeen, twenty five or thirty one Brendan fell into the habit of talking to us like we were kids. I didn't mind that because I'd got used to it over the years but it really got on Glyn's tits.

♦

I didn't have a clear intention of retiring after the Jackson fight, not least because I'd made a monumental fuck up and I wanted to make it right. But I was under no illusion at all that getting another tilt at a World title was going to be a real uphill struggle, and there were times when I doubted my own ability to do it. The old guard in Britain of Sibbo and Mark Kaylor had been replaced by the next lot, Chris Eubank, Michael Watson and the like and I wasn't quite sure where I fit into it all.

Maybe I was tired, maybe I'd somehow lost my edge, because I'd spent the first thirty seven fights of my career having a great laugh, boxing with a smile on my face and riding on a wave of ambition. But three defeats, only one of which I could accept without losing sleep over, had taken its toll. Maybe it was time to think about doing something else. But then what else could I do?

In the event, over the next couple of years the decision was largely taken out of my hands. I didn't get a fight for a year after the Jackson fight, and even though I beat John Ashton in Sheffield it wasn't a great win and I didn't really feel the buzz that I'd always had before.

And in September the following year I was stopped for only the second time in my career by Frank Grant, in a British title bout at Elland Road in Leeds. That was it. Enough.

After that fight Brendan knew that I didn't have anything left in me. I was as fit as ever but there was something not there. The spark had gone. I was thirty three and emotionally knackered. So I announced my retirement to the gathering press, who probably guessed what was coming and I went home.

♦

And so began a whole new chapter in my life. In fact the second half of my adult life – retirement. Retirement at thirty three, there aren't many people who could do that. So the rest of my life was ahead of me and the world was my oyster, notwithstanding two things. Firstly I had a three year old son living with me, and secondly I was not awash with cash. I'd spent most of what I had earned over the past fifteen years on houses, three girlfriends, I lent a few people a fair bit, oh and of course the jewellery shop. But I thought I had enough for me and Oliver to get by and enough to give me the time to work out what I was going to do next.

And by far the best thing was the time I could spend with Oliver. I'd relied so much on mates when I was still fighting and now I could do it for myself. I'd missed the chance to be a big part in Natasha's first few years and I was so proud of her now as the perfect daughter. But there was no reason for me to miss out on Oliver's early years. I got to watch Playschool on TV and eat banana custard so there were great benefits, although there were some dirty jobs to do. Oliver was a clever little sod and had a well developed sense of humour from a very early age. Potty training was his favourite wheeze when he would drop his shit anywhere within two feet of the potty but never once in it. So I abandoned that and he went straight on the bog.

But there can't be many prouder moments than dropping your boy off at school on his first day and I had a tear in my eye more than once at the start of the day. Oliver was the best thing in the world for me and I couldn't see it any other way.

And I still had people waving and shouting at me all the time so I didn't feel lost. There was always someone to have a coffee with and when I had a baby sitter sorted for the evening there were plenty of people to dance with in Josephines or Annabellas. Sometimes people said to me what a great time they'd had following me, and because the support had always been so close to me I knew an awful lot of them personally. It was really nice for everybody to still take an interest and want to talk to me, even though I was no longer fighting. Now and then someone would say to me, 'why did you quit Bomber?' but I think they were just being nice.

When Oliver was at pre-school or school I often went out for a run or down to Glyn's new gym on Carlisle Street where I enjoyed watching the boys sparring and working on the bags. And the more I went down there the more I realised that I actually missed the old game a little bit more than I thought. I hadn't really worked out what I wanted to do, maybe run a gym of my own, maybe do some training, maybe even television work, who knows? But I hadn't got my arse in gear on that and I was just biding my time. So after I'd done a couple of runs I did some bag work one day. And soon enough, Glyn asked me if I'd spar with one of his lads.

I think the year off had done me good. Just like when I went to Tenerife in the middle of all the hype, sometimes you don't realise that you just need to get away from everything for a while to get things into perspective. Not boxing had given me the opportunity to spend some precious time with Oliver, but now he was out during the day so I really needed to work out what I was going to do with my life next, particularly before my money ran out.

The more I ran and the more training I did, the more bag work and the more sparring, suddenly it came clear to me what I wanted to do. I wanted to box. And I was only thirty three for goodness sake. Lots of sports people were at the top well into their thirties, Ian Callaghan and Pat Jennings were forty when they retired I think. And in boxing George Foreman made a comeback long after his chicken roasting machines had taken the cooking world by storm. So why not me? I asked Glyn.

*"You........are off your fucking head,"* he suggested.

*"That's no good reason. Give me a good reason."*

Glyn just shook his head and walked off. I knew he'd agree.

So reinvigorated with my enthusiasm to get back in the ring I wrote to the British Board of Boxing Control to ask them for my licence back. And then I waited. And waited.

Four weeks later I received a letter telling me I'd have to go down for some psychological tests of some sort so that I could be assessed. The Board take licences seriously and I think that because I'd lost badly on my last fight, and because of the well publicised rows I'd had, they wanted to see whether I was all there and okay. Fair enough I suppose.

I went down to a medical centre in London for what turned out to be the first set of tests. And I sat through some maths stuff, some word stuff and other bits. I thought it was all okay and waited to hear from them.

In the meantime I carried on going down to Glyn's gym at Carlisle Street to keep myself in trim. One morning he said to me:

*"Hey Herol, do me a favour and get in the ring with this lad."* And he called over the boxer, a bloke named Cornelius. He looked a pretty athletic character so I got myself ready and stepped into the ring with him.

He was a smart boxer and I enjoyed having fifteen minutes with him and as the session went on I really felt like I was getting my form back. I felt just like I did fifteen years ago when

I was sparring in Brendan's gym. I had all the bounce and spark. It was still there. I moved around, ducked a couple of shots and started to do my old tipping and tapping on the lad. I felt like I'd never been away and he was working harder and harder to keep up with me. I looked outside the ring and saw Glyn looking at us and for a brief moment I thought he was smiling! I was loving it. I kept on moving and started to do my old thing, dropping my hands and moving my head, and by the end of the session I had run him around. He touched my gloves, thanked me and climbed out of the ring:

"*Good, good, good. That was good,*" I said to Glyn.

"*You know who that was don't you?*" he asked.

I shook my head.

"*That's Cornelius Carr.*"

"*Oooohhh.*" I had no idea who Cornelius Carr was.

"*Look how you just sparred with him and he's got your old title Herol.*"

"*Oh yeah, he's the ABA champion.*" I pretended it had dawned on me.

"*Not the ABA you daft sod. He's the fucking British middleweight champion!*"

Oh. Sorry.

Well if nothing else that was encouraging, even if I'd once again displayed my piss poor knowledge of the sport I loved. So I felt even more confident that I had a couple more fights in me. I was fit and strong and mentally all together. And in a way I was more relaxed than I'd been before. Being in Brendan's gym had been great for me over the years but I had grown up now, and if I was going to give it another shot then I could do it my way, inside and outside the gym. I didn't feel bad about not going back to Brendan's gym, he had enough on his hands with Naz and in any case I think he believed that my time was gone. Maybe he was right.

The medical people at the boxing board also seemed to think that my time was gone and after failing a couple more maths tests I was eventually referred to a new set of people in white coats. This was all a bit frustrating for me because the board seemed to giving other boxers in my position their licences back but I was being made to jump through more and more hoops for reasons unbeknown to me. But if I wanted to get back in the ring I'd have to keep jumping. I have to say I didn't much fancy cage fighting!

After answering an endless questionnaire which seemed to be about what made me happy, angry or sad (I just kept ticking 'b' because I remember someone giving me that tip at school) I moved on to interpreting modern art. Two doctors, both wearing glasses but only one with a clip board sat in a quiet room with me and the one without the clipboard started to turn pages over. The first one was a silhouette of an elephant.

*"What do you see here Herol?"*

*"A butterfy...... no hang on, is it an elephant?"*

The quack turned the next over:

*"And this?"*

*"Definitely an elephant this time."*

And then another:

*"And this?"*

*"A pair of tits."*

The doctor sighed and turned over another:

*"This one?"*

*"Ah I know this one. That's my inner nightmare.... or is it a Picasso?"*

The two white coats looked at each other sternly and then back at me. Clipboard lady said:

*"You really need to take this seriously Herol."*

*"Okay."*

Six months later I was called back and I did much better that time. Which got me on to the eye tests, reflex tests, memory tests and some more maths tests, maybe I hadn't passed that one after all. But the whole thing seemed to be taking forever, although maybe I wasn't helping myself. I understood the mental tests but not the mathematics. And when they started doing memory stuff it was a nightmare. I never had a really good memory anyway. I had difficulty remembering what I had for breakfast. It was a real problem and it was so stupid and frustrating.

Eventually after what seemed like years, well it actually was years, I managed to convince the various boards that I was of healthy body and mind (suckers) and in 1996 they reluctantly gave me back my licence to fight.

So, after three years of recuperation, I was back on the trail again and feeling pretty good about the whole thing. And life at home was good too. Oliver was doing ever so well and I had a new girlfriend, Nina. I was really taken with her and we got on easily from the word go. With my new found maturity I thought that I had every chance of making this relationship work and so I had lots to look forward to professionally and personally and a new lease of life.

But I knew that getting back up the boxing ladder as I advanced into my late thirties would be easier said than done. I had no trainer, no manager and no promoter. There was an obvious candidate to fill the training role. Apart from the fact that I could do a lot of my own training schedule, I knew when and how to run and what to eat, I needed a trusted sounding board and someone who I'd really want in my corner. Who better than Glyn? He was an up and coming trainer and knew the tricks of the trade inside out. Perfect.

As far as a manager was concerned, I think I'd had enough of managers when I was boxing in the eighties, so I decided that was an unnecessary expense. So all we needed was a promoter and I'd come across Frank Maloney, the London manager and promoter a few times before. He always had an eye for an opportunity and so he agreed to promote my fights.

The first fight that Maloney got on for me was in November of 1996 against an American guy called Terry Ford at the Sheffield Concord Centre. It was great to be fighting in Sheffield again after all these years and things were back to normal. Well almost. I did all the usual running, skipping, ring work and weights, but away from the training there was no

Brendan, and in the final two weeks I couldn't go to Rita and Dave's because they were Brendan's friends and I don't think he agreed that I should be coming back. I didn't want to contact Rita and Dave so I decided that I had to do it on my own, with Glyn of course.

As I ran the streets of Sheffield lots of people waved at me, but there were quite a few in the city and in the press who thought it was too risky for me to come back. We didn't know much at all about Terry Ford, other than that he had won sixteen out of twenty fights so he was no mug. But a defeat would be a disaster.

But I didn't really have a choice. I was excited about getting back in the ring, but in the three years I had been out of the game I hadn't really come up with a good plan of what I could do as an alternative. And when I looked in my bank account there wasn't a lot left. I had borrowed some money from a mate in London whose hotel we used to stay in, but I didn't want to ask him for more. And I didn't have a record or a memory of who I'd lent money to. So the only place I could go was to ask Graham if I could have some money out of the jewellery business. But, once again, I'd been sloppy with my deals and I didn't actually have a share in the business. I couldn't get any more money out of it, I'd had dribs and drabs over time but I suppose a lot had been reinvested in stock or whatever so I didn't have a leg to stand on. Or a pot to piss in for that matter. So as well as doing what I loved it was also a case of 'needs must'.

Johnny was supportive of my return and he told me I had too much ability to struggle at this level and I should show some of the old vintage. But underneath his warm support I could sense that he wasn't completely sure, particularly when he said:

*"I'll support you bro whatever happens. There's lots of other things you could do."*

When we arrived at the Concord Centre there was a buzz about the place but as I was starting lower down it didn't have the big fight feel of days gone by. But good old Johnny was at the ringside with his gleaming smile! He was summarising for

Radio Sheffield and starting out on his alternative career. And as I sat in the corner and Glyn gave me his encouragement at least I knew I had my mates around me.

But I felt sort of ring rusty and by the time I'd sat down at the end of the second I hadn't made a whole lot of progress. Glyn squirted water at me and said:

*"Come on Herol, you've got to get more points in. Get more jabs in, he can't touch you."*

He was right. Terry couldn't touch me but still I was labouring. My timing was all over the place and my range was about two inches out which is as good as a mile in this game. I didn't seem to have any power even though I was nine pounds heavier than Terry. And despite the training schedule I'd stuck to, my legs felt heavy. I scored more regularly as the fight wore on and at the end of eight rounds I won it by a unanimous decision. But it was no spectacular comeback. Glyn looked down at the canvas and then straight up at me:

*"It's not there any more Herol. Herol, for fuck's sake that's not you."*

Brendan was at the fight as well and he was interviewed afterwards by the Sheffield Star's lad. I didn't expect him to be glowing in his praise, but neither did I think that he'd have anything against me trying to make a comeback, but he said:

*"I might be wrong, but I think there was nothing there; he should not be fighting in my opinion. I get my living from this game and my advice is to pack it in. The worst thing you can have at this stage is people slapping you on the back and saying you've done well."*

Well there was no danger in Glyn doing that. And that's the mark of a true mate, someone who isn't going to bullshit you, no matter how hard it might be to take.

♦

I know Glyn (and Brendan) had been right about the Ford fight but I wasn't willing to chuck it all in now. I couldn't. I'd waited long enough to get my licence back and I needed to make a success of it. My legs were a little weary after the fight, but I was determined to give it another go. If I thought that time was running out when I was thirty, at thirty seven then it definitely was.

So I was happy to get another fight and four months later I was on my way down to London with Glyn, to the Elephant and Castle to fight a lad called Craig Joseph. It was already proving to be an arduous slog back and I'd only had one fight, but I was armed with a new pair of turquoise and blue tartan shorts that Brenda had come up with, so one or two of the pieces were starting to fall back into place one by one. But Glyn, being a man of no little integrity said that he didn't want to go into my corner. He had trained me, but he had also tried to tell me that I didn't have it in me any more so he thought he'd be a hypocrite if he took money off me in the corner. He wouldn't hear my pleas but he was there to support me. That's a true mate. He didn't take money off me, but he spent his own money coming down. He's as honest as the day is long.

The Elephant and Castle wasn't exactly Vegas, it wasn't even the Concord in Sheffield, but it was packed with nine hundred boxing fans that had come out to see us. A guy from London came in my corner and Glyn sat in with the crowd.

Craig was a tougher opponent than Terry but I got into my swing a bit better, ever so slightly at first but then as the fight went on I started to move. The crowd were a bit restless but I wanted to be professional and not get into a scrap. Soon enough I got him in a spin and at one stage in the fourth round he charged at me and as I stooped he went clean over my shoulders. In the sixth I marked his eye and the crowd started to warm up. So then I got going. I jabbed him in the face, kissed my glove and then hit him again. The crowd loved that and a cheer, not wild but a cheer nevertheless, went up at the end.

During the fight Glyn heard a lady sat in front of him say:

*"This bloke fights just like Naseem Hamed."*

He waited until the end of the fight but he couldn't help speaking to the lady and he said to her:

"*Excuse me love. I heard your comment love about him boxing like Naseem Hamed – it's the other way around. Herol Graham doesn't box like Naz – Naz boxes like Herol.*"

He said to me later on:

"*They didn't know because they weren't boxing people, Herol.*"

Top man.

Frank Maloney collared me before I got out of the ring and said:

"*I don't want you to speak to anyone else, let's do another fight.*"

"*Okay.*"

And the Board of Boxing had still been watching over me until then but after this fight they left me alone.

♦

It was great to have a better fight under my belt and Maloney seemed happy enough so it was a case of 'so far so good'. And it was good to see Glyn happier with me as well. He still wasn't convinced that I was doing the right thing, but the way he stood up for me when he heard someone talking about me in London made me think that he was still fighting for me whatever he said.

So when he asked me to go down to Devon with him to support one of his lads in an exhibition I was more than happy to, particularly as I loved seeing exhibitions.

The place we were heading for was a one horsed town called Clumpton and it was absolutely in the back of beyond. There were about five hundred in the crowd, half of which looked like the Wurzels and they were there to support a local lad who was top of the bill called Des Gagano. Glyn was in the corner with a boy called Ritchie Wenton but it was only when we arrived after a five hour drive, the last hour behind a hay wagon, that we discovered that there were only three bouts on the card.

Then this bloke, who I guessed must have been running the show spotted me (not hard as I had the only black face within a hundred mile radius) and he came up and said:

*"Hello Herol, great to see you here. Thanks ever so much for coming down to support us."*

*"No problem bro."*

Then he stroked his chin, looked sideways at me and said:

*"I don't suppose…… you'd be happy to box a round for us, see we only have three fights on, and it'd be great to have a European and Commonwealth champion for the lads and lasses to watch."*

*"Sure."*

The bloke was taken aback by my keenness to join in.

*"Oh that's fantastic Herol. I'll find someone to fight you. Or do you think Glyn Rhodes will help out."*

*"Sure he will."*

So I went to break the good news to Glyn.

*"Sure I fucking won't!"*

*"Aw come on Glyn it'll be a laugh."*

*"Are you joking? For who exactly?"*

*"For everyone."*

Wrong answer.

*"No. I'm not doing it. Fuck off."*

As Glyn climbed into the ring he was still muttering on:

*"You're off you're head. This is fucking silly. I haven't trained for ages."*

As we met in the middle to the cheers of the scrumpy and pasty chomping fans Glyn mouthed to me:

*"Take your time and make it look good,"* before turning and mumbling *"Fucking silly."*

I don't know what made me do it, my new found *joie de vivre* or just that I thought it so funny how cross Glyn was. But for whatever the reason I thought it would be a laugh to drop him with a body shot after ten seconds. As he struggled to his feet he looked at me with what I could only describe as pure hatred. But then five seconds later I accidentally caught him and his eye came out like a golf ball.

*"What the fuck are you doing, it's a fucking exhibition, we're supposed to be making it look good!"*

I could see in his eyes that he wanted to go for me and leather me. I could have been his best mate but at that very moment he would have battered me if he could have.

We were well past Bristol when Glyn next spoke to me.

♦

I won another fight in London against a lad called Chris Johnson and by the end of 1997 it seemed like it might really be happening for me again.

Finally after several failed relationships I got married. Nina was the one for me and we tied the knot in a very glitzy and glam wedding. And Oliver was growing up into a great little lad. I went to watch him play ice hockey for Sheffield Samurai against Nottingham under 10s and I was so proud.

So now I was a 'respectable' married man with two wonderful children and a career back on the right track. The next fight I had lined up for me was a super middleweight bout against a really big name, Vinnie Pazienza 'The Pazmanian Devil.' Like me, this Italian American was making a comeback. He had held the light middleweight World title and beaten Roberto Duran at least once. The fight was staged at Wembley in December and was promoted by Jess Harding and some jazzy marketers called Panix Promotions.

The build up was brilliant and hilarious at the same time. The fight was billed as:

# Good V Evil
## The Taming of the Devil

I was 'Good' if you're in any doubt. And there was this superbly tasteless poster produced with a picture of Vinnie on one side climbing out of a small bonfire clutching two beautiful women's severed heads and with the devil looking on. On the other side was yours truly, with a halo, an angel looking on and wearing nothing but my Lonsdale Belt (my dangly bits were covered by my boxing glove). It was brilliant. So brilliant in fact that we all received a severe reprimand from the Board for bringing the sport into disrepute, making charges of 'grotesque sexism and blasphemy.'

So it was my duty to make up for all this by 'taming the Pazmanian Devil' which I did with a unanimous decision in front of a pantomime crowd.

Glyn was delighted and admitted he was happy to say that he was wrong when he told me that I didn't have it in me any more. I'd proved it to myself and a few others that I could still mix it with some top fighters. And I wondered for a moment what they would be saying in Brendan's camp back up in Sheffield. Did they still think I should pack it in? Three fights back and three wins and each one better than the last.

The following night as I walked through the snow back to my house in Millhouses after a few drinks with Johnny and Brian I was a happy man.

And happier still when I got home for Nina to tell me that she was pregnant. Merry Christmas everybody.

◆

1998 arrived and with it I had a better feeling than I'd had for a decade. I'd got myself into a good place after a difficult time coming to terms with the Jackson defeat and then struggling to get my licence back for almost three years.

When I started to make a comeback in 1996, everyone outside Sheffield, not to mention a few inside, had written me off and said I couldn't do it. But the last two fights had proved it to a few of them, as well as giving me more confidence in myself.

I carried on working hard at Glyn's gym and started to watch what was happening on the world scene. Charles Brewer, who was known as the Hatchet, had won the vacant IBF World super middleweight title and defended it against a guy called Joey DeGrandis. He was still quite young, about twenty eight and he was looking for his next fight. But the truth of it was, true to his name he had bludgeoned his way to a lot of his wins with a punch like a sledgehammer and nobody was very keen to fight him. Apart from me. And with a little encouragement my name went up there and I was nominated to take him on. It wasn't such a big surprise to us because although I'd only had three fights since my comeback, Pazienza was well respected; and even though I say it myself I'd lost two very close World title bouts and I was still a bit of a pull – just about. I didn't have the time to box journeymen so it made a lot of sense for me to go for it as soon as possible. And given Brewer's reputation there wasn't such a big queue.

So I got the Brewer fight because he wanted a fight and nobody wanted to fight him. I was more than happy to go for it and I knew I had to box over there in the USA, so I would have to beat him on his own soil. At the beginning of March I headed out to a training camp in Miami to prepare for the fight at the Boardwalk in Atlantic City. Glyn was coming out later because he had a show on in Sheffield and a lot of his lads were boxing. So he sent an eighteen year old kid called Regan Denton out with me. He thought it would be company for me but also a great experience for the kid. Lennox Lewis was at the training camp too and what a fantastic opportunity for a young kid that would be, to spend time with Lennox and even me!

Regan was a nice lad, a bit quiet at first and keen to learn, and he was understandably awe struck when we arrived at the camp and hotel. It must have been a dream come true, Miami at eighteen. And the States are always hyper, everything happens around you at a hundred miles an hour. So I kept my eye on Regan and made sure he was okay. I also felt a responsibility to help him with his training and his diet, because if he wanted to be a boxer then I hoped that I could give him some guidance. He was a bit surprised when I woke him at five on the first morning to go for a run, but as it was so hot out there early morning was always the best time to run. The air was very close and so I told him to keep hydrated and take in plenty of water and less salt. When I saw him reaching for the salt pot at lunchtime I said:

*"Hey, hey look after yourself man. You don't need any more salt. There's plenty in the fish and the vegetables, just drink some more water."*

So at the next mealtime I made sure there wasn't a salt pot on our table and there was an extra bottle of water. That'd be good for Regan. And after dinner we rested for an hour before we did an evening training session.

It looked like Regan was really enjoying himself and I was glad to help. Then after a week I got a call. It was Glyn:

*"Herol, what are you doing?"*

*"Getting ready to go sunbathing."*

*"No what are you doing with Regan?"*

*"What do you mean?"*

*"He's just rung me up and he sounds like he's nearly in tears!"*


Ten minutes earlier Regan had called Glyn and the call went like this:

Glyn:

*"Hiya Regan how's it going?"*

*"Fucking terrible. I want to come home."*

*"Why mate what's wrong?"* asked Glyn.

*"It's Herol. He's a fucking nightmare!"*

*"What do you mean?"*

*"He's mad. I can't stand living with him any more! He's making me do everything, running in the morning, training in the evening, going to bed early."*

*"That's what training camp is,"* said Glyn.

*"But he won't even let me have salt and vinegar on my fish and chips. He's a fucking nightmare!"*

*"I know he is. Living with Herol Graham IS a nightmare. Just get on with it."*

*"I can't."*

Glyn knew me well enough because we'd shared hotel rooms many times in the run up to fights and he said to me:

*"Herol – how anyone can live with you I do not fucking know. Just go easy on the poor lad and I'll be out in a week. Don't upset him any more."*

"I'm just helping him," I protested.

*"Well don't!"*

Glyn came out the following week and we went from Miami Beach up to Atlantic City. And while we were there he gave a motivational speech that even Brendan would have been proud of. Well most of it. Glyn has a big heart behind the rough and tough exterior and he said:

*"This is your best chance now Herol. You've been up there at the same time as Marvin Hagler, Sugar Ray Leonard and Roberto Duran. There are some major legends there and Herol Graham, a kid from Nottingham was up there, and he deserved to be up there. Without Herol Graham there would be no Brendan Ingle, no Johnny Nelson, no Naz, no Glyn Rhodes, none of them other guys. There are people who've won titles that aren't half the boxer you are. And I've come from being a little trainer in Sheffield to training the British, Commonwealth and European Champion for a world title shot. Fucking hell Herol, it doesn't get any better."*

I was going to give him a hug but I thought better of it because I'm sure he'd have hit me.

♦

Physically and mentally I was in great shape. The mental side of it was always the most crucial for me, I knew I could handle the build up physically, the only worry I had was a tight calf. I'd been running on the beach a lot at Miami and it felt a bit sore. Running on sand isn't what we'd do nowadays but I thought it would help to build up my stamina in the heat. I trained hard because I knew this was my last chance and if I didn't take this then that was it.

But I had to get my head right because I knew what Brewer could do.

It was a fantastic atmosphere at the Boardwalk and there were a few from the UK there too. To be on the undercard of the World heavyweight championship was great. There were fifty thousand in the crowd. And I did have some support from over there as well because not everybody liked Brewer and some people, as well as me, wanted him to lose. And I could see why. At the weigh in he was quite rude and arrogant and playing the big American guy. He just sneered at me, 'who are you?' and saying, 'I don't know how but I'm going to beat you.' I just smiled at him. He didn't shake my hand with much friendliness and I didn't warm to him at all. By the time we got to the fight I wanted to slap him around a bit.

I knew this was my last chance. If I lost I knew that nobody else wanted to fight him and so it was the opportunity of a lifetime. And as the massive limo picked us up at the hotel to take us to the Boardwalk I had a familiar sense of destiny, combined with the shits.

As always I was nervous as I climbed in the ring in the massive stadium and as the announcer made his noise I was ready for the fight. The bell went and Brewer moved on to me straight away to try to pressure me so I knew I had to move him around. So it was all movement and movement and, with the experience of Jackson's one shot demolition always sharp in my mind, I was on the lookout for Brewer's sledgehammer. As we moved around I realised I was picking him off. And in the first couple of rounds I was back to my game, doing this and that, I threw him over, spun him around and tripped him over. I was doing all sorts and he hated it. He kept looking at the referee for help but the ref couldn't help him. He kept gesticulating but the ref kept telling him to get on with it.

I caught him with some good shots and in the third I hit him and he went sprawling. I thought 'shit – I've got him.' That wasn't even a shot and he went down and he had to take a standing count. It was a long count, it seemed to me that the ref waited before he started the count but maybe I was just anxious. He saved it.

It wasn't the type of fight that a lot of Americans like to see. They love a brawl and I was making Brewer miss while boxing him. As time went on he tried to pressure me in the corners and on the ropes and he just nicked me on the face, which got the crowd rising for him and by the end of the fifth he knew he was on top for the first time. But I came out again and gave him one or two jabs – it was all exciting and I could feel my heart buzzing. I knew I had to do well because it was a world championship fight and it felt to me like I was doing okay.

He came on to me again and I threw a shot and spun him around and he went down again. He really hated it and he kept away from me for a while. At the time I didn't realise he'd done something to his ankle but he quietened down quite a bit and he wasn't at all sure what I was going to do. I kept on hitting and at one point I virtually had the fight won and thought the ref would stop it but he didn't. The crowd would have hated that.

Brewer clung on and then he started pressuring again and moving around me to try to get me into the corner. He was a good hooker and as he moved me around he caught me and I slipped onto the ropes, then he caught me on the chin and I felt that one. I could feel my calf tightening up from when I was running on the beach and had stretched the tendons and I went a bit floppy and sat on the rope and the next thing I knew the ref jumped in and told me I was finished as I was trying to get up. I said:

*"What?"*

I could hardly believe my ears. It was all over. I had been hit and it was a good shot as well but I could have easily carried on without getting badly hurt and the biggest threat was my calf. It was the tenth round and the first time I hadn't been moving very well. It was the first opportunity the ref had to stop me fighting, but he'd had ample opportunity to stop Brewer. I was on the ropes but I wasn't hurt. And I could still make him miss. He was hurting more than me because of his leg injury and wasn't fully mobile himself. It felt to me like the referee just couldn't wait to stop it.

The whole irony of my third World title defeat became clear when the big screens showed me being interviewed with hardly a mark on my face as Brewer was taken out in a wheelchair. If we'd known how bad his ankle was then I could have gone for him a bit more.

I wanted to win that fight so badly that it hurt me. And I knew how much the people around me and back in England wanted me to win that fight.

I knew I'd lost my final chance to become a world champion and as I watched them push Brewer out of the arena I asked myself what I had to do. Enough.

There was no sign of the limo that brought us, so we had to catch a bus back to the hotel. And on the following morning as Glyn and Regan packed their cases I just sat on the end of my bed with my chin in my hands watching golf on the telly. They took a walk round the mall and came back to find I was still there, watching the TV. So they went down to the bar for a coffee and when they came back Glyn said:

"Herol?"

I looked up and he said:

"Thank fuck for that. I thought you were dead!"

I smiled up at him and replied:

"That's it Glyn. It's over."

# 14

# <u>Dark Clouds</u>

*"On stage I make love to twenty-five thousand
people, then I go home alone."*

## Janis Joplin

The worst thing about my profession is that when you retire
boxing drops you like a bad habit. In other sports there seem to
be more options but boxing drops so many people. To suddenly
stop one day, having done it since you were sixteen years old is
a big shock. Everything changes. Your circle of friends change
because you are no longer in the gym, you aren't a boxer any
more. I was eight when I started and I had devoted my whole
life to the sport and so I had nothing else. I didn't have any
friends from before boxing and so for the first time in my life I
really needed to do something else. And it was definitely it this
time. There's a big difference between retiring at thirty three
and retiring at thirty eight. As well as having to contend with my
generally ageing limbs the medics had found that I had a
detached retina and so there was no way I could have another
go. I was finished.

All of a sudden I was a thirty eight year old who needed to
get a job. But what could I do? I couldn't do anything else. So I
went to see Glyn at his new gym down at Hillsboro. I went

down there a few times and enjoyed being in there training and just generally being in touch with the sport. There was a big part of me that didn't want to, or was too frightened to let go for good.

The year before Glyn had received a call from the landlords telling him that a film company wanted to come down and look at the gym, and it turned out to be the crew that were filming The Full Monty. All the practice scenes were filmed there because his gym was an old school and Glyn was unusually excited. Some of the lads had got parts as extras and Glyn managed to get himself in too. Until there was a minor bust up. He'd made an arrangement for the filming to run until three thirty so that he could get the bags set up for a paid training session he had every day at four.

Unfortunately for the crew they ran over time one day and when Glyn arrived at ten to four to see all the filming stuff all over the place and the gym upside down he went ballistic. His four letter and loud protest kind of dampened his relationship with the director and so his chance for stardom was scuppered and film goers worldwide were deprived of a glittering new talent. Their loss.

In June of 1998 Nina and I had our first arrival, a beautiful little girl called Jessica and for a few months my life was taken over once again by the chaos of having a baby, amazing and knackering in equal measures. It was another special time for me and it gave me renewed purpose. But unlike the situation I found myself in with Oliver, I wasn't bringing Jessica up on my own so I still needed to find something to do to keep myself busy and get some money coming in.

But as I approached my fortieth birthday I found myself getting down for no particular reason for the first time in my life. Maybe the realisation had hit me but I felt empty, almost as if I had left something behind. I could have arguably continued for a few more years if I didn't have the eye problem and I was finding it hard to accept the position I was in. This type of thing happens to lots of sports people, particularly those with short careers. It's so difficult to be up in the spotlight for so long to find that someone then turns the light out. And when they did I felt lost, abandoned and saddened. I really found it difficult to decide what to do next and I think that put some pressure on Nina. We were getting along okay, but she could see that I was increasingly up and down and the fact that we needed to get some money in didn't help. We had a lovely house but you can't live on fresh air.

I tried to get some of my investment out of the jewellery business but as I didn't have a contract or any shares I didn't have a leg to stand on. And I didn't have the confidence to ask questions so eventually I put it straight in my mind to say goodbye to that. But it could have been even worse. On one visit to the shop I had my car broken in to when it was parked outside. When I realised what had happened I was shitting it because my Lonsdale Belt was in the boot. The front passenger window had been smashed but when I opened the boot the Belt was still in there thank God.

♦

The following year a couple of good blokes I knew called Graham Bartholomew and Graham Teesdale agreed to open the Rotherham Fitness and Boxing Gym with me as the trainer. That was the perfect opportunity to get my teeth into something. It was just what I had been waiting for and so my mood picked up straight away and it put a smile back on my face. Nina was happy with that as I could start to get more money into the house. We built it up pretty quickly, partly through me being well known I guess but mainly thanks to the hard work that the two Grahams put into it. Soon enough it was a busy gym with sometimes up to a hundred and thirty users of all ages. It was a great environment and had such a good buzz.

I had always done a lot of skipping throughout my boxing career and am convinced that it is one of the very best ways for anyone to keep fit. So while I did that with all my clients at the gym it gave Nina and I a second idea for a business. After a bit of careful planning we launched Skip Fit where we would go out to schools and kids' organisations to talk about health and fitness and run skipping classes. Nina had the business and financial brain and I had the enthusiasm and energy and love of people, so together it wasn't a bad combination and we had a thriving little enterprise for a few years.

Those next few years went by with my time split between the gym, Skip Fit and three more wonderful additions to the family, Samuel in 2002, Molly in 2003 and little Harvey in 2005. The birth of all my children was special and they continue to fill my life with a sense of purpose and meaning. So I was busy and for a while I seemed to be coping okay with my new life away from the professional fight game.

The gym was still bouncing in 2005, but on the building side it was in need of a bit of love and attention to say the very least. It was an old building, a bit like an emptied church or school hall and to be honest it was grotty. Things were falling down all over the place, and it hadn't been painted for quite some time. I always seemed to be doing little odd jobs and I know Graham and Graham did too. But unbeknown to us the whole structure of the building was dodgy.

One unusually warm August day I was in the gym doing a training session with a couple of lads while a few others were in there working out along with two or three children. The sunny weather had lifted my mood; it always does which is natural being a Caribbean boy. The gym was buzzing and the music was loud and giving the place a great rhythm. I was standing on the edge of one of the rings watching my two lads sparring, when suddenly I heard a shout. The music was so loud that I couldn't hear exactly what it was, but it was something along the lines of:

"WATCH OUT!"

I looked up to see a huge crack in the ceiling and before I knew it a massive beam came tumbling down. Then before anyone had the chance to realise what was happening the ceiling collapsed! We all dived for cover when one of the main support beams fell within inches of where I was standing and I was trapped underneath it. As I looked around I couldn't see a thing as the gym became shrouded in thick dust. Everyone was coughing and the kids were crying and it was utter chaos. Two guys managed to lift the beam off me and I struggled to my feet so that we could check to see who was hurt. There were one or two minor injuries but thankfully nothing too serious. When the police and the fire brigade arrived within a few minutes most of us were taken to the hospital for a check up.

The gym never opened again and a lengthy court case proceeded. And I felt like my whole world had collapsed, never mind the roof. I was devastated, not just because I had lost my work, but also because it was such a frightening thing to happen. Thankfully there were no major injuries but it was a real body blow.

I loved working at the gym but that didn't work in my favour in the long run. I had been spending most of my time there so I hadn't given enough attention to Skip Fit and now I wished that I'd carried on with that.

So with my main two income streams drying up I was finding it increasingly hard to make money and in turn things were getting tenser at home. Nina and I had started to argue, and as with most couples' arguments, it was often about money. It was really starting to get me down. Most of the arguments I'd had in my adult life had been connected to money in one way or another. And now I didn't have any and I started to feel really bad about that. When I was boxing I'd always provided plenty for my family, but since then it had been difficult no matter how hard I tried. And I couldn't really work out where all the money had gone. We had a lovely house which we had built up together, and we used to go on great holidays, I'd lent a fair bit out, made some poor investments and given some to ex girlfriends here and there. Throughout my boxing career I always seemed to be able to get rid of money almost as soon as the big cheques came in. But since I retired the cheques were no longer in tens of thousands, sometimes they were two figures and I think that was as hard on Nina as it was on me. We had both got used to the lifestyle I could afford as a professional boxer. The kids didn't mind, kids don't really. They had everything they needed and wouldn't understand why I was increasingly getting more down.

I didn't realise at the time, but I think I had been on a downward spiral ever since I had retired and the roof of the gym falling in was almost the last straw. I started to feel desperate and frightened of what the future would bring, and most terrifyingly for me, for the very first time in my life I felt lonely. And my fondness for a glass of brandy now and then started to turn into a crutch.

So I thought that the best thing to do would be to do what I'd always done and to train. It seemed the most natural thing to carry on and so I went on a course and qualified as a fitness instructor and personal trainer and was employed to train clients at Fitness First and then Virgin. I still had other bits of work coming in and was commissioned by EIS to take a couple of boxing classes a week. So there was some money coming in and I thought my marriage was kind of okay but I was always busy doing this and that and Nina was busy with the kids and our communication wasn't right. But the pressure really increased when I was finding it more difficult to make money and the rows at home increased too.

While I still felt emotionally alone, I did have friends around me, and I always had people still waving and shouting at me when I walked around Sheffield. I had a good friend in a bloke called Steve Cheetham. I'd known him for years and he had helped me a lot latterly with my training and he was a real family friend, the kids loved him.

When I was particularly down Steve always tried to lift me up and one day he said to me:

*"I've got us two tickets for a bash in a couple of weeks Herol; it'll be a decent do."*

*"What is it?"*

*"Don't worry what it is – it'll be a good night."*

*"What is it Steve?"*

*"It's a celebration of the life of Brendan Ingle."*

*"Aw Steve, I don't know."*

I really didn't want to go. I hadn't seen Brendan for years and we hadn't parted company on the best of terms. We'd had a special and loving relationship for so long but it went kind of sour, from the time I left Brendan to go with Barney, and then on my comeback he didn't really think I was doing the right thing. I regretted not keeping in touch because he'd been such a big part of my life, but then I was useless at keeping in touch with anyone, they had always kept in touch with me. Up until now.

But Steve was insistent and on the day of the do he rang me to tell me to get smart for a seven o' clock start. I was in Preston doing a skipping class and I said:

*"I don't know if I'm going to make it in time."*

*"Come on Herol, make sure you do."*

It was good of Steve to get the tickets, because he knew that I couldn't really afford to go myself and so I eventually resigned myself to having to go. And maybe it'd be okay. All the lads were going to be there apart from Naz. Johnny was going to be there doing his singing and speeches and such and Steve was convinced it'd be a good laugh.

We arrived a bit late at the do in Rotherham and as we walked down the corridor, low and behold Brendan was stood there outside the banqueting room waiting to be introduced to everyone as they came in. He was shaking hands and talking to someone as I walked towards him and when he turned round and looked at me he looked like he'd seen a ghost.

I said in my best Irish accent:

*"Begorragh. Well hello their Brendan – how're you doin'?"*

He was visibly shocked, but I hope he was more pleased than uncomfortable. His name was called out and he went through.

♦

At home things were going steadily from bad to worse and eventually Nina and I had nowhere to go. We had long stopped getting on together as friends and the way we were with each other was never going to be good for the kids. So we got a quick divorce in 2007 after a bitter split which I regretted deeply.

It was a terribly difficult time as my children were so young and it hurt me so much to have to leave them. Divorce is painful for everyone and I wish it could have been dealt with in a more amicable way but that chance has gone. We were divorced on the grounds of irreconcilable differences. Neither of us could get back from the place we'd got to. There was blame on both sides as there always is in this, and I thank Nina for the good times we had and the four wonderful children she gave me. But I had to leave them and leave the house we had built up together.

I was completely broken and in the worst place I had been as an adult. The day after we split up Steve saw me sat in the corner of the gym at Virgin crying and I told him that I'd had to leave my kids. I couldn't see any hope and it was all very dark, almost black to me. Nina gave me enough money to put a deposit down on a little ex council house on Low Edges. It was okay but not what I was used to. It was so small and empty and not a really nice place to go outside if I wanted a walk.

It was then that I really started to struggle. I had four kids but I couldn't see them when I wanted and it was breaking my heart. When I could see them I didn't have money to look after them as well as I wanted. I was never educated in the ways of the world and I struggle with banking and finance and any of that stuff. I'd been protected for so long and now in my mid forties I was out on my own. I'd never even used a bank card.

Nina had always organised all my work and made sure I knew when to be at the personal training and gym work and skipping classes round schools. I loved being around kids but as I was slowly but surely falling into depression I didn't even want to do that any more. I worked a couple of days at EIS and Virgin, but I couldn't concentrate on everything that was kicking off. Eddie, my accountant helped me. I just wanted Nina to keep the house and everything else for the kids. Nina took care of all the financial side.

But my new house badly needed decorating and it was a dark, cold place to go. In the evening when I sat alone I often started crying and too often reached for the brandy bottle. I was so alone.

On my good days, which were getting fewer by the week I still harboured ambitions of running my own fitness centre. A few mates put some money in to open a gym at Bramhall Lane but when that had been done I think I had lost my strength to be able to manage it. And I spent almost every waking moment thinking about my kids. I told Steve about it and he said that I simply had to make money out of the gym. I had already packed up EIS and Virgin. And now I had the additional pressure of needing to get thirty people in the afternoon and forty at night in the gym and I couldn't cope. Very soon it got on top of me.

Every night I sat in the dark on my own and stared at the television that didn't work. I had a massive collection of CDs. My music is so important to me but I didn't have anything to play them on. I just sat and stared and cried. After the divorce I realised that I might have been depressed for a few years, perhaps even as far back as 2000. I had managed to keep going but was feeling increasingly anxious and isolated. As the years had gone on I thought I'd still be involved with boxing somehow, probably in commentary, but it never came about, maybe because I didn't push myself forward. Slowly but surely I had distanced myself from the world of boxing and that had made me feel even worse. To the outside world I didn't look any different. I was still always laughing and joking around but my laugh was forced. Nobody knew what was behind the laughter. Everybody knew Bomber but hardly anybody knew Herol. And Herol was slowly dying inside.

I was struggling and losing the battle to keep myself motivated and was beginning to let myself and my employers down by not turning up for work and spending days in bed. By the end of the year as I sat and shivered in my house my moral and mental clarity was at an all time low. I'd never been on my own before and I just couldn't do it. All my self belief had gone, completely gone.

A few days before Christmas I looked at my phone and saw that I had a message on Facebook which read:

"Hi Herol, it's Karen. I want to talk to you."

And Karen's number was on the message. I looked at it again. Karen? Karen? Then I put my phone down and poured myself a Christmas drink.

Karen had seen an article where I'd been interviewed after my divorce and there was a picture of me and my kids. She had stayed in London ever since our split back in 1987 but she had followed my career. For years she had people coming up to her saying:

*"Aren't you the bitch who cost Herol the World title?"*

She had been offered a lot of money by the News of the World to do a kiss and tell but hadn't done it.

Two days later I plucked up the courage and the energy to ring her but she didn't answer. But as I sat on my chair my phone rang:

*"Herol?"*

*"Yeah."*

*"It's Karen. I need to see you."*

We spoke on the phone almost every day for weeks and then a month or so later Karen came up and I met her for a coffee at the railway station. She had so much to tell me about her own marriage and divorce, but she could tell that something was wrong with me. We'd grown very close in our relationship and she still knew me well. She knew I liked a meaty conversation but all she was getting was the laugh:

*"What's wrong with you Herol?"*

I looked at Karen and summoned all my strength to avoid crying and I said:

*"I'm alone, I've lost my kids and I'm broke."*

Karen put her arms around me and I sobbed.

♦

Karen could afford to come up emotionally and financially every two weeks to Sheffield to help me. And I needed her. I needed someone who wanted to help me. I was just living on my own in the house and there was nothing there. I was existing. It wasn't homely at all and that made it worse. All I had was the things that people had given me. I was embarrassed to let Karen see the house but she wanted to help so I let her in. She looked at me with tears in her eyes and said:

*"Oh Herol. What has happened to you?"*

The next day Karen went out and bought me a lamp and a picture. She put the picture on the wall and turned the lamp on and while it was only a start it made a lovely difference. Over the next few weeks, every time Karen came to see me she came with her car laden with furniture and clothes for me. I didn't have any proper clothes that weren't training clothes. That's all I'd worn for years. She bought me a new television and a CD player.

In a truly wonderful way Karen was trying to show me the kindness that I'd tried to show other people when I could. She sorted out my finances and kept on buying me little things to make it feel like my house was a sort of home. The lamp was okay but the music system was wicked!

But it was still hard when the kids came. I so wanted to see them but I only had one bed. If Karen was here we'd sleep on the living room floor, but then when she had enough spare money she bought bunk beds for the kids and that was the best thing of all.

Karen was doing so much for me but she was only in Sheffield for two or three days and only once a fortnight. I had become a financial burden on her and she had a demanding job as a freelance PA with two high profile clients. So for two days every now and then I was no longer alone and I could face the world again. But for long periods I stayed in the dark place and I was back to the start. I just couldn't pull myself out of it.

I felt the worst when I spoke to Nina on the phone because it made me feel inadequate and when I woke up in the morning I felt even worse and didn't go in to work. I don't think Nina meant me to feel like that but I felt so much shame and so useless that I couldn't help my own children and it was hurting me more and more. I felt like I was letting everyone down. Karen tried to tell me that I'd not let anyone down and that my kids have had a very privileged life. They were okay. But I hated it when they came to stay with me; I couldn't buy them things. I couldn't even buy the right food.

We had a lot of late night phone calls when I was tearful and Karen could tell when I was off. We talked about the 'black cloud' and Karen knew when it was here or when it was coming. She worried a lot about me and sometimes phoned my mate Shaun, who had a key for the house, so that he could let himself in and make sure I was alright.

One particular night Karen was worried about me but I assured her I was okay. I was okay. And I bid her goodnight. After I'd put the phone down I began to think and fret. I asked myself what I had got from the last twenty five years. Whose fault was it? It's my fault. I'd never been the best at getting things done because people had always done things for me – Mum and Dad, Brendan and Alma, Rita and Dave .....and so I let things drift into a position where I couldn't recover them. And I needed a way to escape. So brandy was the first port of call. And at first it was a comfort. So I had a drink.

But I couldn't deal with the loneliness any more. When I was alone I had too much time to think and too much to think about, and this night was worse than usual. There had to be a reason why this had happened to me. Why was I in this situation? Over the past couple of years I was hoping that something was going to happen for me, but by now I had got to the position of thinking 'well actually nothing is going to happen'. Maybe all the good things coming my way had already happened in my life and I'd had my lot.

And now I was at the very bottom, almost ten years to the day after being at the very top. I was living alone in my house and my marriage had failed. I didn't know what to do next with my career and I was financially on my knees. I was being tormented and I was tormenting myself. I sat crying. I just wanted out. So I sharpened a knife and went to the bedroom with a bottle of brandy. I said to myself:

*"You selfish bastard."*

I was letting everyone down. I'd just do it one more time. I made a couple of phone calls and said a few prayers before beginning to slash my wrists. As I did it I screamed and lay down, thinking I would die in my sleep. I knew there was no comeback.

♦

But in the morning I woke up on my sheets hardened by dried blood and realised I'd somehow failed in my attempt to end the misery I was going through. God knows how. I managed to get out of bed and wondered what the hell I'd done and then I was overcome by a sense of relief that I was still here. I went to hospital and they patched me up and sent me home, even though I told them I had tried to kill myself.

I'd forgotten that I'd told Steve that I'd be in the gym that morning and I just spent the morning driving around before parking up and sitting on the pavement by a fence outside Millhouses Park where we used to take the kids at the weekend. When I hadn't turned up Steve was worried and had set out to find me and he knew where to look. He saw my car first and as he jumped out of his car he knew straight away that I'd slit my wrists. I just wanted someone to talk to.

Karen came up and bollocked me. When someone's doing so much for you and giving all this love how can you do that? Then for the next few weeks when she phoned me she pestered me to go and see the doctor. I lied that I had and then we'd have a row. I felt even more that I was letting everyone down and now I'd done it to Karen. She'd done everything she possibly could to help me but I'd thrown it back in her face. But I couldn't get out of where I was. I felt like I was slowly going mad.

Eventually Karen was getting desperate and told me she wouldn't put up with me unless I got professional help. She panicked about me and when I didn't answer my phone she drove up one night to find me in bed. That love was what kept me alive.

We talked about the black cloud and at times I was shrouded, but we kept on talking. But Karen was never far from worrying that I would try again to get out. She knew that every other day I wanted to die, and all she could do from a hundred and seventy miles away was tell me I had to keep going. Every night we were on the phone for hours.

But I was still on my knees and couldn't see any end to the darkness, no matter how hard Karen tried and how hard I tried. One night when I was hysterical and terrified she rang the police.

I answered the knock on my door to be faced by two police officers:

*"Herol, are you on your own?"*

*"Yes."*

*"How do you feel?"*

*"Absolutely shit and I want to die."*

*"Okay, that's enough."*

I was sectioned and they took me down to the police station, where they phoned Karen to tell her not to worry and that I was okay. I felt so relieved that someone had turned up at my house and I felt like a weight had been lifted from my shoulders.

It had been the hardest phone call for Karen to make. But she had saved me.

# 15

# Redemption

*"To live is like to love – all reason is against it,*
*and all healthy instinct for it."*

## Samuel Butler

I wasn't in the cells for long. The guys who brought me in were top men and they kept Karen informed of my condition. I quickly improved while I was down at the station, but that's the nature of depression. When you have a release of some sort then you can climb out of the depths and these two lads had temporarily given me my release.

When Karen spoke to them on the phone she could hear me laughing in the background and the copper told her I was fine and had asked for some herbal tea, which they didn't have. But Karen knew how quickly I could drop back into the abyss so she told the policeman not to be fooled by me at least until she made it up the M6. She wanted to make sure I wasn't on my own when I was discharged.

Depression is such a difficult thing to describe. I guess it's different to everyone who has suffered from it. People say all the time 'oh I'm really depressed' but what they really mean is that they're pissed off. Depression eats you, slowly and frighteningly. When the black cloud was on the way I knew and it scared the shit out of me. Once the descent starts you just can't stop it. You need to get to the very bottom and then hope it doesn't eat you up entirely. Then how you get out of it is up to you. I had tried to get out of it by killing myself, but there must have been a small part of me that didn't want that to be the end of it all. But I didn't know what else I could do.

People who love you can do their very best to help you drag your way out of depression but you have to work at it yourself as well. And I was under no illusion that I was facing the most difficult and fierce opponent of my whole life.

I wasn't in the slightest bit angry at Karen. She had me sectioned for my own safety and she did it at just the right time. As much as anything I just didn't want to be on my own. Karen couldn't be with me all the time and so that's why she fretted and became so worried. But she had saved me and given me the starting point to try to lift myself up again.

When she came up she brought some books for me to read, some general stuff but also some self help books. She understood more than anyone that I had to do a lot of the work for myself. I couldn't rely on anyone else to do everything any more. Sure I needed help but to deserve that I had also to help myself.

A week later and after everything was getting back to normal again I went to see my doctor who finally realised that I needed a referral and so he put me in contact with a team of psychiatrists who would begin the process of trying to put me back together again. A very close friend of mine, Martin Horner, also paid for some private counselling for me.

So I spent the next few months trying to understand why I had become so depressed and that way I had the best chance of beating it. The thing that tipped me over was having to leave my home and worst of all my children. From that moment on I lost all my energy and fight. I had enough to laugh and smile and wave when I was walking around Sheffield but that's all I had. There was nothing at all behind it.

At the point that I was sectioned I would say that I had maybe an equal split of good and bad days. I knew that a bad day was always just around the corner and sometimes, at the worst times the black cloud didn't shift for over a week. I was missing my kids and so sad that I couldn't see any hope. But I had to keep going for them and for Karen.

Part of my problem in the longer term had been my inability to accept where I was. The divorce was just the tipping point but for a long time I had struggled with what had happened to me throughout my life. Retiring from boxing for good came as a big shock and it hit me much harder than I could ever have imagined. And if I look back even though we had Skip Fit and the gym in Rotherham, I wasn't really ever happy. All I ever wanted to do was box and to have that taken away from me was hard to take. I'm by no means the only sports star or even boxer to have problems with my mind. International stars from all sorts of sports have suffered and there have been documentaries looking at the problem.

Boxing had dropped me like a stone and when I looked back I realised that I'd never really accepted that fully. And so I was always susceptible to mental fragility.

I talked to the counsellors about my childhood and the rape I suffered at the age of eight. That's something that I can never really have proper closure on but how do you accept that? I can't talk about it without becoming tearful so I don't talk about it often. Did that help to drive me into depression? One of the main aspects of that was the trust a child has in a grown up and the betrayal of that trust. But that happening didn't make me lose the ability to trust people. In fact I continued to trust people through most of my life, very much like a child. I always saw the best in people and that hadn't always stood me in good stead. For a lot of my life, although I had plenty of guidance and always people around me I didn't really have anyone looking after me properly and telling me to be careful or how to look after myself.

I had people who called themselves my friends who borrowed money off me with no intention of ever paying it back. I'm not saying I never borrowed off anyone in my life, in fact I borrowed off my parents, but I know I have been a net loser. I was too trusting and too naïve. I've always seen the best in people and always given everyone a chance and I haven't been particularly quick to change that way of seeing people. But I have discovered that the world is full of shysters – whether they're politicians, bankers, salesmen or just people who want to rip you off. The trick is in seeing who you can trust quickly – it's a shame that you have to make that call. Either I couldn't be bothered or I had a genuine trust of people. I haven't led a blameless life, I've nicked bikes and apples as a kid and not always lived up to Mum and Dad's moral code but I have tried. Some people just don't try; all they do is make what they can and fuck everyone else. But then we all have to live with ourselves don't we?

All that angst about not having any money to spend on the kids was multiplied a thousand times when I eventually realised that I had thrown so much money away. And it's a terrible thing when it dawns that you've trusted people who you shouldn't have. But it was all too late for me now and I had to accept that. The sad by product of that realisation is that I will always find it hard to trust people now and that makes the world a poorer place and me more sorrowful. That is something I have to accept.

The Julian Jackson fight has preyed on my mind for a long time. I've laughed it off every time people ask me about it, but that's another big thing on my mind, nagging, nagging and nagging. In a way I'm glad the Jackson thing happened. There were so many people around me at the time, I was being torn in all kinds of directions and I didn't know the true value of myself or them. When things went sour, a lot drifted away and only a handful stayed by me. There're the people I count as my friends like Brian and Glyn and Steve. The others were just acquaintances. And even if I'd won the World championship then, the money might have drifted as well. I just had no idea how to handle money so whether it was twenty thousand or two hundred thousand you could bet your backside it would be somewhere else pretty soon. If I told you how much I'd spent wildly or lent out and never saw again you'd call me stupid, but that's exactly what I was. And I accept that.

But I do believe that what goes around comes around. I believe that big style. If you lose out in life and it's not your fault, then down the line you'll get something good. And if you've spent your life shafting people then maybe you'd better watch out.

People who are spiritually rich don't worry about making money and don't have to shaft anyone, and they always seem to get by. Something always turns up. Somebody might give you something. There seems to be an element of luck about it but generally you will reap what you sow. It's Karma man. Isn't it a fantastic thought that all those people who shit on others are heading for a mammoth's turd.

I'm still a spiritual bloke. At the best times I thanked God and I prayed at my lowest ebb. Who knows if there is a God? I really think that most of us accept there's only one way to find out and it's funny how many atheists search for some spirituality weeks before they die.

♦

So accepting where I was became a huge part of my therapy because once I had accepted that, and accepted all the worst things that had happened to me I could start to move on. Karen was a wonderful support and I knew that if she hadn't contacted me on Facebook a couple of years earlier I might just be dead. I was so grateful. And now I had to take the second chance I'd been given. But the rebuilding process will be a long and tough battle. Part of that is in me finding out just what I want to do. I have always loved kids and that's maybe something that I could work in.

As I started to rebuild, I worked briefly as a teaching assistant in a big school in Sheffield. The work in the school was great but the political system in there didn't work for me, it was like nothing I'd ever seen. I loved helping the kids who were struggling with their reading or with their sums. It was really good for me and I had my own way of getting them on my side, but for me it didn't mean filling in form A or form B. I enjoyed it and some of the kids started coming down to the gym near Bramhall Lane, and when I saw their parents I could tell them what to eat and when to eat as well. That's just the sort of opportunity I want. I heard a statistic recently that for the first time in history there are almost as many people dying from obesity related illness as there are from starvation. That's a horrific thought. Loads of people are eating so much of the wrong stuff that it kills them, at the same time as thousands die every day from malnutrition. It's a tragedy.

I'm not sure the teachers knew what to make of me. I think some of them saw me as a boxer and a big black guy, and I guess boxing isn't high on the list of priorities for forward thinking educationalists. But boxing still saves as many kids who'd otherwise be in trouble as it always has.

I started to struggle a little with the way things worked in the school. The form filling was too much and when there was a bit of snow in the car park no one cleared the snow so that they could park. It was something to do with health and safety. I couldn't get my head around it because I thought it'd be much healthier and safer if someone cleared the carpark and we didn't all spend the day slipping on our arses. That environment was so hard for me to accept having come from such a free environment. There were just too many pointless rules and regulations. They wanted me to fill lots of forms in all the time and soon enough I realised it wasn't for me.

Steve had warned me that I wouldn't like the bureaucracy and he was absolutely right. But it was important for me to do that and it was part of the rebuilding process. And it was no waste of time because I got to work with kids and carried on forming my ideas of what to do next. And it also gave me a sense of routine for a while which was important because even when I could see a black cloud coming then I still had to get in to work, which I always wanted to do because of the kids. So sometimes the cloud didn't actually arrive.

I need to find a light at the end of the tunnel and something I can do. A lot of people know me and I have to make the most of that, but I'm also in the process of being reprogrammed!

When I'm doing something that I really want to do I know I'll be able to look back at this part of my life and say that it has gone.

I've always been interested in the science side of sport which has developed massively over the past decade and a couple of years ago I decided to see how long I could skip for. The world record is about twenty seven hours and when I was down the gym one day I put my music on and started skipping. And I carried on, on and off, for the next twenty four hours. I probably had a few hours off in total but at times I didn't stop for four or five hours. I told Steve what I'd done and that I was interested in making a world record attempt, so he put me in touch with some science lads at Sheffield Hallam University and I went down to see them.

The two guys in charge were called Alan and Rob and they had some Masters students who were keen to support me as part of their degree project. They were great lads and over the next few weeks I saw a fair bit of them.

Alan and Rob did some initial fitness assessments which included a routine health screen, lactate profile and maximal exertion test, which basically involved me running like shit until I was knackered. After that they did a skipping test and hooked me up with a mask that measured my oxygen uptake during skipping. It was quite a laugh. Alan asked me to skip at three different speeds to help them work out the most economical skipping speed where I'd burn the fewest calories. They worked out that the best speed for me to skip at was ninety per minute and they worked out that if I could do that I'd only burn about twenty thousand calories if I made it to twenty eight hours! Twenty thousand calories, that's about a weeks worth of food for a grown man.

The record attempt was set up to be held at the Ponds Forge centre in Sheffield on the day that there was a national junior swimming championship there so there'd be lots of people. But we didn't have a lot of time to prepare so Alan and Rob decided that rather than do long stints which would risk injury we should concentrate on shorter sessions and feeding protocols. So the science lads set up a training programme on that basis.

I knew one of the lads, a guy called Matt as I'd seen him down at the EIS. He was a sound lad and well up for the project.

On the first session he wanted to check my energy expenditure again to see how economical I was skipping. They monitored my heart rate and then after I'd done a session they looked at how quickly it recovered and then the resting rate. Matt looked at his gizmo then looked at me:

"*Blimey Herol. Forty six!*"

I'd got my resting rate down quickly and I don't think that Matt had seen one that low before, particularly on someone of fifty years old! He seemed dead excited about it.

Over the next few weeks I went in and did everything they asked of me, usually hooked up to a mask and all sorts of equipment. And they tried to help me whenever I asked for something. They had a television and dvd set up and managed to put some of my favourite music on it which passed the time. Then one day, a lad on the team called Ed came up with some old boxing dvds which he thought would help me. That was all okay until the clip of Jackson knocking ten bells of shit out of me came on, not once but six times:

"*Bloody hell what are you trying to do to me?*"

Ed rushed over and put the music back on.

I was having a good time doing all this stuff but I had to do a lot of bike work and that killed my arse. So I said to Matt if I had to do much more of that I'd get him some day. I don't think he believed me because the bike work seemed to be increasing. All I needed next was for Ed to come up with a dvd of the Kalambay fight and a tape recording of the malicious phone call and the torture process would have been perfect.

The lads seemed to be pleased with me and when I left each session they gave me instructions of what I had to do on my own. But I lost them so I just did my own thing. I wanted to tell Matt that I'd done something so when he asked how I'd gone on I replied:

"*Pretty good, I've run sixteen miles and skipped for five hours.*"

He just shook his head and hooked me up again. He didn't appreciate my nutritional habits either. I often turned up to training without having had breakfast and then when I'd finished I had a tiny sip of water before going to a sauna. Matt and Ed started to make me take on more food and drink while I was training. Matt said that left to my own devices I would have completely dehydrated. I guess old habits die hard. In the old days when I was preparing for a fight I spent the last three days losing weight and draining the fluid out of my body. But that's not the way to do it now. The science lads couldn't believe what we used to do, looking in amazement when I explained how we got down to weight.

We persevered and I trained as well as I could. I liked going in and every time I met Matt I threw a flurry of punches at him stopping millimetres in front of his face. I'm glad he never stepped forward as I'm not as quick as I was!

On the day of the attempt we set a skipping mat up in the corner of the main hall and right in front of some big entrance doors. I was happy with that because it meant that there'd be loads of people passing through which would hopefully relieve the boredom of skipping for hours on end. The downside was that we were next to the massive glass windows and as the day became sunnier it got warmer and it was a bit like being in a greenhouse.

I felt sorry for the student who was walking around the centre in the Sheffield Children's Hospital Big Teddy outfit. It was like Pudsey Bear off Children in Need but when the guy took the head off he was sweating like a donkey. We were trying to raise as much money as we could but the bloke who was carrying the bucket and guiding the teddy round must have had a wicked sense of humour because he kept on taking him up and down the stairs to different levels. Every time a crowd of people appeared on the floor above, the hapless Teddy was dragged up there.

But I was finding it warm too. The effect of the windows and all the people around me increased the temperature quite quickly. I loved having all the people there and kept encouraging kids and their mums and dads to join me on the mat. And for a few hours it was sweet. The problem was that I was sweating at two litres per hour (nice) and we couldn't replace the fluids I was losing through sweat. Eventually I stopped sweating which indicated that I was getting dehydrated and I soon cramped up. I worked through the cramp for some hours but then had to call it time.

I was gutted that I hadn't done it, but I had tried my best. I think we just didn't have enough time to prepare. But I haven't given up the idea of doing it again. I'm going to get a world title of some sort if it's the last thing I do, and I don't fancy trying to fit four hundred straws in my mouth!

♦

Neither the work in school nor the skipping had taken me right away from the darkest places but they had both given me some respite. I knew that I needed to concentrate on things that were positive while I tried to get things sorted out in my head and my life as a whole.

I still had some bad days but by the beginning of this year they were staying away more and more. And some of my friends have helped me enormously. When you're in a fix you really find out who you'd want to be in a trench with. As well as Martin, Steve and Shaun my good friend Rory and his wife Wendy have been a constant source of strength. I met Rory years ago through boxing and we kept in touch. Rory and Wendy have a place in Spain and several times over the past couple of years when I was at a low point, Rory flew me out to Spain to spend a couple of weeks with them. This friendship has meant so much to me, and Rory, as a man of immense integrity, has always told me how it is, warts and all.

Karen was working towards coming up to Sheffield, because she knew that the city had become my home. But maybe I need a complete break now and a clean start, so for the time being we've gone to London. The world's a smaller place, so I'll be up to Sheffield to see the kids all the time, and they can come down to the big city. But Karen and I agreed that it would be easier for us both to survive if we went to London. That's where her work is and the market. And for me, I always said that the opportunity for a fighter in London was far greater than Sheffield and that applies to many things.

To start with I was acting as Karen's house husband, which I'm quite good at. There are plenty of Caribbean shops in London. I can get everything I need to make the perfect dish of chicken and rice and peas (mungo beans of course). And I do my bit to keep the house clean and tidy.

When I first went down Karen was still concerned to leave me on my own all the time and I always like to get out, so I went with her on her work now and then. The best trip was a visit to Harrods to buy a cat collar for one of her clients – that's Karen's client's cat of course. Karen's client isn't a cat. I don't think.

And by introducing me to some of her friends I have started to get some personal training work, which is much more lucrative in London. I have seven clients already, largely thanks to Karen. She's been tough with me by telling me that I need to do things for myself. She'll give me a number and say:

*"You have to ring him or her."*

*"What do I say?"*

*"I don't know. You work it out."*

I know it sounds simple but it's helping me to rebuild my self belief. So I go through it in my head and tell her what I was going to do and then she'd tell me maybe what I should do. I'll get there.

And I'm planning an exercise skipping programme for schools using some of the data I can get from the world record attempt, as well as doing fitness sessions for obese women, which is a growing market. Get it?

One of the best things about being in London is that Natasha lives down here too, she's only about three miles away and I sometimes babysit for my beautiful granddaughter Maya.

As I write I haven't had a brandy for three months, I'll have a glass of red wine now and then but no spirits. I had ample opportunity last night when Karen and I went to the Michael

Watson tribute dinner at the Dorchester. It was a fantastic evening and a lot of the old guys were there; Nigel Benn, Chris Eubank and Errol Christie, but no Mark Kaylor – maybe he thought he'd steer clear of Errol! And I had more offers of work with some really exciting meetings to come soon. I'm not counting any chickens but London is the place to be for me to really get to where I want. But I'll always love Sheffield as my home and the home of many great friends. You won't keep me away.

But more than anything it was inspirational to see Michael doing well. He still has trouble walking but he's still fighting on and so will I.

I'm in a better place now. I have good days and bad days but for the first time in four years definitely more good than bad. Sometimes I'm happy and sometimes I'm not, but that surely applies to everybody in the world. I have to accept where I am and I've made good headway there, and that will give me the best chance to get myself out whenever I'm feeling down.

And I have a future to look forward to. I want to make things happen for my children too. The kids have amazing memories so I know that they love me even though I can't do everything I want for them at this very moment.

I'm still laughing.

And for the first time in a while…. the happiness is there behind.

# SPECIAL THANKS

My children Natasha, Oliver, Jessica, Samual, Molly and Harvey, and my granddaughter Maya. You are my world and my reason for living. I love you all

My Mum and Dad, for being the best parents and giving unconditional love

A massive thank you to Karen Elizabeth Neville and her children Dane Junior and Pele, who put her touch to this book and who has been instrumental in me reclaiming my life

Rory and Wendy for holding me up when I was falling down and truly making a difference

Winston, Noel, Paul, Leonnie and Elaine - my great Brothers and Sisters

Brian Anderson for being a true friend

Brenda and Trevor for the shorts and Dressing Gowns and the unquestionable support before every fight

Shaun Hessey & Petermans Forklift Trucks for being a valued friend and for sponsorship

Johnny Nelson for being there when it mattered

Steve Cheetham, a friend of immense proportion

Martin and Anne Marie Horner for their unfaltering support in many areas of my life

Brendan and Alma Ingle, the biggest thank you for everything that you ever did for me

Barney Eastwood for giving me a chance

Naseem Hamed for never losing faith in me. Thanks Bro

Roy, Frank and Alan Smith for putting me on the road to boxing

Rita and Dave Marriott the most amazing hosts and friends

Bob Bonsall for being a friend and playing a big part in my life

My accountant Eddie and his wife Yvonne for financial and moral advice and support

Glyn Rhodes for always being there, as a boxer, friend and counsellor

## I ALSO WISH TO THANK

Graham Teesdale and Graham Bartholomew for helping to launch the Rotherham Boxing Gym

Bill Bradshaw an avid and loyal supporter

Samuel Cope for being a friend and a brother

Paul and Liz Holmes for their hope and inspiration when I really needed it most

Paul Elliott for the financial support with the gym

Ryan Rhodes, Jason Channer, Scott Endersby, Mick Mills and Danny Teesdale for their sparring and friendship

Sorry for any others I may have missed

*Herol*

## HEROL GRAHAM PROFESSIONAL RECORD

*Won 48 (KOs 27)*        **Lost 6**        *Drawn 0*

| Date | Opponent | Location | Result |
|------|----------|----------|--------|
| 1998 | Charles Brewer | Atlantic City | L TKO |
| | **IBF Super Middleweight Title** | | |
| 1997 | Vinny Pazienza | Wembley | W UD |
| | **WBC International Super Middleweight Title** | | |
| 1997 | Chris Johnson | Kensington | W TKO |
| | **vacant WBC International Super Middleweight Title** | | |
| 1997 | Craig Joseph | Southwark | W PTS |
| 1996 | Terry Ford | Sheffield | W PTS |
| 1992 | Frank Grant | Leeds | L TKO |
| | **BBBofC British Middleweight Title** | | |
| 1992 | Sumbu Kalambay | Pesaro | L UD |
| | **EBU (European) Middleweight Title** | | |
| 1991 | John Ashton | Sheffield | W TKO |
| | **BBBofC British Middleweight Title** | | |
| 1990 | Julian Jackson | Benalmadena | L KO |
| | **vacant WBC Middleweight Title** | | |
| 1990 | Ismael Negron | Dewsbury | W KO |
| 1989 | Rod Douglas | Wembley | W TKO |
| | **BBBofC British Middleweight Title** | | |
| 1989 | Mike McCallum | Kensington | L SD |
| | **vacant WBA World Middleweight Title** | | |
| 1988 | Johnny Melfah | Bethnal Green | W TKO |
| | **BBBofC British Middleweight Title** | | |
| 1988 | James Cook | Sheffield | W TKO |
| | **vacant BBBofC British Middleweight Title** | | |
| 1987 | Ricky Stackhouse | Doncaster | W TKO |
| 1987 | Sumbu Kalambay | Wembley | L UD |
| | **EBU (European) Middleweight Title** | | |
| 1987 | Charles Boston | Belfast | W TKO |
| 1986 | Mark Kaylor | Wembley | W TKO |
| | **EBU (European) Middleweight Title** | | |
| 1986 | Ernie Rabotte | Las Vegas | W TKO |
| 1986 | Ayub Kalule | Sheffield | W TKO |
| | **EBU (European) Middleweight Title** | | |
| 1985 | Sanderline Williams | Belfast | W PTS |
| 1985 | Roberto Justino Ruiz | Kensington | W TKO |
| 1985 | Jimmy Price | Shoreditch | W KO |
| | **vacant BBBofC British Middleweight Title** | | |
| 1985 | Jose Rosemain | Kensington | W KO |
| 1984 | Liam Coleman | Sheffield | W TKO |
| 1984 | Jose Seys | Kensington | W TKO |
| 1984 | Irving Hines | Wembley | W KO |
| 1984 | Lindell Holmes | Sheffield | W TKO |
| 1983 | Germain Le Maitre | Saint-Nazaire | W TKO |
| | **EBU (European) Light Middleweight Title** | | |
| 1983 | Carlos Betancourt | Kensington | W KO |
| 1983 | Clement Tshinza | Sheffield | W KO |
| | **vacant EBU (European) Light Middleweight Title** | | |

| 1983 | Tony Nelson | Wembley | **W** RTD |
|------|-------------|---------|-----------|
| 1982 | Hunter Clay | Lagos | **W** PTS |
| | **Commonwealth (British Empire) Light Middleweight Title** | | |
| 1982 | Fred Coranson | Liverpool | **W** PTS |
| 1982 | Chris Christian | Sheffield | **W** TKO |
| | **Commonwealth (British Empire) Light Middleweight Title** | | |
| | **BBBofC British Light Middleweight Title** | | |
| 1981 | Kenny Bristol | Sheffield | **W** PTS |
| | **Commonwealth (British Empire) Light Middleweight Title** | | |
| 1981 | Prince Rodney | Sheffield | **W** TKO |
| 1981 | Pat Thomas | Sheffield | **W** PTS |
| | **BBBofC British Light Middleweight Title** | | |
| 1981 | Lancelot Innis | Liverpool | **W** PTS |
| 1980 | Larry Mayes | Liverpool | **W** TKO |
| 1980 | Joey Mack | Sheffield | **W** PTS |
| 1980 | George Danahar | Sheffield | **W** PTS |
| 1980 | Glen McEwan | Sheffield | **W** PTS |
| 1979 | Errol McKenzie | Sheffield | **W** PTS |
| 1979 | Billy Ahearne | Barnsley | **W** TKO |
| 1979 | Lloyd James | Sheffield | **W** PTS |
| 1979 | Gordon George | Sheffield | **W** PTS |
| 1979 | Mac Nicholson | Newcastle | **W** PTS |
| 1979 | George Walker | Southend | **W** PTS |
| 1979 | Dave Southwell | Burslem | **W** PTS |
| 1979 | Dave Southwell | Reading | **W** PTS |
| 1979 | Jimmy Roberts | Bradford | **W** TKO |
| 1978 | Curtis Marsh | Southend | **W** KO |
| 1978 | Vivian Waite | Sheffield | **W** PTS |